Architects: the Noted
and
the Ignored

Architects: the Noted
and
the Ignored

Niels L. Prak
School of Architecture
Delft Technical University

JOHN WILEY & SONS
Chichester · New York · Brisbane · Toronto · Singapore

The illustration on page ii is of 1st and 45th Street, New York.

Copyright © 1984 by John Wiley & Sons Ltd.

All rights reserved.

No part of this book may be reproduced
by an means, nor transmitted,
nor translated into a machine language
without the written permision of the publisher.

Library of Congress Cataloguing in Publication Data

Prak, Niels Luning, 1926–
    Architects

    Includes index.
    1. Architects. I. Title.
NA2750.P68 1984   720   83–6988
ISBN 0 471 90203 9

British Library Cataloguing in Publication Data:
Prak, Niels L.
    Architectural designs
    1. Architecture
    I. Title
    721   NA2510

    ISBN 0 471 90203 9

Typeset by Photo-Graphics, Honiton, Devon and
printed by The Pitman Press, Bath, Avon

CAL

NA
2750
P68
1984

For the people who made this book possible:
— the late Marinus Jan Granpré Molière, my
teacher, whose theories I tried to refute;
— Pierre Bourdieu, whose theories I tried to use;
— Peter Gleichmann, who showed me the uses of
sociology;
— Roelf Steenhuis and René Ackerstaff, my
students, who asked such difficult questions;
— Elisabeth Prak-de Waha, my wife, who cheered
me on from the sidelines.

Contents

alterations, do-it-yourself architecture and vandalism — different countries

3. **The Evolution of the Profession**

Low level of technical competence gradually improved during the Middle Ages — fires and building regulations — patrons claiming the designers' role — geometry, the 'secret' of the lodges — design decisions during construction — master-masons: contractors and designers — a change of forms: the artist-designer — Alberti on the preeminence of design — rise in status of the architect — pattern-books — gentleman-architects — the business of building and the necessity of supervision — Soane on the architects — architects' associations — larger practices — rising quality of the built environment — loss of functions of the architect — no monopoly for architects — the universal artist

4. **Case-Study: Halen**

Background of the architects — difficulties of realization of the project — description of Halen — common facilities and the philosophy behind them — communal living — the social composition of Halen — other housing projects by Atelier 5 — architects' criticism of users' alterations in Wertherberg — points still to be discussed

5. **Society and Culture**

The subculture of Liberals — acculturation in the home — peer groups, roles and their visible signs — larger social aggregates — the class-system — Veblen's leisure class — speech habits — cultural capital — art as a symbolic system for emotional orientation — training in taste — the cultural elite — highbrow and lowbrow — legitimate culture — cultural lag and the trickle-down effect — the art-museum and its public — varieties of taste in the different classes — economic and cultural elites — reasons for continuous innovation in the arts — tradition in visual art — the negative freedom of the artist — artists criticising competitors — art, propaganda and religion — conservative preferences of the economic elite — the natural public for advanced art — the goals of the artist and his road to fame — the goals of curators — the 'configuration' of the art-world — parallel in the social sciences — Halen and Wertherberg partly explained

6. **Architects and their Belief-systems**

The practical and the artistic tasks — preference for the artistic task — the pecking-order among architects — a preference for the artistic task instilled in architectural school — history as the 'celebration of architecture' — well-known architects as teachers — presuppositions of architectural theory — Mies' school in Chicago: transmission of a creed — learning in an architectural office — originality in design — mannerist variations and acceptance of the new — competitions — architects as 'patrons' — 'in praise of architecture' — practical architects; the philosophy of Welton Becket — architecture as advertising — imitation of the masters — clients for artistic architects — varieties of taste among patrons — architecture for the cultural elite — ideal projects — great artists do not have to be so careful

PART II

1. Introduction: A Summary of the Argument

Of the huge number of buildings built every year, only a few attain a worldwide reputation, and even fewer are finally canonized in architectural history. This book discusses the relations between the few famous 'artistic' architects and their more practical colleagues. It shows that the distinction between artistically relevant and run-of-the-mill design is a central and not an accidental feature, consciously pursued by the artistic architects. The overrating of aesthetic above practical aspects is promoted by the trade journals and by the critics in the daily press and is instilled in the architectural schools. The critics, the art historians, but primarily the architects themselves are responsible for the social support-system which creates and maintains an architectural elite. Though many are called, few are chosen; the majority of ambitious young architects get bogged down in the harsh realities of the building industry: the price per cubic foot, the resale value, the reluctance of developers and realtors to experiment. But the latter cannot entirely neglect aesthetics, for neither they nor their clients want to look like philistines. Therefore they trail at a comfortable distance behind the development at the 'artistic front'.

Usually the relation between well-known architects and the mass of their unknown colleagues is seen as a one-way street. A few highly gifted individuals set the course for the architects of the future and the others follow suit. An entirely different perspective is gained when this relation is seen as reciprocal: if most architects follow the trend or trends set by the leaders, the leaders will see themselves as 'pursued' by their followers. Imitation is not only a compliment, it can also be experienced as an encumbrance.

The growth in architectural publishing, in particular after the Second World War, has increased this pressure. The same buildings appear over and over again in architectural trade journals all over the world. The rapid spread of architectural 'hot' news speeds up its 'vulgarization' and at the same time diminishes its emotional impact as its novelty wears off; both factors exert a pressure towards innovation. But when an architect presents a solution which is really revolutionary, he often runs up against the lack of understanding on the part of the client. Most clients want to play it safe; they exert a pressure towards conservative design. Only exceptional architects can afford the luxury of resisting this pressure and only exceptional clients encourage their architects to experiment at their expense. In the field of business acquisition, the architect has a position different from the one in his peer group, and the tension between these two positions explains a great deal of architects' behavior. Of course it is obvious that it is at the root of the envious admiration of the ordinary practitioner for the 'Great Makers'; less obvious is the influence of this configuration on the behavior of the stars themselves.

Architects can be ordered on a scale from the practical to the artistic. At the practical end are firms doing primarily industrial, technical and commercial work; they specialize in fast, efficient service, reliable costing and economic construction methods. The stars are at the opposite end of the scale. The majority of architects are somewhere between these two extremes, but would prefer to move towards the artistic side, even though the practical is more remunerative. Why? Because artistic success confers infinitely more status and holds out the lure of immortality, whereas the practical side can only bring in more money.

If all clients tended towards conservatism, architects could only experiment on their own homes, and innovation would never get off the ground. There is however a group of clients which allows and even encourages architects to experiment, because it has a stake in innovation: the cultural elite. It consists of people who 'know' about the newest developments in art and architecture, i.e. people who are educated in matters of taste. Critics, journalists, writers, historians, museum directors, artists and architects belong to it. This elite not only 'knows' about taste, it also makes it, by its access to the media, to exhibitions, prizes and awards. Though internally divided about the future, it makes a common front against the 'bourgeois' taste of the economic elite.

Architecture often serves as a mark of identity. What somebody is, what he believes in, is partially visible from his clothes and his home furnishings; if he could exercise any choice in his home, then that is an indicator too. We see at a glance whether we have to do with someone who is 'revolutionary', 'progressive', 'modern' or 'conservative' in taste. Works of art and architecture help to establish our cultural identity, but thereby also become signs to the world at large. The varieties of tastes may seem completely arbitrary when they are looked at by themselves, but they start to make sense when they are again seen as related to a field of different positions. *Avant-garde* taste serves to identify members of the cultural elite by its distinction from the 'bourgeois'.

Architecture in particular has a large potential for identification, because it creates a 'place'. Such a place may symbolize what you want to be by looking like the place *where* you would like to be. If you identify with the future, it may look like the future; if you identify with the past, it may look old-fashioned; if you identify with rural values, it may assume a rustic, neo-vernacular look. For those who can choose their homes or their architects, a building may bring Utopia just a little nearer.

To believe in a futuristic Utopia you have to believe in the future itself. Like religion or political beliefs, this belief is influenced by circumstance. In the thirties, as today, increasing unemployment and the growing threat of war made the belief in the future wane and increased the belief in the past. This became visible, then as now, in a growing nostalgia in architecture, both on the popular level (stylistic revivals) and on the *avant-garde* level (e.g. la Tendenza, the Kriers, Stirling, Bofill).

The waning belief in the future has also prevented the creation of a rallying point in the *avant-garde* of today. This in turn has increased the tendency to diverge. For, though the cultural elite may make a common front against outsiders, it is sharply divided internally, because, amongst other things, to innovate means to be different from the others.

The theory developed here can help to understand the present 'crisis' in architecture. The diversity of post-modern architecture can be explained if it is placed against the ubiquitous — but rarely mentioned — background of ordinary buildings and of the novelties of yesteryear. Post-modern architecture is not unified by what it tries to achieve, but by what it tries to avoid.

Architects Meet to Note Failures of Modernism

By PAUL GOLDBERGER

IT was not like most architectural symposiums. First, the setting: the participants sat at a U-shaped table in the great hall of the Harvard Club on West 44th Street, lined up like the opposing sides at an international diplomatic negotiation. Second, the purpose: it was a private meeting last Monday evening between the partners of Skidmore, Owings & Merrill, the firm of architects that has come to be viewed as the very embodiment of the American architectural establishment, and a group of so-called "postmodern" architects whose much-publicized houses, apartments and institutional buildings have been designed with the deliberate intent of shifting public taste away from the steel-and-glass modernism Skidmore has made so popular.

That the event took place at all was remarkable; it was, in every sense, a confrontation between architecture's establishment and its anti-establishment. But it was also a sign that design directions in architecture have begun to shift dramatically. Skidmore, Owings & Merrill, architects of Lever House, 1 Chase Manhattan Plaza, and 9 West 57th Street, is a firm that has paid little heed in recent years to new developments in architecture. It built its success by convincing businesses that its sleek glass and steel architecture is the ideal corporate expression.

Skidmore's architecture was fresh and new in the 1950's, but it has seemed tired to most critics in the last few years, as design leadership has passed toward the sort of architects who made up the group on the other side of Monday's table — those whose work rejects the austerity of modernism in favor of an architecture that is more ornamented, more concerned with fitting buildings into their surroundings, and more willing to re-use the styles of history.

The event was not thrust upon Skidmore: the firm invited the editors of the Harvard Architecture Review to put together a program that would inform it of new developments in architecture. Jeffrey Horowitz, editor of the review, acted as moderator of the event, which included presentations by Michael McCarthy, Raoul deArmas, Donald Smith, Thomas Killian and Jan Pietrzak of Skidmore, and Michael Graves, Robert A.M. Stern, Jorge Silvetti and Steven Peterson, representing the post-modernists.

The event began with each side presenting slides of its current work. The buildings Skidmore showed were not precisely like the ones for which the firm has become famous — they showed somewhat more eccentricity than the stark boxes of years past. A new project for the Irving Trust Co.'s operations center in lower Manhattan, for example, instead of being a tower in an open plaza, is a bulky structure with elaborate setbacks, a rounded corner, a central atrium and a coating of stripes of white, silver and clear glass.

That was not enough for the post-modernists, who rejected the new designs as they had rejected the firm's earlier work. "The kinds of buildings Skidmore builds are boring — tall or short, fat or thin, if you've seen one you've seen them all," said Mr. Stern.

The major work the post-Modernists presented in opposition to Skidmore's designs was the new Public Services Building for Portland, Ore., designed by Michael Graves and now under construction. It is a massive structure of stucco, set on a heavy, dark base with lighter, colored elements above. It is full of exaggerated classicizing elements, though it bears no literal resemblance to any classical precedent, and if it calls anything to mind, it is the immense, ornamented storage warehouses that moving companies used to erect in Manhattan decades ago.

The battle was not a little false, since no one — not even the Skidmore team — defended modern architecture in quite the austere form it was offered by its founders. At one point, Mr. deArmas called modern architecture "exclusive and limiting and often without grace," words that could have been spoken by post-Modernists just a few years ago.

So the first thing proved is that the shortcomings of Modernism are generally acknowledged, even by the style's advocates. But there was still an enormous gap separating the two sides.

Skidmore's partners were arguing in favor of evolution, not revolution; they frequently sought refuge behind the claim that it was their conservative clients who demanded the stark modernism they produced, ignoring the fact that it was they who helped mold modern taste in the first place.

But now the avant-garde of an age past has become very much the establishment of an age present, and if offers many of the same defenses. The fact of the matter is that large-scale, corporate architectural practices have difficulty responding quickly to stylistic change. Real innovation rarely comes in the form of high-rise towers for conservative corporations — it comes in the form of the smaller buildings being designed by the post-Modernists.

But still, it is true that around the turn of the century there was a much closer correspondence between design innovation and the making of major buildings. The professional leaders of that age, architects like McKim, Mead & White, Cass Gilbert, Burnham & Root, were designing buildings that shaped their times as much as did, say, the work of more innovative architects like Frank Lloyd Wright.

Whether the same could be said of the current work of Skidmore, Owings & Merrill is doubtful — and last Monday's events proved that there is still a long way to go before the professional leadership of the architectural profession and its design leadership are one again the same.

© 1980 by The New York Times Company. Reprinted by permission.

Part I

2 Building

The demand for architectural services is but a part of the demand on the building industry as a whole. The latter fluctuates with the state of the national (and international) economy, a state which is in permanent disequilibrium, according to the post-Keynesian economists[1].

The relations between the building industry and the general economy are still far from clear[2]. Building for business usually follows the general trend, and often even precedes it, as many industrialists consider new or expanded facilities the first items to go when they fear a recession. Residential construction has often lagged behind in boom and slump periods, because the interest rate rises sharply in booms, pricing houses out of the market, whereas in a slump it may become advantageous to invest in houses built with cheap mortgages and yet rented or sold at relatively good prices. The uncertainty of employment is the bane of the building industry, as any carpenter, electrician, contractor or architect knows; it is one of the most frequent themes of complaints:

...it cannot be emphasized too strongly that fluctuating demand is not harmful just to the industries. The inflationary effects during peak demand and the unemployment in the downturn are deleterious to the whole economy. Inefficient working that can result from fluctuating demand increases costs and, in the long run, clients pay the cost in higher prices, in less satisfactory design and in delayed or postponed projects[3].

But of course it is impossible to create an island of continuity in the stormy seas of capitalism. Some national governments (of Sweden, the Netherlands) have tried at times to use the building industry as an instrument of anti-cyclical economic regulation, but without too much success. Building techniques may be relatively simple compared to the manufacture of cars, television sets or computers, but the social and economic ramifications of the building industry are exceedingly complex.

One aspect that contributes to this complexity is the durability of the product. Fifty years is a normal period for the depreciation of buildings; no other durable consumer good approaches that length of time. Consequently there is a large stock of buildings around against which any new addition is assessed. Instead of building something new, many potential clients have the option of buying something old, and there is often a very large market to choose from. William Smolkin described in 1972 the narrow margins of a developer considering the construction of an apartment:

Within a radius of a mile or two where he proposes to build, the present apartments, however inadequate they may be, generally have to be 90 percent occupied... The rent at which he brings this product to market should usually not be more than 5 percent above the level of the existing apartments, despite the fact that the existing units were built earlier at lower costs and lower interest rates... Size of the units. The tolerance must be within ± 50 sq ft of the competition. Let me illustrate what 50 sq ft might mean. At $5 per sq ft marginal cost, 50 × $5 is $250 worth of extra cost, which is equivalent to $3.75 a month of rent. More importantly, 25 per cent more cash is required. That is a pretty narrow tolerance in which to live unless the owner does not care how much money he invests or how much return he gets[4].

Some architects subscribe to the philosophy that the cost of a building 'does not really matter', because that will be 'forgotten in a few years time', whereas the glories of its architecture are there to stay; who has ever calculated the economy of building the cathedrals of Chartres or Amiens? This point of view would probably not be shared by a banker. Statutory regulations may forbid the spreading of excessive construction costs to other facilities, and so a building's price tag may indeed become a millstone around the neck of its owner. A case in point is the Woodhull Hospital in Brooklyn, designed by Kallmann and McKinnell, and described in *The New York Times*:

Mayor Koch has ordered a re-evaluation of the new but still-unopened Woodhull Medical and Mental Health Center in the Williamsburg section of Brooklyn, with the possibility of mothballing the $200 million municipal hospital... Mr. Koch finds himself torn between two painful and equally untenable choices for Woodhull. One would be to allow it to open sometime next year with a daily Medicaid reimbursement rate roughly projected at $350 a patient. This would make it one of the most-expensive hospitals in the country, even though it is not designed to provide the high degree of sophisticated tertiary care that is given by the major private voluntary hospitals or by the municipal hospitals, such as Bellevue. The other would be to keep it closed... Even closed, Woodhull would cost the city about $18 million a year in debt-service payments to the New York State Facilities Development Corporation, which built the hospital, and several million more a year to keep the building's computer and engineering equipment from breaking down... Opening it, however, would cost the city far more, because state health officials have insisted that they will not approve a Medical reimbursement rate that will come close to paying the costs of operating Woodhull... As conceived ... Woodhull was supposed to cost $85 million. But miscalculations, inflation, strikes and other construction delays drove its cost to more than $200 million[5].

During construction, a great deal of money is tied up in the building without any returns; the hard-hats may be busy enough, but the money is 'lying idle'. Many clients insist therefore on heavy penalties for late delivery, penalties which affect insurance and union negotiations, and are handed down to the subcontractors; ultimately they are of course reflected in the bids. Inflation has sharply increased the pressure for speeding up construction and has led to such techniques as *fast-track* and *design-build* in which construction starts before all contract drawings are finished and checked against each other[6].

Buildings differ also from other durable capital and consumer goods in their geographical idiosyncracies. Cheap and heavy per cubic foot in comparison to a motorcar, they are difficult to prefabricate economically. Transportation costs severely limit the operating range of any prefabricator. Nearly all buildings are therefore locally constructed. As demand is tied to a locality, so are construction and the concomitant services, such as contracting and subcontracting firms, and architects' offices. The geographical scatter of the building industry has an effect on its technology: as contractors and architects in rural areas have to remain jacks-of-all-trades, they are of necessity unable to specialize and to assimilate the most recent technical innovations. It is one of the reasons for the relatively slow rate of change in the building industry.

The geographical dispersion of the building industry is one reason why there are so many contractors and why most of them are of diminutive size. There were 876,000 contract construction firms in the USA in 1965, of which 75% had fewer than 8 employees, 54% 1–3 employees and only 1.16% over 100[7]. Construction contracting is mostly done on credit and requires little capital outlay; the field has attracted droves of newcomers, particularly in the boom years after the Second World War. With traditional craft methods of construction, there is no economy of scale; a large constructor has no outstanding advantages over a small one. This has kept many small contractors in business; but the industry has also one of the highest rates of discontinuance: 14% in 1964[7].

One way by which the contractor can try to counteract the vicissitudes of the market and the instability of demand is by participating in as many jobs as he can handle. His subcontractors do the same. Although most contractors build up relations over the years with a limited number of 'trusted' subs, these relations are seldom formalized, and nearly every middle-sized contractor asks several subcontractors to bid on plumbing, finishing, plastering or electrical work. Vertical organization from manufacturer to contractor is extremely rare[8].

A large number of trades is involved in any building job: around 25 on a detached single-family house and around 80 on a large apartment building[8]. Only a few of these are employed by the main contractor; in some cases none at all.

Thus nearly every building is put together by an *ad hoc* combination of firms, all exercising different trades and each firm participating in *other* jobs elsewhere. The timetables of these jobs do not tally, and a fair amount of contractors' and architects' time is spent on getting this or that sub on *their* job, away from the rush job elsewhere. The whole temporary arrangement is tied together by contracts between the various parties. But it is obviously a very rickety social structure and management is time and again made out to be the weakest area in building. With the division of labor as it is (strongly defended by the unions), weak management is anything but accidental.

The combination of many trades in a single firm would be rather vulnerable in a rural area, but much less so in an urban one, because of the larger market. The advantages for control over the building process are obvious, and the bigger firms indeed cover a larger number of trades; yet even there it is rare for general contractors to have in-house painters, plumbers or electricians.

Big builders do try to get a firmer grip on the process of construction by assimilating other functions. The entire process can be subdivided into initiative, acquisition of land, design, finance and construction, according to the Dutch economist Hendriks[9]. By taking over initiative, land acquisition, finance and design, builders can ensure themselves a more regular flow of work. Many large construction companies in Europe and the USA have grown during the building boom of the fifties and sixties and have created developing firms as subsidiaries to keep their business going. The turnkey project or package deal is another fairly recent development with a similar background[10].

The conditions of the architects parallel those of the contractors. Theirs is also an atomized profession spread all over the country, and for the same reasons. Demand is local, the product is locally made, so if a client wants to discuss it and requires some supervision, he needs a local man. In 1970, there were 56,284 architects in the USA[11]. In 1972, architectural firms with 0–3 employees made up 54.1% of the total number of architectural offices and they got only 17.6% of the total annual receipts. The offices of 50 and more employees in that year made up 1.5% of the total number of offices, but they grossed 22.1% of the total annual receipts[11]. The large architectural offices handle a disportionately large share of the business, just like the big contractors. In 1958, the 100 largest offices made up only slightly over 1% of the total number of offices, but were responsible for 9.1% of the total volume of building construction[12]. The share of the big firms continues to increase, at the expense of the smaller ones. The larger firms come to rely more on draftsmen and clerical staff and less on qualified architects[13]. Though there are more architectural students than ever before, there will probably be less work for architects in the future.

The architect heading his own small office is of necessity a jack-of-all-trades, contacting clients, doing design- and often working drawings, writing specifications and certificates of payment, supervising jobs. In larger offices, there is a division of labor which can in principle be handled in two ways. Either the office is organized as a federation of small offices, each job having its own draftsmen, job captain and designer, or it is organized on the principle of the assembly-line: the job goes from the design department to the drafting room for contract drawings, yet another group of people does working drawings, etc. The 'federal' type has usually a joint clerical staff and some other centralized functions, such as spec-writing, job supervision or public relations[14]. The large and very large offices are all run on the assembly-line method, as far as I can see from the few available data.

The 10,500 private and public architectural offices in the USA of 1950 employed 19,000 registered architects and 90,000 unregistered professional employes[12]. About 30% of the latter were only 'not yet registered', but hoped to make the grade in the near future. This expectation of finally running one's own office or becoming a partner has led to rather anomalous labor relations, peculiar to the architectural office:

In many cases, the classic management–labor division doesn't exist; management and labor have gone to the same schools, hold the same degrees and share the same basic goals and concerns. Most architectural employees aspire to be principals; many feel that they are long before they get there. A recent study by P/A's research department shows that 83 percent of the architectural employees listed as draftsmen, for example, have at least three years of college education; more than half hold degrees, and three out of four degree-holders have degrees in architecture[15].

These people consider their present employment as a temporary stage in their careers, and are consequently less inclined to ask for a raise. And their employers, too, often consider their draftsmen as people preparing themselves to strike out on their own. A French study described the attitude of principals very clearly:

At the same time as they cry out against the demands for more pay by their draftsmen, and against social security costs and the intervention of the State, just as (any) owner of a small business, they tarry to call up a necessary community of thought between all the people working in the office, they think even of the employees as doubles of themselves, more preoccupied by architecture than by salaries and working hours[16].

It is this attitude, combined with the 'privilege' of working with a great master, which let some well-known architects get away with working conditions which would not be accepted in more mundane professions. Le Corbusier, for example, paid his draftsmen for the competition project for the League of Nations with a dinner, a railway ticket and autographed copies of *Vers une architecture* and *l'art décoratif d'aujourd'hui*[17]. Frank Lloyd Wright ran his office (and his household) for years with people who paid *him*, rather than the other way around[18]. And it is again this attitude which is behind the opinion of Robert A. Class, Director of the Management Division of the AIA:

Efforts toward unionization of architectural employees have so far been confined to small pockets of unrest. So long as employers continue to recognize that the intellectual and creative capacities of trained professionals are more important than the mere productive capacity of warm bodies, there will be little need for union activity[19].

If he is correct, then this attitude will be a considerable help to principals in running an economic office. But some employees *have* discovered that they are not all going to the top and that they had better unionize to protect themselves[15].

Big offices continue to grow at the expense of the small ones. This tendency is enhanced by the appearance of new techniques, such as computer-aided design, network planning, fast-track and design-build[6]. The small offices cannot afford to hire new specialists, conversant with these innovations, and do not have sufficient staff available to implement such a technique as design-build. As materials proliferate, buildings become larger and time-schedules shorter, more and more architects, even of middle-sized firms, have a hard time keeping up. So there are often complaints about their work:

A great number of architects live on Cloud 9 so far as their idea of the future is concerned. They're not keeping up with such techniques as project management, prefabrication, systems building and the like[20].

One effect of the mounting complexity of construction has been the invasion of the architect's field by other specialists. Actual construction is nowadays frequently managed by non-architects. Programming seems to be on its way out. Architects are obviously far from happy with this loss of territory. Vincent Kling on the program writers:

Every encounter we have had with so-called space planners, programmers, interior design coordinators and efficiency experts in office planning has left something to be desired. The largest office building we have done, for a governmental client, was programmed by such a group, but when it became time to move the people in, we had to rework almost every individual layout... Having an outside programmer undertake work that any architectural firm of substance does for itself and the client automatically sets up tension in the progress of the work... I don't feel that the advantages of a predigested written program, delivered by a nonarchitectural firm and saving the architect some leg work in looking at nuts and bolts, offsets the disadvantages of being detached from the investigation process during which time understandings, personal relationships, spontaneous outcroppings of clients' emotions and fresh responses of the architect are most likely to occur[21].

Besides programmers and construction managers there are also the package dealers, home-builders and engineering firms which are helping themselves to a slice of the architectural cake. Morris Lapidus voiced the concern of many architects when he wrote in 1967:

In all these instances and many others, the role of the architect is being offered by a firm not practicing architecture *per se*. They do not furnish the kind of impartial, ethical and professional services that are normally considered to be in the province of the practicing architect. So common has this become that the profession of architecture has become quite concerned. It has reached a point where The American Institute of Architects recently decided to evaluate the services being offered outside the profession, compared to those which the public, and more specifically the individual clients, have come to expect from the architect[22].

The losses of today are part of an ongoing process of division of labor. The eighteenth century architect Balthasar Neumann designed city plans, fortifications, canals, bridges and sewage systems besides the buildings for which he became famous. Vital parts of architects' projects today are designed by outsiders: the structural, mechanical and electrical work since the nineteenth century, the ventilation and the foundations since the early twentieth century[23]. The complaints about encroachments of civil engineers resemble those of today. The British architect W.H. Leeds wrote in 1862:

Mathematics have perhaps been too much neglected by some of the Architects of this country. The consequence has been the establishment of a new branch of art whose... professors are called Civil Engineers. As Art is open to all, we would not quarrel with these gentlemen, some of them possessing talents of the very highest nature, if they would be content with practicing strictly in their vocation. In their designs, even the best that they have produced, though cried up by their partisans, which they have in high places, there are many violations of architectural propriety, so that it would surely not be asking too much of them to submit to the advice and correction of those that have made the art of design the principal study of their lives[24].

By now, the quarrel with the structural engineers has been settled. It is the first specialty that a growing architectural office takes on as an in-house service. Relations of architects with their structural, mechanical and electrical consultants are usually satisfactory from the architects' point of view; one reason for that might be that these consultants are usually appointed by, and serving under the architect, in contrast to the programmer and construction manager.

Architects not only use specialists, they often become specialists themselves, doing primarily — or even only —

schools or shops and stores. More often than not, such specialization has not been sought by the architects themselves. It is the natural by-product of the process of selection. Many clients, before picking an architect, visit a number of recently finished buildings of the type they have in mind. If an architect has satisfied a particular client, he is likely to receive a similar commission.

There is also another form of specialization. Architecture is considered to be both a practical profession and an art. Some architectural firms concentrate primarily on the practical side of their profession, either by choice or forced by the nature of their briefs. These firms are outstanding for their fast, efficient service, for cost control, for smooth relations with the municipal authorities and for finishing their jobs on time. They build primarily for business: plants, offices and shopping centers. Monumental buildings, such as museums, town halls or churches, go often to another type: the artistic architect.

The 'practical' architect is oriented on service, the 'artistic' architect on creation. The reason for the differences between these two types will be further explored in chapter 6.

This form of specialization is not so clearly visible as that of the school or shopping center specialist. One reason for it is that all architects claim to be practical *and* creative, and the differences are usually papered over. Also, the transition between one type and another is gradual; many firms can make this claim with good reason.

But clients and architects are well aware that there *is* a difference. Phyllis Bronfman Lambert described how she made a successful effort to convince her father to hire a more artistic architect:

In 1954 Joseph E. Seagram and Sons at last decided to build on Park Avenue. I was living in Europe when Seagram's intent to build reached me in Paris in July through a rendering of a very mediocre building. I flew to New York and started to learn all I could about the good buildings built since the war, and I consulted with architectural critics. I felt that my task was to explain to my father, the president of the company, what the business's responsibility could mean in terms of architecture and to convince him of the new architectural thinking that started to mature in the twenties[25].

Ms Lambert's campaign ended in commissioning Mies van der Rohe and Philip Johnson (Fig. 1). And it had the effect she was after, for it put Seagram's on the architectural map. But building a monument has also some drawbacks, as Morris Lapidus — a practical architect who does not consider himself to be in the same (artistic) class as Mies — noted in an interview:

... the people in Seagram's achieved status because they sat against this impeccable historic background which no one could question; they had instant status... I visited the same chairman of the Seagram board many years later... sitting in his huge office in the Seagram Building of Mies van der Rohe. And here is this little man, only about five foot five or six. In the Chrysler building, he was seated behind my very modest

Figure 1
Seagram Building, New York,
1958. Architects: Ludwig Mies
van der Rohe and Philip Johnson.
According to Morris Lapidus, it
gave Seagram 'instant status', but
left the director perplexed (Ezra
Stoller photo)

but beautifully carved desk and he felt that he had arrived. Now, I see
him sitting behind a huge desk in a huge room with probably a half
million dollars' worth of art upon the walls, the finest woods and the
richest carpets, a little man in his huge office. In this conversation, he
said to me, 'Morris, you remember my first office which you
designed?' And I said, 'Yes'. He said, 'I enjoyed that.' Then he said,
'What do you think of this one?' and there was such a feeling of
uncertainty in his voice. He said, 'I look around me and I say, "What
does all this mean?"'[26].

Only artistic architects can confer instant status — at a price.

The distinction between artistic and practical architects is
all-pervasive. It determines the pecking order among architects
(discussed in Chapter 6): practical architects treat their artistic
colleagues with respect, artistic architects treat their practical

counterparts with contempt. Practical architects often express a desire to become, or to be seen as artistic; the reverse never happens. The preeminence of the artistic side has an effect on the management of offices. The 'art-work' — elevations, renderings — gets a great deal of attention, and even working drawings are often made with a view to aesthetic appeal not warranted by their use. The RIBA described this in its 1962 report *The Architect and his Office*:

Many offices were clearly wasting an enormous amount of time doing everything in ink with stencilled lettering, drawing in every course of brickwork and every glazing bar on working-drawing elevations and indulging in acres of shading, cross hatching and even coloured washes on prints ...[27].

The artistic ambitions of many architects tempt them to adopt the mannerisms of the 'misunderstood genius' and to try to circumvent their clients' criticism. I quote the RIBA report again:

Some... offices took the view that the less their clients saw of the projected design the better — particularly if committees were involved; others made a point of showing plans but never elevations or perspective; others again plainly regarded the whole problem of client relations as an unavoidable nuisance. These attitudes were characteristic of the architect who appears to look on his work more as an exercise in self expression (which he can get away with if he is lucky) than as a service to the community[28].

Artistic ambition has effects beyond rendering, color washes and beautiful models. It extends into the daily management of many an architectural practice, inducing the principal to consider labor relations, deadlines or cost estimates as matters of secondary importance, coming after his 'creative work'. It explains also the resistance to change of many architects. The RIBA report writes:

Some offices clearly subordinated the client's needs to their own aesthetic prejudices. We did not grade these highly. The 'adequate' offices strove conscientiously to achieve a balance even if they did not always succeed. Only two of the (44) visited offices had made themselves competent in modern techniques of work study and were using these to lead to a deeper understanding of the needs of the building user. We thought this was excellent but deplored the fact that such a small proportion had taken the initiative in a field which goes to the roots of the architect's stock in trade[29].

The ambition to 'create' rather than to 'serve' is probably also one of the root causes of the complaints of other professionals about architects. The RIBA report summarized a number of complaints of builders, quantity surveyors and engineering consultants about architects:

  (i) inability to coordinate the work of several people;
 (ii) inability to work to a timetable and cost limit;
(iii) inability to produce a coordinated set of clear drawings[30].

It is on these points that outstanding practical firms concentrate and get results. They can manage their office, and construction as well if necessary, they work to a timetable and within budget. George Heery about three schools which his firm designed in Florida:

Major accomplishments in these projects were significant time savings within relatively low construction costs and a high degree of flexibility in very human spaces[31].

These firms offer feasibility studies, marketing studies, site analysis and assist the client with his mortgage, contracts and public relations. Having a fair number of in-house specialists on their payrolls, they are of necessity large firms: Welton Becket; Daniel, Mann, Johnson and Mendenhall; Giffels and Rossetti; Smith, Hinchman and Grylls; Albert Kahn, etc. Their names are hardly known outside the USA, in contrast to their more artistic colleagues.

There is a good reason for that. With the increase of the payroll, an architectural firm loses some of its freedom to maneuver. To keep the business going, the principals have to accept all comers and be prepared to accept compromises. This is great for the satisfaction of the clients, but not a recipe for artistic masterpieces. Architects are well aware of this; *Fortune* reported on it in 1966:

... there is a curb on growth inherent in most of the best offices. The conscientious few — backed by much experience — take the view that the quality of work declines as the office grows. The best architectural firms stubbornly want to get smaller rather than bigger. Mies's office has only thirty people and he sighs, 'I always wanted a staff of five'. Louis Kahn has even fewer: when his staff went up to thirty-two several years ago, he told a visitor, 'It frightens me'. Philip Johnson, with determination, whittled down from fifty-five two years ago to thirty-five today. I.M. Pei and his three partners employ about seventy-five people, but Pei is obdurate about climbing over a hundred, despite a waiting line of prospective clients.

The truth is that running too big an office simply is not worth it to a first-rate architect interested primarily in design. Creativity is his main drive. He is able to pick and choose among the proffered jobs, thus be assured of interesting, ambitious clients, and the living is usually comfortable enough[32].

Yet, if he stays small, he will never get those very large jobs, which are so conspicuous in the landscape or on the skyline. For the very large client it is a pity too; the size of his job excludes the services of the more famous artistic architects.

A way around this dilemma is associated practice. The artistic architect designs, and his design is translated into contract documents and managed by the larger practical firm. The General Motors Building in New York was done by Edward Stone and Emery Roth, the General Motors Research Center in Warren, Michigan, by Saarinen in association with Smith, Hinchman and Grylls, the World Trade Center, New

York, by Yamasaki and Roth, and the Public Services Building in Portland, Oregon, by Michael Graves and again Roth.

One more department which many practical architects have and most artistic architects have not is 'business development', a euphemism for acquisition. A big office needs a continuous stream of commissions, and this cannot be left to chance. Large amounts of money are involved in any sizeable job, so there is a lot of elbowing going on. The bare outlines of one such operation were described in *Fortune* in 1958:

June 10, 1955. Chase Manhattan, soon after merger, buys 64,000 square-foot parcel fronting on Liberty Street from Guaranty Trust. New York S.O.M. partner Ed Mathews hears rumors Chase plans to build new headquarters building on site, consults colleagues, who call Owings in San Francisco, Owings flies in, puts out feelers, finally asks David Rockefeller, Chase executive vice president, to arrange informal meeting with Board Chairman John J. McCloy, President J. Stewart Baker, Rockefeller, other top bank officers. At meeting, top S.O.M. task force — Owings, plus New York partners Severinghaus, Brown, Mathews — states S.O.M. qualifications, indicates firm interested in submitting proposals for site. Bankers give S.O.M. green light to work out general plan on time-card basis — i.e. bank will pay labor plus overhead costs, not otherwise commit itself. Owings returns to West Coast[33].

Here the principals and partners did all the bird-dogging, which was natural in a job of this magnitude. On smaller jobs the way may be paved by a business development manager.

For acquisition, brochures are written, slide-shows made up, and architects attend business luncheons, conferences and club meetings, and are willing to sit on committees or boards. Architects are not selected from the yellow pages, so they must work for their own publicity. Here the artistic architects have some advantage over their practical colleagues, for their work is often published in trade magazines, and they can use copies of that as handouts. As the praise bestowed on their work in a journal is obviously not from their own hand, it is much more effective than a self-made brochure.

The building engineer of the American Telephone and Telegraph Company (the biggest client in the USA) enumerated in 1964 the dimensions on which an architectural office is scaled. Note that they are mainly practical:

The factors normally considered in the selection of an architect include such items as the size of the firm in relation to the job, its history, services furnished, ability as indicated by exhibits of work, amount of work designed and constructed in the last five years, proximity to the project, current workload, estimated time for completion of the project, number of technical personnel and the technical, educational and professional experience of the members of the firm[34].

He mentioned also that A.T.&T. tried to raise the quality of design by distributing awards to architects of recently completed A.T.&T. buildings.

The insistence on timetables and budgets by prospective clients is understandable. The art side, the creative aspect of the profession, attracts architectural students with artistic ambitions. The high status of artistic merit makes many architects put 'design' as the first item on the agenda, and makes them consequently treat practical aspects in a somewhat offhand manner. Mishaps (such as the Woodhull Hospital) contribute to the reputation which certainly not all deserve. As a spokesman for the large grocery chain A.&P. put it bluntly:

We look for an engineering firm unless we want fancy doodads[35].

Clients are therefore likely to stay on the safe side. Playing for safety increases when the selection of an architect is made by a committee, and when other people's money is involved.

As one architect noted, selection committees — both corporate and public:

'are as concerned with protecting themselves from criticism as they are in selecting the best firm. If the project is a doghouse, many committees will prefer to award it to a firm that has done eighty previous doghouses, for no one can criticize them for awarding the eighty-first'. A firm that best meets all the client's needs as well as makes itself the 'safe' decision will consequently get its share of projects[36].

Through this mechanism, many firms drift into a specialization on schools, shops or offices.

It is also obvious that if the choice will be 'safe', the architecture will probably be too. Experiments in design are not the thing to expect from a firm which makes itself the 'safe' decision; and the building committee, minding its vulnerability for criticism, would not favor them either. The social relations between the various participants go a long way towards explaining why so much architecture looks run-of-the-mill, or, in harsher terms, drab and dreary.

The process is reinforced by the moneylenders:

A uniquely architected home, for example, in contemporary styling with an abundance of glass panels, open fireplaces, and expanse of redwood deck is not favored by lending institutions just because it may have won a design award or enhances the area. It is more often looked upon as an expression of an individual's idiosyncrasy, on which they are reluctant to advance funds because they are concerned about its resale potential in a stock home market. Thus, penalizing it with a fifty to sixty percent loan instead of a seventy-five to eighty percent loan to value (which is the same as cost in this instance), they are exerting the negative influence of keeping imaginative design within bounds. It appears that only the wealthy or the bold, or both, may transgress those bounds[37].

The inclination towards 'normal simplicity' and away from 'fancy doodads' increases when a developer takes the initiative.

... the main criterion in a speculative builder's choice of an architect will be the goals he has in mind for the building. If, as in a majority of the office and apartment buildings built today, the aim is a maximum profit in a minimum amount of time, then economics will usually dictate the choice of an architect who has proved his cost-consciousness, but shown ability to capitalize on every square foot in the zoning envelope, and who is known to be able to turn out a set of plans at a low fee[38].

The lending institutions tend to concur, which is a help to the developer:

Few things are more sensitive than a borrower seeking money. Sensing that lenders base their outlays on two factors — income from the project and current replacement costs in the area — the borrower has responded to the challenge in a manner to be expected rather than admired. He has jacked up rentals to what he feels the traffic can bear, while reducing maintenance to what the lenders, or tenants, will allow; and he has inflated his construction or land costs so as to arrive at the highest value assignable to his project in order to offset the lender's paring.

While this has been reduced to a mathematical game for both sides, few bonuses are granted the builder who goes out of his way to create something of great merit or which reflects advanced design. Why should he, he reasons, since the real compensation lies elsewhere, and he is rarely in business for aesthetic satisfaction[39].

With all these constraints, prospects for artistic architects look bleak. But they do get a chance, once in a while, even in the speculative market:

After the success of the IIT buildings, Mies, then aged sixty, began a wholly new career as a designer of prestige apartment blocks and administrative offices — largely as a result of a meeting with a young property developer, Herbert Greenwald, who was rather more interested in erecting monuments ('putting his stamp on the scene', Blake quotes Mies as saying) than in making more and more money[40].

Greenwald commissioned Mies to design the Promontory and Lake Shore Apartments on the waterfront at Chicago, (Fig. 2). Some of the background of these projects was illuminated by another architect:

Victor Gruen ... was reminded of the time when the builder of the Lake Shore Apartments in Chicago, the late Herbert Greenwald, had expressed his admiration for Mies van der Rohe, who designed them. 'You know', he reported Greenwald as saying, 'he's a genius, and not only that, I can build him for $2 less per square foot than any other architect'. Mr. Gruen was very surprised by this, in view of the expensively pure exterior of the towers. 'That's true', he recalled Greenwald replying, 'but inside he lets me do what I want'.

Mr. Gruen: 'When you went inside the Lake Shore building, it became evident. The elevators were the cheapest things in all Chicago. Except in Greenwald's own apartment, the heating was terrible. The air conditioning was nonexistent, in spite of the completely glass walls — it had to be left out at the last minute, because something had to give — and the people in these apartments had to carry their garbage cans across the halls to the stairways, which would not be acceptable in a public housing project, and generally speaking the inside was shoddy and shabby. Yet you could find enough people who were, interestingly enough, so artistic that they wanted to live in that sculpture even with all the unpleasantness — like, for example, frying and freezing in it and being blinded by the sun'[41].

Figure 2
Lake Shore Apartments, Chicago,
1951. Architect: Ludwig Mies van
der Rohe. The expensively pure
exteriors were not matched by the
interiors (Ezra Stoller photo)

Greenwald was out of the ordinary, but not so far out as the first quotation suggested. He was undoubtedly pleased by the architectural renown of his apartments, but he was also a realist — the system wouldn't allow him to be anything else. Gruen's analysis of the character of the inhabitants seems correct; it tallies nicely with the data on Halen, discussed in chapter 4. Greenwald had discovered a hole in the market: there were enough Chicagoans with intellectual and artistic leanings — and yet not very much money — to want to live in one of his 'monuments'. So the expensive exterior fulfilled a clear function: it betokened to renters and visitors alike that a very special group of people was living there. The choice location helped of course too.

The problems of financing construction have an influence on more than design alone:

Taxes and wages went up, up and up some more. As wages became inflated, individual efficiency went down with the law of diminishing returns. New, larger and more productive equipment continued to be developed, effectively braking inflationary costs of machine operation. Work that had to be done by a man's hands however, became more and more expensive to the point of pricing itself out of the market[42].

The upward movement of construction costs, usually ahead of inflation, caused contractors and developers to exert a downward pressure on quality: cheaper materials, simpler and above all faster methods of work. American journeymen have protected themselves in their union contracts against speeding-up; but most of their European colleagues lack such protection. The continuous complaints about deteriorating standards of workmanship in new buildings are probably not unfounded; there is enough pressure to account for them.

The situation is aggravated by the peculiar forms of ownership:

The entrepreneur who puts together a new building often has to haggle for the site, the financing, the tenants, the contractor. He is inclined to tell the architects to give him something that will come in cheap, be painless to maintain, have the maximum ratio of net rentable area per floor, lots of glass, etc. (and that will thereby provide an excuse to shave the fee).

These are important entrepreneurial services and can earn a fat fee. However, the entrepreneur cannot afford a fee at the high surtax rates, so he takes ownership instead. What better way to make him a responsible developer? However, he has already figured out that he can maximize his after-tax profits by selling the fully rented building at a handsome capital gain to some conservative investor, who did not want the bother of putting together the deal. Since the first owner has quick resale in mind from the beginning, he has only a minimum incentive to consider quality. To the conservative investor, if the income is assured, his main concern is satisfied. Pride in a building built to last and remain a good neighbor is not encouraged by this system of taxation[43].

Nobody really feels responsible for the technical quality: neither the developer, nor the contractor, nor the final owner. It is the tenants who have to cope with leaking roofs, malfunctioning drains and peeling paint. Even the lending institutions, whose money runs a risk being tied up in a low-quality project, show often little interest in checking this development:

Since lenders do not reduce their loans for poorer quality construction by the same percentage ratio as the savings to builders, they indirectly encourage the cheaper construction[44].

A number of factors coalesce to make a building a harder and riskier operation now than it was thirty years ago.

Construction workers under continuous pressure to produce more for their wages, regardless of quality, have lost a part of their professional pride in their work. They, too, can read the handwriting on the wall and see that developers are not really keen on durability. Operations have been rationalized and streamlined to save another dollar; a bricklayer who has never made an arch, a plasterer who has never turned a cove (except perhaps as an apprentice) is unable to do so when the occasion arises.

Quality control was always a problem in the building industry. It grows worse when buildings increase in size, whenever larger crowds of journeymen are involved in the job and when the pipelines between the main office, the job superintendent and the crews become longer and longer. The organization for any building was always *ad hoc*, but the network of communication can wear so thin that it disappears. People no longer know what the other fellow is doing, and they often do not care to know.

The same dangers threaten the architect's work. If he uses outside consultants for structural and mechanical engineering, a number of the construction drawings will be made outside his office; will they match with his own work? In a small office, or in a large one organized on the 'federation' principle, there is a specific group of people who know themselves to be responsible for a particular building. But an office run on the assembly-line principle has often only a job captain and a supervisor with such a responsibility; they are unable to check and recheck details and dimensions to make sure that everything fits together.

Technical complexity has grown enormously. A job superintendent of today cannot see at a glance that the reinforcement of a certain part of a floor is insufficient for the load; he has to rely blindly on the structural engineers. And they, in turn, have to rely on the draftsman, who more often than not will never see the job.

As buildings grow in size, they are of necessity drawn at an ever smaller scale. The German sociologist Peter Gleichmann has pointed out that such schematic drawings become very unreal to the people drawing them; an abstraction enhanced by the ever larger number of people operating on or with these schematics and unable to communicate face-to-face with each other[45].

The problems are compounded by the relative 'uniqueness' of every architectural design. The teething troubles of a new car model are thrashed out in pre-trial runs and sometimes in a model which is not quite up to standard, but will be in next year's edition. But a building is a one-shot operation; contractors and architects may learn from some mistakes, but in the next job everything will be different and offer an opportunity to make new mistakes, in wholly different areas.

The present problems of building construction were not consciously created; no one has actively *designed* the technical and social constraints[46]. Weight of building materials and costs of transportation led to a localized and atomized industry; economic circumstances forced contractors and subcontractors to participate in several jobs at the same time, thereby preventing a tightly organized and integrated form of production. Decentralized control and the concomitant weak organization were, in my opinion, bound to lead to complaints about management when building operations started to grow in scale, and hence to the appearance of the construction manager as a corrective. With hindsight, each phase in the process follows naturally from the preceding one — but there was no plan, no 'conspiracy' to rob architects' prerogatives.

A process which involves so many people, connected by such a tenuous and opaque network of power relations and often working with such sophisticated and risky techniques, is bound to misfire from time to time. Mishaps may occur in deadlines and cost, as in the Woodhull Hospital, or in technology.

Buildings designed by the best-known American architects have been suffering ignoble ailments. principally cracking and leaking roofs and glass walls. The most notorious of these is the John Hancock Building in Boston, by the office of Ieoh Ming Pei, who this year was awarded the American Institute of Architects' gold medal, the top tribute of his fellow architects.

Hancock commissioned Pei in 1967 to build a skyscraper in the Back Bay. Pei and his principal design partner, Henry Cobb, devised a sixty-two-storey tower proportioned as slimly as a fashion model, sequined in reflective-glass panels. Before the building was occupied, hundreds of the glass panels cracked and some fell out, scattering shards below, which made it necessary to cordon off the sidewalks. All 10,344 glass panels were then removed, and the building was rewalled in stronger glass at a cost of $8.2 million. Later, Hancock spent another $17.5 million to stiffen the building's lean frame, and to install two 300-ton adjustable counterweights near the top to help stabilize the structure against the push of wind. Hancock's employees and tenants finally moved into the building in 1976, but some of the new windows have since cracked, too[47].

Of course lawsuits for reclaiming the damages followed in the wake of each building failure. Insurance premiums soared:

Malpractice insurance is now the second-to-third-largest business expense for many architects and engineers, and is inexorably driving up the cost of building[48].

Building failures and shoddy speculative construction are not peculiar to our age; they have been around since the building trades became a specialty. Europe was littered in the late Middle Ages with the debris of collapsed churches. Only the most solid and durable buildings of the Middle Ages are still standing today, giving their builders an undeserved reputation for solidity.

Poor construction endangered not only the owner but also his neighbors. Municipal authorities attempted to regulate and control building operations from the Middle Ages. As the medieval city consisted of mainly wooden houses, often built close together, fire was the main hazard. In 1212, London issued regulations which tried to combat the inflammable thatched roofs. [49].

The modern building codes date in substance from the last quarter of the nineteenth century, and were created as a corrective to the speculative housing of the Industrial Revolution. By establishing minimum standards and by allowing control of drawings and calculations and on-site inspection, the building codes have provided a check on the tendency to continuous reduction of quality and ever greater risktaking in construction. Though they could not prevent all mishaps, they have prevented quite a few; the knowledge that their work would be minutely examined in the building department has made architects and engineers watch their step. Building codes are by nature conservative; but the view that they hamper technical progress should be balanced by a consideration of the very real benefits that they have brought.

Restricted by building codes and zoning regulations, inhibited by the requirements of his engineers and confined by his brief, the architect is far from a free agent. He holds some strings, but certainly not all, and probably not the most important. Because his contribution to the building is far more visible and tangible than that of the engineers or of the building code, he is inclined to overrate it.

It seems to me that the major source of power of the architect lies in his straddling two large and vital cultural domains. He is both an artist *and* a technician. The former confers a cultural status on him which he uses to keep the pure technicians, the engineers, at bay. As a technician he relates to the world of finance and construction; it makes his position much more complex, but also much more secure than that of a poet or sculptor. His command of two specialties gives him a strategic advantage over engineers and over other artists. Of course he is often decried by the artists as a philistine who sells his artistic integrity for some shekels, and by the engineers as a half-baked technician. But the two tracks do reinforce each other. Engineers cannot provide anything remotely resembling the 'instant status' of the Seagram Building or the Lake Shore Apartments, and artists are technically unable to design a building of some complexity. Both domains require hard work; this is clear for the technical but it also holds for the artistic. The architect has to keep up with the latest stylistic developments, be conversant with what goes on in architectural design elsewhere and how this is regarded by his peers and the critics (this will be further discussed in chapter 6).

His position at the interface has given him his power over the other advising professionals, the structural and mechanical engineers. They are *his* consultants, and *he* advises the client which firms should be asked. Being one of the earliest outsiders to get involved in the planning process, he has also a considerable amount of power over contractors: he usually advises the client which firms should be invited to bid.

Of course his power is considerably diminished if he has a

builder as client, or works as an employee in a construction firm. Developers, too, often have direct connections with contractors, which reduces their architects' grip. It made at least one well-known American architect, John Portman, do his own developing[50].

Associations of architects in all western countries have tried to reinforce their position of establishing a legally enforced monopoly in their field. Nearly everywhere they have only been partially succesful (the exception being Belgium). Some countries protect title and practice, but are lax in enforcing the law; others protect the title only. There are historical and socioeconomic grounds for the failure to achieve complete protection. In the past, architects were only involved in a minute portion of all building operations. The houses of New England colonists, the extensions of Georgian London or the vast tracts of nineteenth century speculative housing were all built without architects. Farm buildings were (and often are still) constructed and designed by a local carpenter, or by the farmer himself. Only in the twentieth century have architects succeeded in acquiring a larger share of the total market. But the original self-builders did not let go of their prerogatives without a fight. Thirteen states in the USA exempt farm buildings from the obligation to have an architect as designer, ten states exempt all single-family dwellings[51]. The large financial interests of home-builders and the obviousness of their case prevented the architects' complete victory.

Civil engineers could press a good claim too. They had also been operating in the construction field for ages, building bridges, hangars, garages and sheds; why should they have to accept architectural interference?

Perhaps the greater conflict has arisen over claims for exemption for structures designed by engineers. These claims have usually been asserted on the grounds that engineering projects often involve buildings incidental to industrial, transport, power, and other enterprises for which engineers can supply all necessary services. Whatever the justice of such claims may be, many acts have been forced to exclude such incidental structures from their jurisdiction or to permit design by either profession[51].

All protective regulation of the profession is due to the lobbying of architects' associations. Their lofty pronouncements of today, dealing with public welfare and national culture, show no trace of their more pedestrian objectives. When they were founded, they sometimes showed their hand. The following is from the foundation manifesto of 1903 of the Bund Deutscher Architekten, the German parallel to the AIA:

We see the greatest danger for our artistic life, the most malicious opponents of our own efforts, in the unscrupulous speculators, who without ideals, swayed only by greed, exploit the otherwise beneficial freedom of enterprise. In the extensive new suburbs of our cities we meet everywhere the cold commercial spirit, the blunt spiritual poverty of the building bunglers... The artistically creative architect has long ago lost his influence on the construction of the streets in our new suburbs — here is the realm of the contractor, educated in a lower technical school, who can assume the title of architect with impunity, because this designation appears advantageous to him; and the pitiful members of our class, who perforce have to work for these people, have to content themselves with a pittance... Here is a wide field of endeavour for our association: what matters now is to gain influence on the customs in building and on the building codes, by industrious activity, also of the local groups, by enlightening lectures, by the press, and in particular by the delegation of representatives of our class to the municipal committees, to obtain justice for our real and esthetic demands and to reconquer a rich field for artistic creation[52].

An architects' association is a conscious effort to structure the profession and gain some social control; it is designed, planned, propagated and organized. The majority of social relations are, however, unplanned: the outcome of an ongoing tug-of-war between the various groups concerned. The lines of communication have lengthened when more and more actors appeared on the scene, and the operation of construction has become remote and abstract.

Not only for architects and contractors, but also for clients and users. Bronfman, the president of Seagram's, felt somewhat alienated in his new office; but at least he had decided himself that that was what he was going to get. What about his employees? Were they consulted?

Most people today have to work, shop and play in architectural environments on which they did not have any influence in the planning stage and with which they have the most tenuous of emotional relations. These buildings were ostensibly created for them, but more often than not on the philosophy of what was 'good for them'.

The pinch is felt hardest in the home. A number of families can afford to buy their houses, so the developers have to pay attention to people's likes and dislikes in architecture:

The product must not violate local market expectations as to what a house should look like. These are some of the things that are involved: the design motif should not be Early American in California and should not be 'California' in the Northwest suburbs of Philadelphia. The roof pitch should not exceed a one-foot deviation from the expected norm in any area. The roof pitch of a house is enough to make it somewhat difficult to sell, e.g. a straight roof when the market expects a hip roof is enough to kill the sale. The absence of brick as a primary exterior material on a house is enough to keep the house from selling in a market where brick is the expected norm... The cookie cutter approach to houses does not work in the market place where the customer has a choice and where the price makes any difference[53].

A far cry from 'good, modern architecture'; no wonder that developers in the housing markets turn to practical architects — *if* they use an architect at all.

The users of public housing have no such options; they have to accept what others thought up for them. Before the Second

World War, public housing contributed only a minute fraction to the total housing market. The destructions of the war and the backlog in building construction set large public housing programs in motion after 1945, particularly in Europe. A much larger segment of the population used it; when its standard of living rose in the sixties, it no longer accepted everything that was being offered, and protest movements and tenants' associations got under way. They were enhanced by the changes in the social structure of housing supply. Before 1939, public housing in Germany, Holland and Scandinavia was usually organized by relatively small, locally based housing associations. Their boards, consisting mainly of working-class people, collected the subsidies from the government, selected the architects and approved the plans. With the sudden increase in their activities after 1945, these boards were gradually emasculated. State officials, trying to limit the rising costs, clamped down on standards of design; more professional men were invited as board members to try to wrangle a better deal from the officials; and the associations grew in size. The upshot of it all was that the lines of communication between the individual tenant and the authority which decided on the plans lengthened considerably; here, too, there was an increase in alienation. As in building construction, this alienation was the unplanned but inevitable outcome of a series of steps, each of which taken by itself was logical enough. Tenants' associations which arose on a purely local level, often by block or street, succeeded in obtaining a right to criticize and to participate in decisions affecting their homes in Germany and Holland.

In the USA the scale of public housing is much smaller than in Europe. Public housing is believed to be 'socialistic' — it is — and held at arm's length. Renters are considered to be 'job-mobile, not saving, having no choice', whereas home-owners are seen as 'independent, nontransient, taking better care'[54]. The high status of ownership (much higher than in Europe), the relative weakness of planning and the larger amount of available open space has led to a specifically American solution for low-income housing: the mobile home park, in which no home is ever moved an inch (Fig. 3).

We would suggest that the largest group of trailer dwellers are young lower middle class working families who are looking for a better way of life but cannot yet afford to buy a permanent home in the suburbs. The residents of trailer housing, thus, may view their home on wheels as an inexpensive escape into suburbia which will enable them to save for a permanent home while being able to immediately get one foot in the suburban door. Thus, the attractiveness of mobile home living lies not in its 'mobileness', but, instead, in having a place to call one's own home and perhaps a small garden and a lawn on which family barbecues may be held[55].

This quotation suggest that the idyll of suburban life is just around the corner; but reality is somewhat different.

Figure 3
Mobile home, Minneapolis. The cheapest version of the suburban dreamhouse. Shutters added by the owner to make it look more like a house and less like a trailer

Many manufacturers encourage their employees to push units down the assembly line through an incentive system which rewards speed, but not quality of workmanship. The manufacturers worry more about 'flash', such as so-called colonial laterns and 'Spanish' decor, than they do about whether the floor buckles. The dealers make their money by selling finance paper to the banks, so it is to their advantage to puff up a deal with as many extras as possible. When it comes to making repairs guaranteed under the warranty they disappear into their own plastic woodwork.

Many park owners are little Hitlers. They know that space in mobile home parks is limited by unreasonable zoning laws, so they treat residents of 'Moburbia, U.S.A.' with scorn. Some require their tenants to purchase heating oil, and even milk, from vendors who give the park owner a kickback. Park rules are often Draconian. In some parks, a tenant has to have the owner's permission to have the tenant's own mother stay overnight[56].

The mobile home is not a building, and thus falls outside the standards of the building code. Europe has its trailer camps too, but they are generally inexpensive second homes for recreation, and now allowed for permanent occupation.

One advantage of an owned home is that you can change it to suit your personal needs. With relatively new rental housing this is not permitted, and there, too, rules are often Draconian. Landlords of older housing projects are often more lenient, requiring only that the original state be restored when the tenant moves house.

Changing the house is the usual way to get around the standards imposed by the architect and original owners. It is the most universal form of architectural criticism. A famous example is the housing project at Pessac of 1925, designed by Le Corbusier and changed beyond recognition by the tenants. Its analyst, the architect Philippe Boudon, has ascribed the changes in part to the 'open plan', thus turning them into another feather in the cap for Le Corbusier[57]. To me they look more like an incisive criticism.

Another method to obtain a home to your own liking is to build it yourself. It was once the prevalent form of house-building, and it still is in all the underdeveloped countries — i.e. in most of the world. As more and more building was brought under the building code and more land under planning and zoning regulations, this form of architecture-without-architects became increasingly difficult in the western countries. It never died out completely, however, and the recent wave of criticism of the built environment has increased the interest for it[58].

Finally, the harshest form of criticism of the built environment is vandalism. Only a part of vandalism can be imputed to a critical attitude towards the buildings *per se*. For instance, when a high-school kid smashes the director's window in the school it is the man he reacts against, not the building. But a part of vandalism can be ascribed to the buildings, and in particular to the value-system they embody:

When men act against their physical environments as they do in the case of industrial sabotage and vandalism, their activity contains within it conceptions of the origins and meaning of that environment. In the past we have been too ready to assume that the activity was somehow entailed by the nature of the environment (e.g. its drabness, its monotony) or by certain territorial or biological givens (e.g. ideas of maximum density) or by particular proxemic necessities (e.g. the need for particular amounts of personal space). We have thereby paid too much attention to the characteristics of the environment and not enough to the conceptualisations of the actor... We should take care therefore not to attribute some primitive aesthetic sense to working class childen who smash up their council flats or the public flower displays. They may aesthetically prefer the flats and the flowers to the town slums and open bombed sites which they knew before, but they do know now that the flats and the flowers are not theirs. It is their meaning and not their intrinsic quality which is being reacted to. No amount of objective environmental manipulation will dissipate the destructive behaviour in this situation[59].

The building industry is treated in this book as if it were uniform throughout the western world. There are of course important differences from one country to another[60].

The size of construction firms varies considerably. Very large firms occur only in large countries like the USA or in the United Kingdom, which offer sufficient scope either within their own boundaries or in their former colonies. Western Germany has very few main contractors; the coordination of the subcontractors there has to be done by the architects.

The average technical quality of building is high in Germany, Switzerland and Scandinavia, fair in the USA, the United Kingdom and Holland, and low in France and Italy. The stringency of the building codes (they vary enormously from town to town even within such small countries as Holland or Belgium) varies with building quality, being on the average high in Switzerland and low in Italy.

Most European countries have stricter zoning regulations than the USA. Partly this is due to historical development; planning is an old-established activity in densely populated Europe. Partly it has to do with national political ideals; rugged individualism was never so idealized and promoted to a national philosophy in Europe as it was in the USA. Much more attention is therefore paid in Europe to the context of a new building, how it relates to its neigbors.

Most western countries have legislation protecting the title of 'architect' (Holland excepted). Only Belgium has created a legal monopoly for registered architects, but the legislators show a tendency to move in that direction in other countries too.

The involvement of architects in the total built volume varies considerably. It approaches 80% in the USA, in Great Britain and Switzerland, and goes below 30% in France and Italy.

Architects' offices are small on the average all over the western world; large firms occur only in the USA and in the UK. Several countries make it their custom to organize competitions for every public building: Finland, Germany. In Switzerland, such competitions are obligatory. This system promotes the creation of new small offices, because the competitions are often won by young architects.

All western countries have architects working as officials. Great Britain is exceptional in having such a large proportion: 40% of the total number of architects.

Most architectural offices in western countries are run on similar lines, the architects being responsible for design, specifications, estimates, working drawings and supervision of the construction. The UK is again exceptional in having quantity surveyors for estimating and spec-writing. In France, detailing and working drawings are done by special firms, not attached to the designing architect. Programmers and construction managers are beginning to appear in Europe too.

The difference between the various countries are profound, but they do not touch the main theses of this book. In outlook, ideals, self-image, in education, mode of practice or degree of specialization, the similarities are more striking than the differences, I contend.

In this chapter, the positions of the architect were examined: in relation to his clients, to the construction industry, to his consultants and to his competitors. Each of these positions has an effect on architectural design. The strong position *vis-à-vis* 'his' contractors and 'his' consultants has encouraged some architects to take a rather casual stance about the technical problems in these areas; details are not checked for ease of manufacture, structural work and ducts have to be fitted in as an afterthought. The weak position *vis-à-vis* the client forces many architects to adopt forms more traditional than they would personally prefer, and is one of the reasons why so many become 'practical' rather than 'artistic' architects. The 'power' of the architect was estimated to stem from his dual competence: a technician in comparison to a pure artist and an artist in comparison to a pure technician. Many threads come together in the architect's hands: form, construction, cost and supervision. But the position looks stronger than it really is: the organization of the building team is weak and temporary. There is a similarity here to the influence of buildings on the behaviour of the users: a real influence exists, but it also looks more than it really is. Perhaps we may guess that these two points both contribute to the illusion of many an architect, i.e. that he is marked out as a social reformer. Having some real power, and being close to much more which escapes him, might make any man dream of a position of true leadership. The exaggerated claims in this area have certainly helped to make the architect the obvious scapegoat for the quality of the built environment, when criticism started to rise in the seventies.

Economic prudence acts as a check on architectural experiments. This tendency towards the routine in design is probably reinforced by the modern techniques of *fast-track* and *design-build*, which can only be practised on highly conventional buildings. The 'freedom' of the architect, already severely circumscribed, is diminishing in many areas.

3 The Evolution of the Profession

Buildings of some volume and solidity have always been made by professionals, but the architect — a trained and registered specialist, who works full-time on the design and realization of buildings — is a creation of the nineteenth century. There are some constants in the process of building (such as the independence and atomization of the various parts of the workforce), but the architect is not one of them.

Chaos prevailed after the fall of the Roman Empire, as wave after wave of tribes invaded Europe, each wave resisted by the settled inhabitants and, once it had found its niche, itself resisting all newcomers. Permanent unsafety forced people to leave the cities and try to subsist in the countryside.

A new social fabric only gradually emerged. The early Middle Ages are full of local raids, shifting alliances and toppled rulers. Slowly some feudal lords gained a modicum of control over their vassals and established a semblance of regional government.

The well-organized Roman building industry survived in the Eastern Empire but disappeared in the West. The hamlets that arose, on the moors, at the water's edge, or under the protection of a castle, were of the most primitive kind: mud huts, the thatched roofs supported by poles, and a few of the more solid houses framed in timber. Building technology reached an all-time low[1].

It slowly recovered when the dust settled on the battlefields. Villages grew into towns, old Roman cities were restored, providing a field of operation large enough for such specialized craftsmen as carpenters to find work in. Roman techniques, such as the manufacture of rooftiles, bricks and glass, lost during the age of the great migrations, were rediscovered. By the end of the twelfth century the technical level of the Romans was approached again in the larger towns, though only in a modest proportion of the buildings. There were carpenters, joiners, tilers, slaters, thatchers, plumbers, glaziers and painters, organized in local craft guilds.

A leading role in the gradual improvement was played by the most expensive and durable buildings constructed in stone (and later also in brick). Building in stone had never entirely stopped, but it had become exceedingly rare. It was of course reserved for the most powerful clients: the noble lords and the bishops and abbots of the Church. The great cost and rarity of stone or brick buildings made it impracticable for the masons, bricklayers and stonecutters to unite in local guilds, according to Salzman: there would not be enough work for them[2]. Probably for that reason they associated in the lodges, which travelled from job to job.

Construction in durable materials was encouraged by the conditions in the towns. The unsafety of the times made defensive military constructions mandatory, in the form of stockades, earthworks and even sometimes brick walls. Towns offered freedom to serfs and safety to all the inhabitants, both powerful inducements; the area within their walls became densely settled. Sparks from the fires for cooking or heating easily set fire to the thatched roofs; once a single house caught fire, a whole area and sometimes the whole town burned down. Large fires are reported in 1161 in London, Exeter and Canterbury; Winchester was largely destroyed in 1161 and again in 1180. Municipal authorities issued building regulations, first to forbid thatched roofs (London 1212)[3] and later to prescribe incombustible partywalls. The wooden cities slowly 'petrified'.

As safety increased and economic conditions through agrarian inventions improved, the standard of living rose and commerce started to flourish. The traditional patrons for the 'best kind of buildings', from the nobility and the church, were joined by the rising class of merchants. All medieval patrons, but particularly those in the early Middle Ages, tended to claim that they had built this particular abbey or that particular church. (To a certain extent they still do so today.) The claim preempted the role of the professional designer, and not always entirely without justification. For who is the 'designer' if Ratgar, abbot at Fulda, orders a copy of St Peter's in Rome — even corresponding in the dimensions — to be built as his abbey church[4]? Between 800 and 1100, about a dozen copies of Charlemagne's Chapel in Aix-la-Chapelle were built, some of them (in Bruges, Liege, Louvain, Muizen, Nijmegen and Ottmarsheim) closely resembling the original (Fig. 4), some of them (in Germigny, Mettlach and Hereford) attested as intended copies by documentary evidence[5]. Who other than the patrons who ordered them could be called the 'designers'?

As building technology became more sophisticated in the later Middle Ages, design grew in importance and complexity

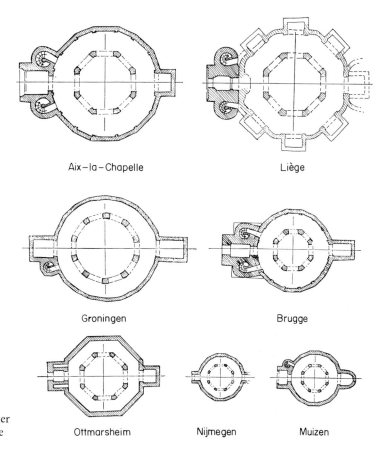

Figure 4
The plan of the royal chapel at
Aix-la-Chapelle (798) and its later
imitations, all drawn to the same
scale

Aix–la–Chapelle   Liège

Groningen   Brugge

Ottmarsheim   Nijmegen   Muizen

and the hitherto nameless 'architects' stepped forward from the
wings. Nearly all of them had been trained for seven years as
masons and stonecutters and had worked for an additional two
to three years as assistants to another 'architect'. Their
professional competence, apart from a first-hand knowledge of
stonecutting, consisted chiefly of a versatility in practical
geometry and drawing. This was the jealously guarded 'secret
of the lodges', which gave them their lead over the other
craftsmen[6]. Geometry allowed them to design the complex
vaulting systems, to determine the exact shape of a keystone on
the ground and to cut a series of details such as pinnacles or
gables of different sizes but of the same proportions. The
power that geometry gave them to perform these complex
tasks, and the obvious fact that the stability of a wall or column
depends on the proportion between height and thickness, led
them to the erroneous belief that their mathematical knowledge
also held the key to structural solidity[6].

The lack of theoretical knowledge of the strength of materials
also facilitated a rather off-hand design procedure. The
medieval designer did not provide his client with a coordinated
set of plans, sections and elevations, as his modern counterpart

does. Design progressed with the job: the plan and a general idea of what was going to be built (sometimes illustrated by a model) was first decided upon, then excavations and foundations were made, and building started. On larger buildings, such as cathedrals, construction dragged on for decades; the original architect often did not live to see the completion of his work. His successor felt free to vary — and sometimes alter considerably — the original design. It has been demonstrated recently that even such an apparently coherent building as Amiens Cathedral has a nave of a height considerably larger than originally envisaged[7]. Details such as mouldings, rib-profiles, window heights and subdivisions, setbacks and pinnacles were all decided upon when the time arrived for their construction.

There was no standard system for the division of responsibilities in the Middle Ages. Often the master-mason who made the design was also the contractor for all the work in stone or brick, hiring the working crews, paying their wages and buying the materials. Sometimes the materials were bought directly by the client. A general contractor was unknown; only rarely was the master-mason responsible for other crafts besides his own. The client contracted the carpentry, roofing, and plumbing, glazing or painting separately and directly with the different crafts concerned. Rarely too was an architect hired only for the making of drawings.

Larger jobs often had a clerk-of-works who took care of the financial handling of the materials and wage-lists. He was an administrative official and not a technician; on churches and abbeys a cleric often fulfilled this function[8].

At the end of the Middle Ages, around 1400, Europe had again a well-developed building industry at its disposal. It differed from its Roman counterpart in its lack of a strong hierarchy of command; the individual craft guilds and lodges were more independent from one another. This necessitated the control and coordination by a clerk-of-works. Technically, Roman construction was equalled and in some respects surpassed. Stonecutting (and to a smaller degree carpentry) had reached a level of technical virtuosity that was never to be surpassed again, and actually fell off considerably in the Renaissance and after.

The technical proficiency reached in the Middle Ages and the social organization of the crafts in separate guilds were the solid foundations of the building industry in the period after 1400. Technical innovations between 1400 and 1800 were few and far between. Tools, techniques and materials were only marginally improved upon: glass panes became gradually larger and more transparent, bricks more regular in shape and size, water-driven sawmills replaced handicraft. As roads and canals improved, transport became gradually cheaper. The once abundant supply of wood became depleted as more and more people used it on an ever larger scale for ships, buildings and to keep themselves warm.

The period between 1400 and 1800 is not marked by major changes in building technology, but by a change in forms. The medieval construction techniques and the medieval guild organization were used to create Renaissance architecture. It made little difference to contracting or to building operations, but it made a difference in design and therefore in the position of the designer.

A new type of designer arose: the artist-architect. He did not have a solid training in masonry, stonecutting or carpentry, but he shared with the master-mason a knowledge of geometry and projective methods (albeit a more limited and less practical knowledge) and the ability to draw. The master-mason continued to exist (and to design); in fact it was to him that the artist-architect had to confide the execution of his drawings. The technical abilities of the various crafts on the one hand, and the lack of a strong hierarchy in the building industry on the other, allowed the artist-architect to interfere in the process of design. No single group had obtained a monopoly over design and construction; there was no general contractor, no set formula for a designer. The lead of the master-masons in geometrical abilities over others had only an effect on their handicraft colleagues, but not on painters or on other people trained in geometry and drawing.

The master-masons very naturally demurred, and advanced their technical knowhow as the basis of their claim on the design function. The artists countered by claiming the superiority of design over technique. Leon Battista Alberti wrote around 1460:

It is the Property and Business of the Design to appoint to the Edifice and all its Parts their proper Places, determinate Number, just Proportion and beautiful Order; so that the whole Form of the Structure be proportionable. Nor has this Design any thing that makes it in its Nature inseparable from Matter; for we see that the same Design is in a Multitude of Buildings, which have all the same Form, and are exactly alike as to the Situation of their Parts and the Disposition of Their Lines and Angles; and we can in our Thought and Imagination contrive perfect Forms of Buildings entirely separate from Matter, by settling and regulating in a certain Order, the Disposition and Conjunction of the Lines and Angles. Which being granted, we shall call the Design a firm and graceful pre-ordering of the Lines and Angles, conceived in the Mind, and contrived by an ingenious Artist...
The Arts which are useful, and indeed absolutely necessary to the Architect, are Painting and Mathematicks[9].

Alberti always had technical help in the execution of his own architectural designs: Luca Fancelli on his two churches in Mantua, Bernardo Rossellino on the Rucellai Palace and Giovanni di Bertino on the facade of Santa Maria Novella in Florence, Matteo de Pasti on the Tempio Malatestiano in

Rimini[10]. Some of the most famous artists of the Renaissance occupied themselves with architectural design. Leonardo sketched a number of churches, Rafael designed a church and a palace and was for some time in charge of the new St Peter's, and Michelangelo had a successful and distinguished career as an architect.

The divorce between handicraft and design was accompanied by a dramatic rise in status. The artists of the Renaissance, and the architects among them, succeeded in transferring their work from the 'mechanical' to the 'liberal' arts, from bricklaying, weaving and joining to mathematics, rhetoric and theology. Architecture turned from an almost exclusively practical profession into a more learned one.

The split in the profession had effects on professional practice. Coordinated sets of plans, sections and elevations became more necessary and more usual and gradually replaced models. Working details were still decided during the course of construction, or left to the discretion of the contractor, who also remained responsible for the stability of the building[11]. As architectural design began to depend on forms and theory rather than on practical experience, books began to appear: a trickle in the fifteenth and sixteenth centuries, a river in the seventeenth and a flood of them in the eighteenth. Most of them dealt with the 'good examples' of 'ancient' (Roman) architecture and the proportions of classical columns and entablatures, but also with theory and interpretations. Patrons of the Middle Ages in England and Germany had hired French master-masons to get a Gothic church; in the seventeenth century they could use a book. The could also try their hand at design themselves. Some architects even encouraged them to do so, provided they had the necessary Taste; James Gibbs wrote in 1728 in the preface of the portfolio of his designs:

... such a Work as this would be of use to such Gentlemen as might be concerned in Building, especially in the remote parts of the Country, where little or no assistance for Designs can be procured. Such may be here furnished with Draughts of useful and convenient Buildings and proper Ornaments; which may be executed by any Workman who understands Lines, either as here Design'd, or with some Alteration, which may be easily made by a person of Judgment; without which a Variation in Draughts, once well digested, frequently proves a Detriment to the Building, as well as a Disparagement to the person who gives them. I mention this to caution Gentlemen from suffering any material Change to be made in their Designs, by the Forwardness of unskilful Workmen, or the Caprice of ignorant, assuming Pretenders[12].

Gibbs' book was widely used, not only in the 'remote parts of the country', but also in the American colonies. The well-known type of the New England church with its illogical combination of a colannaded portico surmounted by a steeple is taken from his book[13].

Though architectural design was clearly defined, the profession of architect was not. There were gentlemen-architects, artist-architects and craftsman-architects[14]. The greatest German architect of the eighteenth century, Balthasar Neumann, was originally a military engineer and cannon-founder, the most famous English eighteenth-century architects were Wren, a mathematician, and Vanbrugh, a soldier and playwright. Architects like Le Vau, Inigo Jones, Wren, Chambers and Adam engaged in speculative building as a sideline to their other professional activities[15].

But if the profession was permissive in its standards and rather vague at the fringes, it was clear enough at the center by the eighteenth century. In the larger cities, an architect was a man engaged full-time in the design and supervision of the execution of buildings. He had been trained in an architect's office. He was an artist first and a technician in the second place. Being only engaged in construction in a supervisory role, he could take on several jobs at once, thereby meeting the rising demand of the growing middle class. Though he could act as a speculative builder on his own account, his clients expected him to be independent on their jobs, for he had to control the quality of work of the contractor. The control function gained in importance as the lump sum contract ('by the great') and the general contractor became more and more usual in Britain[16]. Low bids to get the job could easily lead to skimping on materials and hasty execution. Building became more a business than a craft. Workmanship in the later eighteenth century tended to decline as large-scale speculative development and speed of construction both increased[17]. Competitive tendering appeared in the eighteenth century and became an accepted way of contracting in the first half of the nineteenth century in Britain, increasing the need for outside control[16]. Master-masons and carpenters continued to offer complete services including design, for they could use the pattern books as well as anyone; in fact, a large proportion of the eighteenth-century literature was aimed directly at them[18]. But it was natural for the 'true architect' to mark off his own position by contrasting it with that of the builder. John Soane has left us a remarkably modern description of the architect as he saw him in 1788:

The business of the architect is to make the designs and estimates, to direct the works and to measure and value the different parts; he is the intermediate agent between the employer, whose honour and interest he is to study, and the mechanic, whose rights he is to defend. His situation implies great trust; he is responsible for the mistakes, negligences, and ignorances of those he employs; and above all, he is to take care that the workmen's bills do not exceed his own estimates. If these are the duties of an architect, with what propriety can his situation and that of the builder, or the contractor be united?[19].

Architectural design became more of a business too. With the rising standard of living, an increasing number of clients

required architectural services. The importance of small patrons, committees and boards waxed, that of kings, nobles and
the church waned. With a single patron, the architect had been
entirely dependent on his whims; he was often on the patron's
payroll. With a multitude, the architect had to set a standard
fee.

By the end of the eighteenth century, British architects
discovered that they had common interests in setting professional standards, in distinguishing themselves from the builders
and contractors and in adjusting their fees. The first architects'
club was founded in 1791[20]. A German architects' club was
founded in 1799 in Berlin[21]. They were soon followed by
associations on a national scale: the RIBA in 1834, the French
Société Centrale des Architectes in 1840, the American Institute of Architects in 1857[21].

The increase in number and variety of the clients for
architects had an influence on design. Since the late Middle
Ages there had been a contrast between conservative and
innovative architects; a contrast sharpened in the Renaissance
when the artist-architects naturally assumed the innovative role
and the craftsmen-architects the conservative one. But by and
large, stylistic unity more or less prevailed till around 1750; and
a culturally fairly homogeneous clientele with an acknowledged leadership (e.g. the courts in France, Austria or
England) corresponded to that unity and was its main cause. As
more and more people from different social strata started to
employ architects, this stylistic unity disappeared, because the
clients had different stylistic requirements. The nineteenth
century is dominated by the 'battle of styles', and twentieth-
century architecture — though sometimes schematized into
'modern' *versus* all the others — is also stylistically pluriform.

The professionalization of architects was enhanced by new
technical developments, e.g. the use of cast iron, but particularly by the increase in size of commissions and in their speed of
execution. There were large building complexes before 1800,
such as palaces and abbeys, but they had usually taken decades
to construct. With the advent of the Industrial Revolution
many new buildings were needed: mills, warehouses, railway
stations, hotels, museums, penitentiaries; and they were often
needed in a hurry. Only larger offices with sufficient professional staff could meet such demands.

... the most illuminating sidelight of all upon Victorian success is
furnished by the story often related of Sir Gilbert Scott at the height of
his immense practice, showing that his jobs were almost too numerous
to remember. He left London by train one morning at six; when his
staff dawdled into the office a few hours later they found a telegram
from him at a Midland station asking briefly, 'Why am I here?' ... On
another occasion Scott paused to admire a church, and asked for the
architect's name. 'Sir Gilbert Scott', was the laconic reply. It is not
surprising to learn that he left a fortune of £120,000[22].

D.H. Burnham, the Chicago architect, had 180 employees in 1912 and branch offices in New York and San Francisco[23].

If the term 'architect' is restricted to the full-time professional designer of buildings, then the architect's contribution to the total built volume remained minute till the latter half of the nineteenth century. It increased only when the general level of quality of the built environment was gradually raised at the end of the nineteenth and beginning of the twentieth century; until that time the villages and cities of the western world resembled in many respects the villages and cities of Asia and Africa today. Rapid urbanization in the wake of the Industrial Revolution gave rise to large tracts of speculative building and heavy overcrowding; the epidemics caused by the poor sanitary conditions made no halt at the edges of the slums and led to stricter building codes and zoning regulations as corrective measures. These in turn involved a growing number of architects in housing and planning. Ultimately, the expanding role of the architect derived from the gradual rise in the standard of living in the western world. People no longer accepted primitive housing conditions and they could afford not to accept them.

At the same time as the architect's field of operations was expanding, his field of competence was contracting. The specialists mentioned in the last chapter made inroads on his territory: the structural and mechanical engineers, the heating and ventilating engineers, the programmers and construction managers. It now becomes apparent that the architect as a professional designer only opened the row. He was the first of the specialists to profit from the division of labor. The medieval master-mason often held design, structural design, contracting and construction management in his hands. One by one these tasks fell to different (and often opposed) specialists. The social network increased — and increases still — in complexity; relations between the various parties concerned became more tenuous and communication more difficult. It is only from the limited perspective of today that one could view the architect's function as a 'given', which emerged in the late Middle Ages and has to stay the same forever. The one thing that seems certain is that that will not happen.

The new specialties did not change the field overnight. Masons and carpenters continued to design for centuries side by side with the architects. Today there are package builders who perform more or less the same job. The Austin Company, an American construction firm which offers 'undivided responsibility', i.e. design, contract and execution of the project, has been in business since 1881[24]. At the beginning of my private practice I calculated my own structural work, like many of my contemporaries.

Each new specialty arose as a corrective, in answer to a new need which could not be adequately met by the then operating practitioners. Each led to a shift in the balance of power, to new adjustments... and to new problems, e.g. the often criticized split between architectural and structural design, which fostered a spate of unbuildable paper projects. It is possible to envisage other, different divisions of labor in the construction industry which would be as adequate as the one we have today. If design were subsumed either under finance and developing or under contracting, the power of architects would probably be diminished. The architect reached his present precarious position partly through historical accident.

The relative arbitrariness of the present division of labor, and the after-life — or, in the case of the package dealers, the new life — of different forms of that division, goes a long way to explain why the architects have almost nowhere achieved a monopoly. Their title is often protected, they get all kinds of advantages, but it is still possible to create architecture-without-architects. And that will probably remain.

The sharp distinction between design and technology arose in the Renaissance. The medieval architect was just as interested in tools and construction methods as in design solutions, as the sketchbook of Villard de Honnecourt shows. In the fifteenth century design became a special activity which could be entrusted to an artist rather than a mere technician. The status of the artist-architect rose together with that of other artists. The high regard in which the artistic aspects of design are held by all architects has a long history and can be partly explained by the dramatic improvement in their position in the Renaissance.

Architects owe to the past their position and some of their ideals. Like every other professional, they have their dreams of superior competence and omniscience. But these often do not take the form of a complete mastery of the building field, doing their own contracting, structural and mechanical engineering, etc., but rather of being an artistic all-rounder, doing their own interior decoration, murals, architectural sculpture, etc. Many architects would like to be an *uomo universale*, a universal man in the sense of a universal artist, like Michelangelo. Once again, this is a belated legacy of the Renaissance, originating in the controversies between artists and craftsmen, a struggle in which the architect won the legitimacy and status he still enjoys today.

The 'invention' of buildings and the rendering of that invention in some visual form — a sketch or a model — rightly regarded by architects as one of their central activities, are indivisible. As long as there have been large monumental buildings, since the days of ancient Egypt, there have been architects. The combination of these data has given architects an illusion of constancy, extending to other areas of their professional endeavor. The last chapter tried to shake that illusion by looking at the larger framework of building activities in general. This chapter serves a similar purpose by discussing the changes over time.

Constancy ceases abruptly when we look at these other areas. The rarity of stone construction may have led to the medieval travelling lodges and the stonecutter-architect, risen from the ranks. The diffusion of drafting techniques in combination with the rise in status of painters conversant with these techniques produced the artist-architect of the Renaissance, who needed constructional assistance. This in turn paved the way for the amateur-architect: Perrault, Lord Burlington, Thomas Jefferson, Dr Thornton. The architects rode into fame on the coat-tails of the painters, but at a price.

Remnants of the past survive till this day. The Austin Company is the legitimate successor to the designing contractors of the nineteenth century, such as Thomas Cubitt, and ultimately to the stonecutter-architect. The speculative activities of Chambers and Adam are resumed by John Portman, the architect-developer. The artist-architect has all but disappeared, but the contrast between him and his craftsman competitor lives on in the opposition between artistic and practical architects, one of the main themes of this book. This opposition is also due to the second major historical change in the profession: the tremendous expansion of its sphere of influence. Before the nineteenth century, professional architects were only called in for a tiny fraction of the total number of new buildings. The full-time professionals of before 1800, all of them concerned with buildings of some note, were all 'artistic' architects. The illusion of constancy — which it is in the interest of architects to maintain — leads to a slurring over of the differences and to the belief that every architect is in a sense a successor to Palladio.

The expansion of the field in the nineteenth century and its growing complexities gave rise to a spate of specializations. There are now offices for commercial work, for industrial work, for schools and for hospitals. The traditional job of architect, i.e. the design of monumental buildings, fell to a small group of specialists, the artistic architects. It is through them that the profession traces its ancestry to Ictinos and Wren; it is from them that all the others derive their claim to be cultural standard-bearers. This claim will be critically examined in the following chapters.

4 Case-Study: Halen

Halen is a cluster of 79 terraced rowhouses on the outskirts of Berne, Switzerland, built between 1959 and 1961 (Figs. 5 and 7).

It is very well known among architects and draws visitors from all over the world. Partly this is due to the worldwide favorable publicity which Halen got: it was covered by *Werk*, *l'Architecture d'aujourd'hui*, *Architectural Design*, *Architectural Forum*, *Deutsche Bauzeitung*, *Deutsche Bauzeitschrift*, *Casabella*, *l'Architettura* and *The Architect's Yearbook*. Yet is is by no means a very original project. Its

Figure 5
General plan of the Halen housing development, Berne, Switzerland, 1959–1961. Architects: Atelier 5

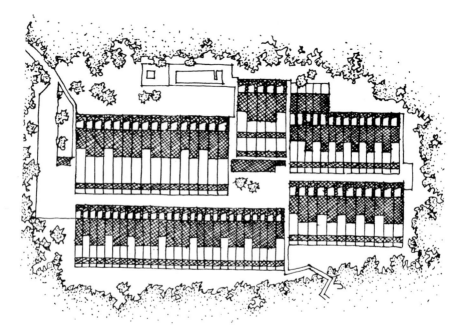

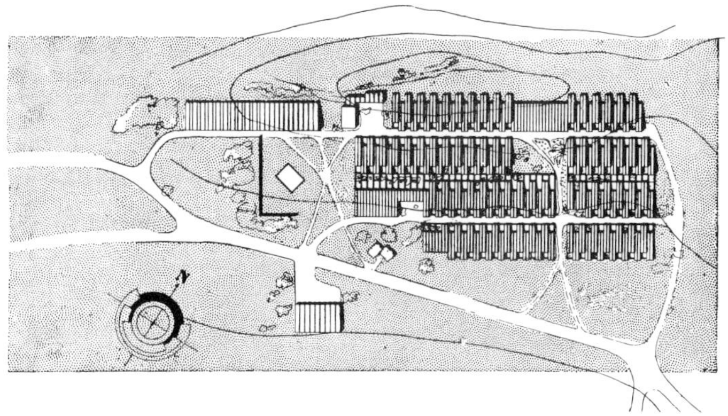

Figure 6
Plan for the Ste Baume housing cluster, 1948. Architect: Le Corbusier. The narrow lots and the high density were meant to minimize the environmental impact on the beauties of the site. This could be applied to the Halen site as well.

architects, Atelier 5, have repeatedly indicated the sources of their design. The general layout is a variation on Le Corbusier's plan for a village for pilgrims, Sainte Baume, and the housing units are derived from another unbuilt project by Le Corbusier, Roq et Rob[1] (Figs. 6 and 8).

Ironically, this popularity may well be due in part to Le Corbusier's own executed plans for mass housing. His '*Unités d'habitation*', built in Marseilles and Berlin, looked rather grim to many architects. Much as the Swiss master was admired, his 'solutions' to the housing problem were often criticized for their overwhelming size and scale, and (in Marseilles) for their inferior detailing and finishes. Halen showed that it was possible to build in the Corbusian idiom, and yet retain a 'normal' domestic scale and a decent standard of workmanship. Another reason for Halen's popularity lies probably in its idyllic site.

The idea for Halen arose in 1954, when four young employees in the office of the architect Hans Brechbühler started to look for a lot to build their own houses on. They found the Halen site, and an architect from another office who was interested, and decided to join forces and work on a larger project, involving more housing units.

Brechbühler was a functionalist architect, who had worked in Le Corbusier's office in Paris in 1930–1931. The partners of Atelier 5 believe that their:

...orientation on Le Corbusier is essentially due to Brechbühler, which has provided us perhaps with more open lines of action, an easier and simpler starting point ... in the university, one is faced with more influences ... this has probably allowed us to form such a group, a rather exceptional fact in the fifties[2].

In 1955 they began to draw plans for Halen[3]. The project met with difficulties from the start. Permission to build was only granted after a plebiscite among the rural population of the village in which it was located. The first real-estate firm withdrew after a year. Rudolf Steiger, another functionalist architect and former employer of one of the partners, mediated

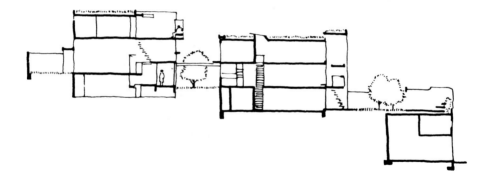

Figure 7
Section of Halen

between Atelier 5 and Göhner, a large contractor and developer. Göhner loaned them money to buy the site. However, banks were still unwilling to mortgage the project; in 1958 Göhner assumed the role of client for Halen, on condition that the architects share in the financial liability and undertake to sell the houses. This proved to be fairly difficult, for although construction was finished in 1961, and a model home was opened in 1959, the last unit was sold only in 1963.

Halen is built on a 7.6 acre lot. Buildings and private gardens take up 3.3 acres. The lot slopes to the south with a 9′ slope, and abuts on the road along the Aare river. Across the river lies a public park. The home-owners of Halen are assured of permanent green view. The wood (1.5 acres) was there before construction started, so the project was always surrounded by mature trees: an idyllic and extremely desirable site indeed.

The houses are surrounded by lawns. The one on the northwest side is nearly level and is used for sunbathing. It has a swimming-pool and a few ping-pong tables. Cars are parked in a large underground garage.

The project contains 79 housing units, most of them belonging to one of two types (differing slightly in width) and all looking alike. All houses have completely secluded private gardens, separated by 6 ft high partywalls. All roofs carry a 1 ft layer of topsoil, grown over with wild grass and weeds, to avoid the usual bleak view of roofing paper from the upper stories.

Materials and finishes are extremely simple. The concrete ceilings and loggias, and the concrete block masonry of the children's bedrooms, are left exposed and painted white. In the living-rooms and the parents' bedroom, the walls are stuccoed.

There is a small number of common facilities: the heating plant, a launderette, a self-service gas station, the garage, and the park with the swimming pool and some children's play equipment. Le Corbusier had put a considerable number of common facilities in his *'Unité d'habitation'* in Marseilles: e.g. a florist, a barber's shop and a post-office. But by the time of the construction of Halen most of these had folded, as they

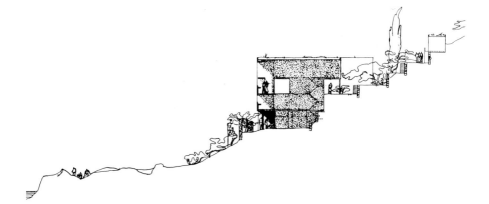

Figure 8
Section of the 'Roq et Rob'
housing cluster, near Cap Martin
on the Mediterranean. Architect:
Le Corbusier. Similar to Halen
are: the narrow elongated plans,
the grass-covered roofs, the
'*brise-soleil*' in the two-story
loggia, the covered walkways

were not economically viable, and this was well known among architects. It was probably for that reason that Atelier 5 only allowed one grocery shop and a small café on the central square.

The common facilities have a symbolic as well as an economic significance. Morgenthaler, one of the partners of Atelier 5, describes them thus:

Halen has been and still is an exception to other housing developments because of its most logical use of a given situation in order to create comprehensive and tangible common interest among its future dwellers. It has been the policy of Halen to share necessary services as much as possible up to the point where they would intrude upon the privacy of the individual or group ... 'Halen' stands as an exception because the sharing of common services has been used not only to achieve economic efficiency, but also to allow each inhabitant to identify himself with the total environment as a 'place to live and communicate'[4].

The text of the Thormanns (Fritz Thormann is another partner) is even more specific:

In this small area with its innumerable possibilities a spontaneous community is easily created. The child feels secure, the frame is both large and small enough. It is claimed that life today is isolated, and this is said to be bad. It is difficult to judge if this assertion is really true. In Halen, however, it is certainly true that people like to break out of their isolation. They enjoy making contacts whenever possible. The experiment with the bottle. To be repeated with guaranteed success as often as required. To find company sit alone in the Square, any Sunday or in the evening, with a bottle and four glasses. Few of the people who start to cross the Square reach their houses. The group grows. Sometimes it becomes late. Visitors say: The houses are so uncosy that they have to live outside[5].

Roger Perrinjaquet, who has studied the project in depth, has drawn attention to the 'utopian concept' behind Halen[6]. It is conceived as an 'ideal village', opposed to the harsh realities of the modern city, a 'community' ('*Gemeinschaft*') set against society ('*Gesellschaft*'). Surrounded by natural vegetation, its inhabitants huddle together on their 'ideal island'. In a 'normal' suburb, villas compete with each other and show the status of their owners. Here, all houses are alike and symbolize the possibility of social harmony among people. The similarities with Ebenezer Howard's Garden City — a cooperative village with the facilities of a town — and even more with Robert Owen's 'New Harmony' and the *phalanstères* of Fourier are obvious.

However, the original home-owners were not so keen on communal living as the architects had hoped. Atelier 5 had therefore to start up the social life by setting and example:

... That is also the merit of M(orgenthaler), who was one of the oldest among us. He has shown that one could sit down with a bottle of wine and that other people came to sit down with us to talk ... Thus we have raised people's consciousness. We have taught them what living together means[7].

The 'education of the people' by architects is another recurrent theme in modern architecture.

The concept of a socially harmonious community as a contrast against the divided society at large makes sense only if it encompasses a representative variety of people. It should cut across the dividing lines within the larger society. The architects were aware of this:

That was also our opinion: the objective of Halen ought to allow a (social) mix[8].

To demonstrate this variety, the professions of the owners were listed in a propaganda booklet of 1964:

13 architects
 2 interior architects
 3 art teachers
 1 painter/art teacher
 2 graphic artists
 1 painter/graphic artist
 1 cartoonist
 1 choir director
 1 pianist
 3 editors/journalists
 1 playwright/writer
 1 teacher/writer
 1 teacher's training college instructor
 3 university professors
 1 university assistant
 2 doctors of technical science
 1 doctor of chemistry
 1 doctor of law
 1 physicist
 1 (pharmaceutical) chemist
 2 engineers
 2 physicians
 2 agricultural engineers
 2 foreign diplomats
 7 government officials
 1 secretary of the World Postal Union

```
1 secretary of the Swiss Trade Union Federation
1 expert on sports fields
1 florist
1 printer
2 managers
1 chainstore manager
1 antiquary
1 bookkeeper
1 optician
1 shopkeeper
1 caretaker[9]
```

The list shows clearly that a social mix was not attained. There is only one representative from the working class, the caretaker, and he was appointed to look after the maintenance and the installations of the project. The middle class is also under-represented with nine people. Architects, artists, writers and people with a university education are heavily *over*-represented. This is also visible from the social statistics of the Berne Municipal Statistical Office of 1970. Of 152 adults (over 25 years of age), 98 or 65% have had a secondary school or further (university, art academy, etc.) education and no more than seven (4.6%) have had only a primary school education. The averages for all Berne suburbs are 15.8% and 47.5% respectively[10].

Atelier 5 admitted in 1977 that the goal of the social mix had not been achieved:

We had thought that people who could hardly afford an individual house would come to live at Halen ... today there live people who could afford ten (of such houses).

Perhaps the working man was afraid of not finding the same circles (i.e. his own kind).

So one could say, with a little exaggeration, that Halen has become a ghetto for people whose ambition is to live lavishly[11].

Atelier 5 attributed this failure to the proximity of Berne. But they continued to believe that they had found a 'different architecture' which would ultimately induce people to live a different life.

And they were allowed to try again. Atelier 5 got commissions for similar housing projects in Brügg, Lutry and Burgdorf in Switzerland, in Park Hill, near Croydon (a London suburb), and in Werther, near Bielefeld in West Germany. All of these were due to the favorable impression which Halen made on other architects and planners. And Atelier 5 continued to bask in the favor of their colleagues. In 1970 they were invited to participate in a competition for housing in Lima, Peru. Judged by their peers, they got the first prize. Apart from this last project, which was intended for very poor people, the other projects catered mainly for similar clients as Halen.

With the important exception of the German project, Wertherberg. This was low-cost housing, heavily subsidized, built by a housing association and sold to its members, mainly white- and blue-collar workers. These people belonged therefore to the lower middle class, and not to the upper class, as in Halen.

Here Atelier 5 ran into another difficulty. As in Halen, the houses in Wertherberg were again built of simple materials, with a lot of exposed painted concrete. The inhabitants did not like this. They started to hide the concrete and cinderblock behind trellises, wooden boarding and even imitation brickwork. They 'decorated' their houses with wrought-iron lamps and window-cages, their entrances with glass brick walls and corrugated plastic sheets in many colours (Fig. 9).

The architects had allowed for changes, and even encouraged them. The Thormanns had written about the exteriors of Halen:

Each house is entirely the property of its owner and within the law he is free to do with it as he likes. It can be changed, broken down or painted red[12].

and about the interiors:

Architecturally rooms are as far as possible neutral. Freedom is given to create the living environment personally chosen. The architect's taste must not be obtrusive[12].

In accordance with this philosophy, Atelier 5 had provided walls around the courtyards and entrances which were easily taken down, and had refused to regulate any alterations.

But they professed to be horrified by what the inhabitants of Wertherberg had done to their design:

The inhabitants start to shape their environment. Nobody is entitled to carp about that. Only the character of the alterations is frightening. They do not aim to increase the usefulness of the project, such as to enrich the public area with new functional elements or to enlarge the conditions of life for the individual (however there are beginnings of this), but they are directed at the 'make-up', at a new facial cream and wig ... Concrete is ugly, masonry is more becoming. To adopt a new, unusual form of living, to use it, to exploit and extend its advantages, this effort could not be produced in Wertherberg. It became important for the inhabitants to import or reimport those values into the project with which they could identify, values which are supplied by television, by the illustrated weekly "House Beautiful" and by the mail-order catalog. With such a supply there remains little room to reflect on your own, real needs ... So much unnecessary cosmetics in Werther are enough to make you cry[13].

In Halen too, the houses have been altered by their owners: supergraphics of house numbers or abstract designs are quite as conspicuous there as face-lifts in Wertherberg (Fig. 10). But these changes have never been denounced as 'superfluous cosmetics' by the architects. Indeed, it is the character of the alterations which they deplore, their 'bad', 'commercial' taste.

Figure 9
Housing at Wertherberg, near
Bielefeld, West Germany, 1968.
Architects: Atelier 5. The owners
disliked the exposed concrete and
covered it with asphalt rolled
siding

The following points are kept for further discussion:

1. Architectural forms are transmitted from one generation to
   the next. In Halen this occurred through Brechbühler, who
   mediated between Le Corbusier and Atelier 5. Architecture
   has a tradition; even modern architecture, which professed
   to be anti-traditional and set such great store by originality.
   Though hardly original, Halen still became internationally
   famous.

Figure 10
Decoration of a wall in Halen.
This is the kind of liberty taken
with the design which the
architects approved of!

2. The architects of Atelier 5 built a successful international practice on the reputation they earned with Halen. They were commissioned to design similar housing projects at home and abroad.

3. The project has a utopian dimension. The contrast between the architecture of Halen and that of a 'normal' suburb is supposed to symbolize a different — and better! — way of life. Architecture makes privacy or social interaction possible, and therefore archiecture is a prime means to further social ends. The architects see themselves as having a moral and educational task, in addition to their technical work. Their sense of a 'mission' was powerfully reinforced by the hardships they had to endure when they developed Halen.

4. Halen has attracted a very specific set of buyers. Artists, writers and people with a university degree predominated amongst them. Apparently you *do* need an education to appreciate exposed concrete. The original owners belong in the majority to the educated upper middle class, and so do the architects and critics who flocked to Halen to extol its virtues and spread the fame of Atelier 5. People from another class — as in Wertherberg — are critical of some aspects of this kind of architecture. This shows, according to Atelier 5, that they have not yet discovered their 'real needs', and that they have to be educated.

In Halen and in Wertherberg the same architects created very similar 'solutions', and commented on the different reactions from the two groups of users. It is this rather unique, quasi-experimental situation, in which some variables have been held constant and the social origin of the users is the — unintentional — main variable, which makes it so interesting and important in the context of the present study. Why are those 'in the know' attracted by exposed concrete and painted cinderblock, and the 'uneducated' repelled by it? This question needs a larger framework: what are the relations between society and culture?

5 Society and Culture

The families in Halen are as much exposed to advertising, television and mail-order catalogs as their counterparts in Wertherberg, because Switzerland and Germany are very similar in this respect. The explanation advanced by Atelier 5 for their differences in taste is probably inadequate.

A taste for exposed concrete — or for colorful corrugated plastic — does not stand by itself. What you like or dislike about building materials is related to your preferences in furniture and clothes, in home decorations and therefore in art, in reading materials (such as *House Beautiful*) and thus in literature. Tastes in the various areas of culture run to a pattern. The American magazine *Evergreen* printed in 1970 a mocking portrait of the Liberal which we can still recognize:

Liberals find pornography 'boring'.
Liberals build bookcases out of cinder blocks.
Liberals give wine and cheese-tasting parties.
Liberals quote Camus.
Liberals don't mind criticism so long as it's constructive.
Liberals attend Bergman festivals.
Liberals often say '*ciao*' instead of 'goodbye'.
Liberals point out Freudian slips.
Liberals check *Consumer Reports* before buying anything.
Liberals read prefaces.
Liberals think it's good for men to express their emotions.
Liberal parents encourage their children to call them by first name.
Liberals approve of premarital intercourse. In fact, they call it that.
Liberals believe in natural childbirth and breastfeeding.
Liberal mothers nurse their babies in front of friends as often as possible.
Liberals own Siamese cats with clever names usually drawn from mythology.
Liberals own separate-component stereo systems.
Liberals try to appreciate electronic music.

Liberals have moral reservations about neutering their cats.
Liberals paint their walls white.
Liberals keep their pencils in Dundee Orange Marmalade jars.
Liberals don't like Danish Modern furniture anymore.
Liberals have 'outgrown' pot.
Liberals attend writers' conferences.
Liberals like: harpsichord kits, existentialism, Volvos, haiku,
Käthe Kollwitz, garlic presses, reform Democrats, Scrabble,
Guernica, Bartok, Cable-stitch Irish turtlenecks, Modigliani,
Bach, WQXH, Tiffany lamps, Ben Shahn prints, Bernard
Malamud, cucumber soap and Gandhi[1].

Apparently there is something which might be labelled 'the
Liberal subculture'. Other subcultures which are recognized —
and therefore 'known' — are those of the flower-power people
and of the blacks. But does it end there? Are all the other people
'ordinary' and 'average'? The subcultures of the white- or
blue-collar workers, of the bureaucratic staff of large
organizations (the 'org-man') or of the very rich are far less
conspicuous; but nonetheless they exist. It is only the extremes
which stand out and become visible; and then only extremes
which are not held in high esteem. It is of course in the best
interest of most people to appear as 'normal' and 'average', and
it is a demonstration of power that they have succeeded in
projecting that image. The Liberal eggheads are not particularly
highly regarded in the USA, which makes it all right to poke fun
at them. In England or Germany, where they wield a larger
social power, a portrait like *Evergreen*'s is less likely to be
written.

Everyone is born in a culture, and even in a subculture. A
child learns to talk from its mother, and inevitably takes over
her accent, her norms and her values. The child's intellectual
and social horizon is expanded in kindergarten and primary
school, but several studies have shown that the early
socialization of the home far outweighs the effects of
schooltraining. For obvious commonsense reasons: the later
educational efforts have to be grafted on the earlier ones, and
the early childhood influences are reinforced every day as the
child comes home again. Children from working-class homes
soon perceive that the use of language and the handling of
concepts in school is different from what they experience at
home, and that therefore 'school is not for our kind of people'.
The majority of middle-class and particularly upper
middle-class children take to school as a duck to water, because
school culture and home culture tally[2].

The division along class lines is only one amongst many.
With his classmates and with his neighborhood pals the child
gets involved in another social configuration: the peer group.
Together with them he does mischief and gangs up against
adults. The norms and values of the peer group are usually
antagonistic to those of the home and the school. The child
learns at a very early age that there are different and inconsistent

value-systems and that it has to prove its loyalty now to one, then to the other, under penalty of being excluded. The ringleader of the neighborhood gang may very well be a docile boy at home.

To adopt the moral code and the values of the moment is not a matter of free choice. Children in the western world are trained and supervised till they are 16 years of age. The continuous social control by powerful and overbearing adults easily arouses feelings of insecurity. The hostile outside world is a social world, peopled by parents, teachers and policemen. You *have* to have a home base, a place of security where you belong. Which means that you are forced to adopt the value-system of the moment. If teacher has disciplined you severely, you flee to mom. If she concurs with the teacher, you run off to your pals around the corner. The inconsistency of the different value-systems allows the child some freedom to strike out on his own, to join the group that will help and comfort him at that particular moment. But of course at the price of conforming to the norms of that group.

Out of this set of different roles a person's identity is built up. He practises his roles until they have become 'second nature' to him, till they have become internalized as a habit.

A role to be adoptable has to have tangible characteristics. The group is as much obliged to 'create' norms and values as the individual member is to adopt them. Children show themselves to be well aware of this when they organize a 'secret society' with a 'cipher' and a 'secret meeting place'. To be 'one of the boys' you must be able to distinguish members from non-members, e.g. by asking for the 'password'. Differences and boundaries are of the essence of group formation. Social identity implies identifiable characteristics in groups.

These characteristics make the group visible to its members, but at the same time to outsiders. They are bound to reflect on them: should they enhance the difference of their own group? or rather imitate? Allegiance to a group is often neither absolute nor undivided; it could not be, for many people are members of groups with conflicting moral codes. Moreover, a major opportunity for social advancement for the individual lies in shifting his allegiance.

Another group, even though you do not belong to it, may be worthy of imitation. It acts as a (comparison) reference group: e.g. the combat veterans for the fresh recruits, the experienced football players for the beginners, the architectural partners for their draftsmen, or the doctors for their nurses[3]. Imitation of behavior reduces the differences between groups; their boundaries become blurred. The imitated may — and often do — try to develop new patterns of behavior which safeguard their group identity. They try to increase the distance which the imitators try to reduce.

Many of the aggregates to which a person belongs, and from

which he derives his social identity, are far less well defined than the face-to-face groups such as the family or the football-team. You may feel proud to belong to a certain profession, a particular firm, a political party or a church, without knowing more than a tiny fraction of the others who share the same privilege.

These aggregates have similar characteristics and are subject to similar tendencies to the small and more visible groups. There are Liberal organizations, but the Liberals are not a group; neither are the managers or the white-collar workers. Yet they do have common characteristics (a 'subculture') by which they differ from others, and which are perceived by others. And they try, too, to imitate those with a higher status and to keep or increase their distance from their social inferiors.

For a good reason. Society is stratified, and the higher up you are on the social ladder, the more power you wield and the more privileges you have access to. High status confers authority on a speaker, easier credit on a borrower and eligibility on an applicant for club membership.

Social stratification can be conceptualized in various ways. The most important — and controversial — is the class-system. A class is an aggregate of people with a similar socioeconomic position in society.

Because 'class' is a politically loaded word since Marx, many people (in particular those reckoned to belong to the upper and upper middle classes) deny the existence of classes. They are helped in this by the vagueness and permeability of class-boundaries. For example, a foreman in a machine-shop (working class) makes more money than a junior clerk in the office (lower middle class). People can be scaled on income, on capital, on education or on status, and the outcome is different each time.

But not *very* different. By and large, capital, income, status and education increase together. The poor score lowly on each of these dimensions and the rich highly. The boundaries may be blurred, but the centers of each large subdivision are clear enough.

The problems of classification arise partly from the repeated efforts (started by Marx) to fit the complexities of the social fabric to the Procrustean bed of a single economic scale. Following a lead from Max Weber, the French sociologist Pierre Bourdieu has suggested that we use three dimensions: the economic, the cultural and the social. Social capital is, for example, the family to which somebody belongs and the status and network of social relations that this entails. Cultural capital is, for example, a person's skills and knowledge, partly expressed in his diplomas and degrees.

The class-system is a sociological grid laid over the existing inequalities in society. It is consequently far less visible and far less 'real' than such groups as the family, the firm, the political party or the church. Most people are not very class-conscious, though in an intuitive way they are usually well aware of the socioeconomic level they have reached (e.g. 'our kind', 'that's not for the likes of us', etc.). Only class-conflicts, such as strikes, raise class-consciousness and class-loyalty ('sticking with your own').

Adults follow a strategy in their allegiances and oppositions, just as children. Whom they support depends at least partly on the situation of the moment. H.G. Wells has expressed this in his description of the loyalties of a systematic botanist:

He has a strong feeling for systematic botanists as against plant physiologists, whom he regards as lewd and evil scoundrels in this relation; but he has a strong feeling for all botanists and indeed for all biologists, as against physicists, and those who profess the exact sciences, all of whom he regards as dull, mechanical, uglyminded scoundrels in this relation; but he has a strong feeling for all who profess what he calls Science, as against psychologists, sociologists, philosophers, and literary men, whom he regards as wild, foolish, immoral scoundrels in this relation; but as soon as the working man is comprehended together with these others as *Englishmen...* he holds them superior to all sorts of Europeans, whom he regards...[4].

The quotation shows that loyalty is restricted. Teachers present a united front towards parents, but inside the school they divide into factions which try to pull the curriculum their way. The managers of a corporation act in concert towards competitors, but struggle internally to get their particular views adopted. The existence of a nearly infinite number of possible groupings inside any medium-sized social aggregate makes social relations complex and hard to understand. But it also allows the individual to shift his loyalty in his own interest; it can be used as a strategy to move up in the power structure — or at least not fall behind.

Power is a relation between people and as such has to be communicated. If a mother never asserts herself, never punishes her children, they will forget that she can make them behave. If you never get a ticket, you willl begin to ignore the no-parking sign. The manifestations of power have an effect on *both* parties involved: the child who sees that 'there are limits', and the mother who feels that she can still 'handle the children'. The role that a person fulfils, the position he occupies, is made real to him or her by the concrete manifestations of that role or position: the white coat donned by the young intern in the hospital, the uniform for the majorette, the leather outfit for the Hell's Angel. And it does not stop at clothes, but pervades all aspects of behavior: language, ritual and manners. Doctors, Hell's Angels and servicemen put on a different behavior and go through various forms of ritual which they would not dream of showing at home. We can speak of 'the bedside manner of the doctor' or 'the professional mannerisms of the lawyer'.

The sociologist Thorstein Veblen drew attention in 1899 to a large number of idiosycracies of the 'leisure class', with which they 'demonstrated' their superior position. They did not have to work with their hands, hence the attention paid to clean hands and unbroken clean fingernails. *If* they strained their muscles, it had to be for something clearly useless, such as sports. They wore clothes which prevented manual work: clean white shirts, lacquered shoes, creased pants; and the women: narrow skirts, sheer silk stockings and high heels. Their cultural activities were visibly 'useless': they learned dead languages, music and art history. Much time was spent on etiquette, and correct spelling and pronunciation. They became connoisseurs of wine and antiques, because these were useless luxury goods which could only be enjoyed by people of their class.

Veblen saw this all as 'conspicuous consumption', flaunted in the face of the less privileged. He did not perceive the reciprocality of the relation between the rich and the less fortunate. The behavior of the members of the leisure class is forced upon them too: a well-mannered person is — up to a point — conversant with art, literature and foreign travel and does not drop his aitches. To feel at home in your own social world you *have* to adopt its *mores* and standards.

Veblen's examples show also that the majority of his marks of distinction have lost their power to distinguish. Since 1899 well-manicured hands, white shirts, sheer stockings and high heels are no longer a privilege of the leisure class. Like sports and foreign travel, they have been imitated by the 'lower' classes. External marks of distinction are easily imitated and are consequently of limited value for demarcation. Therefore they change very rapidly. The obvious example is fashion. The very special 'new models' designed by one of the famous houses in Paris or New York are only briefly worn by the smart set; thereafter you find them in the department stores and by the end of the season in the sales.

Language-use and pronunciation are far harder to imitate and as a result more effective as marks of distinction. A few minutes' conversation are sufficient to identify blacks, New Englanders, Mid Westerners or Southerners for an American, or Scots, Welshmen, Irishmen, Cockneys or Aussies for an Englishman. A 'cultured' voice is a sign that the speaker has probably had an education beyond elementary school; his use of grammar and vocabulary often demonstrates whether he has gone to college.

Black (American) English, originally only rated as a dialect of the poor to be unlearned in school, is nowadays studied by linguists as a language-form in its own right and is often cultivated by black speakers to establish the black identity and emphasize black solidarity, i.e. as marks of distinction in the sense of this chapter[5].

The profession of egalitarian ideals and the enormous number of groups of different ethnic origin has tended to blur speech as a class denominator in the USA — even though the 'true Bostonians' in Marquand's novels immediately recognize each other by ear. In a more class-conscious society like England, it is still a conspicuous element; so much so in fact that upper-class speakers sometimes consciously try to repress their 'Oxbridge' accent so as not to appear standoffish. The philologist Alan Ross, who described in 1956 some of the differences between the linguistic usages of the English upper classs ('U') and the others ('non-U'), raised the question: 'Can a non-U speaker become a U-speaker?'

The answer is that an adult can never attain complete success. Moreover, it must be remembered that, in these matters, U-speakers have ears to hear, so that one single pronunciation, word or phrase will suffice to brand an apparent U-speaker as originally non-U (for U-speakers themselves never make 'mistakes')[6].

Ross' paper on the different linguistic habits of different classes is supported by research. Working-class people have different grammatical usages and are inclined to use abstract words less frequently than middle-class speakers[7]. Obviously language-use is a part of a speaker's cultural equipment and hence of his *cultural capital*.

It becomes clear now how other cultural elements can be attached to this scheme. 'Good taste' in music, literature and the arts is as much a cultural, class-bound attainment as a correct pronunciation. Like that pronunciation (and in contrast to fashion), it has to be acquired in a long and complex learning-process. In music it involves being taken to concerts as a child, listening to records, familiarizing yourself with words as 'B-minor', *'andante sostenuto'* and *'pizzicato'*, perhaps even learning to play an instrument. Familiarity with classical music and with the ritual of concert-going makes a person feel he is a part of the truly appreciative audience. Only in such a situation of security can he venture that he does not care for Bartòk, a statement which coming from a newcomer would be attributed to his 'undeveloped taste' and his 'lack of knowledge of good music'[8].

This holds equally for other class-levels. An Englishman with an Oxford accent in a working-class pub stands out as 'different'; his language is perceived as 'arty' and 'highfalutin'. To be 'one of the boys' you have to speak their language with their accent (or with a working-class accent from somewhere else). It is uncomfortable not to be able to blend with the landscape. A person's sense of identity is built up by belonging, by being accepted by his peers, and by not being thought 'snooty' or 'queer'. Of necessity, he adapts as far as possible to the (temporary) group norms. He needs these norms to *prove* that he belongs, the music-lover as much as the beer-drinker. What he likes in music, reading matter, food and drinks is therefore also an expression of his social personality. His taste, his accent and his knowledge are just as much parts of his identity as his name, age and occupation.

Art, music and literature can do more for him than provide him with standards of conduct or topics of conversation. Their main task is to provide an *emotional orientation in life*. Science gives us a rational and objective orientation, art and religion an evaluative and subjective orientation. A marital conflict can be analyzed by a counselor or a psychoanalyst, as objectively as possible. Or it can be interpreted by a minister; he will appeal to the consciences of the spouses. Or it can be portrayed in a novel or a short story. In neither of these latter two interpretations is rational objectivity the major goal; on the contrary, the primary aim is to involve the listener or reader. Lionel Trilling on the function of the novel:

But its greatness and its practical usefulness lay in its unremitting work of involving the reader himself in the moral life, inviting him to put his own motives under examination, suggesting that reality is not as his conventional education has led him to see it. It taught, as no other genre ever did, the extent of human variety and the value of this variety. It was the literary form to which the emotions of understanding and forgiveness were indigenous, as if by definition of the form itself[9].

The eighteenth-century poet George Crabbe put a similar attitude into rhyme:

This, books can do — nor this alone; they give New views to life, and teach us how to live; They soothe the grieved, the stubborn they chastise; Fools they admonish, and confirm the wise[10].

Because we are emotionally involved in a complex world around us, we are interested in subjective comment on it. How we can or should solve our own emotional problems can be learnt from exhortations, from advice and from examples. The latter are provided on a down-to-earth level by gossip and the neighbors and on another level by literature, the theatre and television. The literary portrayal of emotional situations enlarges and refines our own emotional life. The immediate involvement with the characters of fiction explains why children like to read about other children or young animals, why the bank-clerk finds adventure with Hercule Poirot or John Putnam Thatcher, and the teenager with Batman or Mighty Mouse. Reading involves what the reader has read before and is therefore often as class-bound as clothes. But in its vicarious experiences, its dramas imagined but never really lived through, it goes far beyond fashion and the marks of distinction: it adds to our emotional identity.

Language makes it possible to communicate our feelings to others and to hear about their emotions, and by sharing them to enlarge the context of our own. Through language we can compare and relate different moments and situations. A refinement in language through the reading of poetry or literature incomparably enlarges our emotional horizon.

I believe this to hold for the other arts as well. Music is the language of moods. The composer Aaron Copland once described its emotional content:

Music expresses, at different moments, serenity or exuberance, regret or triumph, fury or delight. It expresses each of these moods and many others, in a numberless variety of subtle shadings and differences. It may even express a state of meaning for which there exists no adequate word in any language[11].

And it can do so in every kind of music: in punk, rock, folk, brass-band or classical.

The visual arts orient us in the visible world around us: a still-life by Morandi on the bottles in our medicine-cabinet, a nude by Wesselmann on female attractiveness, a mobile by Calder on balance, gravity and movement in space.

Cultural consumption is bound up with the class-system. Brass bands and punk are working class, musicals and folk music middle class, and classical music is predominantly upper class[12].

An intimate connection with class-divisions is logical — even tautological — because 'good taste' is itself one of the marks of class-distinction. 'Good taste' does not appear out of the blue; it is something slowly developed over time. In classical music it requires familiarity with the Italian terminology, the musical forms, a goodly number of composers and their works, and with the concert ritual. In literature you have to be able to use such terms as 'stanza', 'sonnet', 'iambic', 'existentialist', 'ego-fulfilment', etc., and to have read a fair number of books, which are used as a standard of comparison: 'comical as Twain', 'symbolic as Melville', 'deep as Bellow'. In the visual arts you need to know the difference between an etching and an engraving, between a wash drawing and a watercolor, between tempera and oil painting, between mixed media and collage; you have again to be able to bandy about quite a few names and to know how to deport yourself in a museum. These requirements are not given by nature, they are cultural acquisitions.

As such, they are desirable assets for the less privileged, who try to acquire them in crash courses, book clubs and subscriptions to records of masterwork series. Bourdieu has pointed out that it is this 'struggle for the higher life' which has given rise to the myth of the 'natural good taste'[13]. The true-blooded cultural elite is bound to look with distaste at the effort to efface the boundary which separates them from the others. Indeed, the familiarity with art, music and literature which he has acquired at home gives the truly cultured mind a self-confidence which the others can never hope to attain; his taste has become 'second nature'. It is this self-confident ease in handling cultural material which separates the cultivated mind from the runner-up. As in his language, the U-person 'cannot make mistakes', and he knows it. The efforts of the middle class at self-improvement look pedantic and comical from his point of view. Just as the nobles in eighteenth-century Europe, he believes himself to be constitutionally different from the common man.

The source of power of the cultural elite lies in its accumulated knowledge, its cultural capital. Members of that elite have been able to invest a great deal of *time* in cultural pursuits. They can judge books, music or works of art against a much larger background than 'illiterates'. This allows them to separate 'true innovations' from 'revivals' or 'plagiarisms', to assess the degree of novelty and to distinguish between innovation of technique, of form and of content.

The situation is comparable to that of the trained professional. A lawyer assesses a case against the law and the jurisprudence; an engineer evaluates an application for a patent (or an idea in the idea-box) against the background of constructions known to him; an editor of a psychological journal considers a paper offered for publication against his knowledge of the field or advances it to a more specialized reviewer. They, too, use their stock of cultural capital to appraise relative merits. They *need* that stock to do their work; and we trust them because we know they have got it.

What can people do who stray into a museum without the requisite armament of 'composition', 'Cubism', 'chiaroscuro', etc.? They have to evaluate a painting in terms with which they *are* familiar:

— *recognition*: what it is.
— *resemblance*: how close it comes to a photograph.
— *technique*: degree to which the painting goes beyond what they think they can do themselves, and the amount of effort spent on it.
— *ease of understanding*: its correspondence with their own esthetic categories[14].

It is obvious from this list that Jackson Pollock, Barnett Newman or Roberto Matta would be rejected on all four categories. Roy Lichtenstein's strip-paintings or Andy Warhol's Coke bottle could still pass muster on the first two, but would fail on the last two categories. On the other hand, 'a sunset on the ocean' or 'a mother breast-feeding her child' would be considered 'very beautiful subjects' by members of the working class, but 'kitsch' by the cultural elite[15]. *Webster's New Collegiate Dictionary* defines 'kitsch' as:

artistic or literary material of low quality designed to appeal to current popular taste[16].

The term embodies the distaste of the cultural elite; there is no word of corresponding aggressiveness to designate highbrow art for lowbrow people.

For the authority of highbrow art is recognized by all, as much as the authority of lawyers or engineers. It is *legitimate culture*.

Table 1

'Legitimate'	
William Faulkner; Saul Bellow	Mickey Spillane; Harold Robbins
Jackson Pollock; Jasper Johns	Norman Rockwell; Charles Addams
George Gershwin; Malcolm Frager	Richard Rodgers; Liberace

Legimate culture is perceived by its patrons and its participants as coherent, even though its parts may be only loosely connected. The poets Apollinaire and Salmon were the earliest and staunchest defenders of Cubism. Movements like Symbolism, de Stijl and Circle involved writers and poets as well as painters. Dada was a joint effort by writers and painters, as was its offspring, Surrealism. The Bauhaus tried to create new forms in the theatre and the movies as well as in art, architecture and industrial design. Poets and choreographers got involved with the New York School of Painting[17].

The universal authority of legimate culture was statistically demonstrated by Bourdieu[18]. It is also evident from communists in France, Italy and Holland voting for subsidies for orchestras, museums and theatres, and particularly from the popularity of book and record clubs which promise to bring you the 'classical pinnacles of world literature and music'. The works popularized by these clubs are all quite old, because they have to tie in with the existing cultural level of their petty bourgeois customers. Hence, for instance, Beethoven, but only the symphonies and concertos, not the string-quartets.

The desire to 'improve themselves' propels middle-class people forward to imitate their 'betters'; their ignorance and consequent lack of understanding holds them back. The process repeats itself on the next 'higher' (or 'more advanced') level. This gradual transmission from one level to another keeps the cultural steeplechase going and has transformed van Gogh's pictures from 'meaningless daubs' into 'classics', fit for giving a cultural air to motel-rooms (Fig. 11).

Artists are of course aware of the cultural lag and the process of transmission. Josiah Wedgwood, who made a living on this mechanism, described it already in 1772:

The Progress of the Arts, at all Times and in every Country, chiefly depends upon the Encouragement they receive from those, who by their Rank and Affluence are the Legislators of Taste; and who alone are capable of bestowing Rewards upon the Labours of Industry and the Exertions of Genius. It is their influence that forms the Character of every age; they can turn the current of human Pursuits at their Pleasure; and either be surrounded with Beauty or Deformity, with Barbarians or Men...

...The Great People have had these Vases in their Palaces long enough for them to be seen and admired by the Middling Class of People, which Class we know are vastly, I had almost said infinitely superior

Figure 11
Sunflowers by Vincent van Gogh,
1888. Once considered to be
meaningless daubs by
authoritative critics, his paintings
have by now become so well
accepted that their reproductions
are found among the standard
decoration of motel rooms

in number to the Great, and though a great price was, I believe, at first
necessary to make the Vases esteemed ornaments for Palaces, that
reason no longer exists. Their character is established, and the
middling people would probably buy quantities of them at a reduced
price...[19].

Pierre Bourdieu has demonstrated how much cultural consumption depends on previously accumulated 'cultural capital'. He and his collaborators questioned 28,000 visitors to
European art-museums on their educational background, their
knowledge of art and their preferences[20].

People with a high-school diploma with Latin and/or Greek
(the European 'gymnasium' diploma) were more overrepresented than those without Latin or Greek.

Catalogs were bought primarily by the most educated
visitors — who needed them least, of course. They, who knew
already so much about art, acquired the additional knowledge
stored in print.

Table 2[21]
Ratio between the proportion of visitors to art-museums of a
particular level of education and the corresponding proportion in the
whole population ('2.0' means that this level is 'overrepresented' by a
factor 2)

	No diploma	Primary school	High school	Higher degree
Greece	0.02	0.30	10.5	11.5
Poland	0.12	1.50	1.04	11.7
France	0.15	0.45	10	12.5
Netherlands	—	0.50	20	17.3

To get into the habit of visiting museums, you have to start
young: only 3% of the visitors went into a museum for the first
time when they were over 24 years of age. The implication is of
course that you have to be taken there by your parents, i.e.
cultural capital is transmitted from one generation to the next.

It is not only the art which keeps working-class people away
from the museum. An exhibition on 'Interior Design in
Denmark', which showed glasswork, ceramics and furniture
such as could have been shown in a department store, drew an
even larger proportion of educated visitors and a corresponding-
ly smaller one from the working class. American art-museums
are more often filled with people than their European counterparts, so this tendency to draw primarily the educated may be
less pronounced, but it seems unlikely to me that it would be
absent, particularly in museums of contemporary art.

Because art is mysterious and inscrutable for them, the
members of the working class are in favor of arrows, explana-
tory texts and guides in a museum, whereas the upper-class
visitors believe that the works should 'speak for themselves'.

Officially, museums are democratic institutions, allowing
everybody to enjoy art. Should they go in for more popularity,
or stick with their own public of 'connoisseurs'? Curators and
critics are divided over this issue.

Alloway:... A museum hopes for attendance and it hopes for some
attention and if it gets it in the mass media it seems to me that this
requires more respect than you are willing to give it at the moment. It
seems to me essential for a museum to have a relationship with the
popular press too and to see that entertainment is part of it.
Glaser: What is the virtue of art news appearing on the 'food fashions
family furnishings' page of *The New York Times* more than it appears
in the art columns of that newspaper? What is the virtue of it appearing
in places where it becomes more and more adulterated and where there
is no serious discussion of the art?...
Seitz: One would assume that the wider the dissemination of art, in
whatever degree of accuracy or adulteration it takes place, the more
will a small group develop an even more hermetic art, which is
desirable. A great many important ideas and important things

inevitably, by their very nature, require a long history of response, and not only because they are complex intellectually. They also require a feeling pattern that is only built up over many, many years of experience[22].

People who have built up such a feeling pattern consider it, naturally, as a part of their personal identity, i.e. as their 'natural' good taste.

Bourdieu and his collaborators have studied the varieties in taste among the different social classes in France[23]. Their results, underpinned by a considerable amount of statistical data, show many similarities with Thorstein Veblen's earlier study of the leisure class, and seem applicable to most western countries.

Taste is partly enforced by economic circumstance. The members of the French working class have to economize: they buy durable clothes and sturdy practical furniture. Out of necessity and by habit they eat cheap and nourishing foodstuff: lard, potatoes, beans, pork, bread; and prefer it to daintier morsels. Their world is dominated by necessity; fashion is beyond their reach and therefore considered 'pretentious'.

The other classes define their position by the distance they can put between themselves and necessity: distinction is shown by the amount of difference from coarse and vulgar needs. That is why they prefer the fragile to the sturdy or the temporary to the durable in dress and in furniture. That, too, is why meals have to be refined, tasty and light, rather than nourishing and heavy; a labourer or a farmer *needs* a lot of food, but those who perform no manual work do not need so much.

The members of the middle class try to move as far as possible from the working class and as close as possible to the upper class. But neither their economic nor their cultural capital is sufficient. They cannot afford many luxuries and they are often unsure about their 'true value'. So they make do with imitation: imitation antique, imitation leather or imitation crystal. The same holds for their cultural tastes: they like film versions of classical books, they read popular works of science or condensed novels to 'improve their minds'. Forever uneasy about what constitutes 'quality' and what does not, they look for certainty in taste. The classical book and record clubs provide them with it. Hence experimental art, music or poetry is anathema to them; it is 'affected' and 'ridiculous'.

Their very struggle for the higher life, their 'pretensions' in speech, dress and manners, in knowledge and taste, is what is most distasteful to upper-class members. These consider working-class taste vulgar, but robust, naive and honest. Middle-class taste is perceived by them as pedantic, a caricature of the real thing. Nevertheless, a considerable amount of upper-class culture *is* assimilated by the middle class and thereby loses its value of distinction. The imitation of upper-class culture by the middle class is one of the driving forces behind cultural change; the upper class has to reset its sights in order to preserve its boundaries. (Of course it does not do so consciously; the banality of the popular leads to instinctive withdrawal).

'Good' taste and 'legitimate' culture are produced, circumscribed and defined by the members of the upper class. 'Form' in legitimate culture takes primacy over 'content'; not what you eat, but how it is prepared and savored; not what you say, but how it is said.

This attitude is shared with the middle class. Content often equals necessity; with the emphasis on form one shows how far one stands above it, how far necessity can be kept at bay. The upper and middle classes differ however in their elaboration of this principle.

One of the reasons for the perplexities of the middle class is that legitimate culture is by no means homogeneous. Is the work of Fautrier or Dubuffet great art or just a hoax? Is Beckett an important playwright or a charlatan?

There are upper-class spokesmen for either view. A constant struggle seems to be going on; whom are they to believe?

The lack of homogeneity in taste reflects the internal subdivisions of the upper class. The economic, the social and the cultural elites all belong to it, but their interests are different and often opposed. The members of the economic elite foot the bills of many cultural efforts. They want to see their values and their status confirmed, yet they are often not culturally up to the mark and they know it. The cultural elite owns or controls the means of cultural production, but is financially dependent on the economic elite, a position of subservience which it resents.

It is easy to imagine the frustrations of many members of the cultural elite. They are the best informed, the most knowledgeable, yet they lack the final decisive power of money. They often consider themselves as a 'relatively classless stratum'[24], for they do not have the economic wealth of the true capitalists. Thus many of them hope for a world less dominated by money. The ambiguity of their position is one reason why so many intellectuals have leftist leanings.

The members of the economic elite can afford anything they like. As in Veblen's time, they like the best; but an ostentatious display of wealth is frowned upon by the settled rich (just as an ostentatious display of learning is frowned upon by the truly learned). Expensive holidays, exquisite wines and domestic servants are all right; with lavish parties you have to watch your step. Homes ought to be furnished expensively but not flashily, e.g. with real antiques and works of art.

The members of the cultural elite, the artists, writers and academics, cannot afford this. Therefore their taste runs to the ascetic, a denial of the opulence of the rich: camping, mountaineering, the museum and the lending library; and in home

furnishings: the spare and simple interior, the modern lithograph rather than the classic oil painting.

These are the broad outlines of the varieties of taste among
French classes and subclasses according to Bourdieu. The value
of his model lies in its comprehensiveness and its statistical
underpinnings. The earlier model of Horkheimer and
Adorno[25] distinguished 'true' (*avant-garde*) art and lumped the
other artistic efforts together as 'culture industry'. Bourdieu
does not deny the exceptional position of the *avant-garde*, but
tries to attain a greater critical distance. He is able to assign a
definite place not only to highbrows and lowbrows, but also to
middlebrows and to relate the various positions. The concept
of 'cultural capital' liberates his model from the univocal
economic criterion of Marx and the Frankfurt School and
shows that cultural power is related to, but not identical with
economic power. Yet his analysis stays close enough to Marx
and neo-Marxist theory to use their conceptualization of
class-relations.

It is this general scheme which can be of use in understanding
the varieties of taste in other western countries. Of course there
are large differences: social capital plays a far greater role in
England and France than in the USA, Holland, Switzerland or
Sweden; the DAR can be seen as the US counterpart of the
British peerage, but its influence is incomparably smaller. The
working class is closer to the middle class in the USA than in
France or England[26]. The proletariat (poor whites and inner-
city blacks) in the USA is proportionately much more numerous than in the United Kingdom. Customs and attitudes may
differ, but all western countries have a working class, a middle
class and an upper class. Bourdieu's model makes it likely that
their different cultural habits start to make sense only when
they are seen *in relation to each other*, as positions in an overall
field. Veblen drew attention to taste as an element in the class
struggle, Adorno and Horkheimer pointed to the effect of the
'culture industry' on the behaviour of *avant-garde* artists, but
the theory of Bourdieu helps us to understand, better than the
others, why people from the middle class not only try to imitate
their 'betters', but also to shy away from their 'inferiors'; it
thereby provides an important clue to the rise of Adorno's
'culture industry' itself.

In particular the concepts of an economic, a social and a
cultural elite, uneasily related to each other, seem to be
applicable to all western countries. Every country has a cultural
elite; it is the inevitable outcome of cultural pursuits and a
differentiated system of education. In the USA its members are
called 'eggheads' or 'Liberals'; Tom Wolfe's 'art-compound'
belongs to it, and so does Mr Wolfe himself. Its values are
celebrated in the *New Yorker* and portrayed in the films of
Woody Allen and the novels of Saul Bellow. Gans distinguished between five cultural levels in his *Popular Culture and*

High Culture[27]; the upper two correspond to the varieties of taste of the cultural and economic elite in Bourdieu's model.

Within the outlines of this model, there is still a great deal of variation and contrast, engendered by the struggles between fractions of classes. The young want to show their mettle against the older generation; newcomers claim a place for themselves amongst the settled[28]. The classic restraint — sometimes going as far as 'studied seediness' — of the 'old rich' is a ploy against the flashy showiness of the parvenu[29].

A continuous tug-of-war is going on between various groups of the cultural elite on what belongs to legitimate culture: in poetry, in music and in the visual arts. All three seem to change continuously, in hot pursuit of novelty, often brought about by changes in technique: other uses of language, other musical instruments (tone-generators, computers), other visual means. In painting, dripping (Pollock) was followed by staining (Frankenthaler) and stencilling (Lichtenstein). After centuries of visual art in canvas, paint, marble and bronze, we have now works in cardboard, fluorescent tubes, earth and garbage.

Several possible reasons can be advanced for the ceaseless innovations. The most obvious is the one implied by Josiah Wedgwood. Forms of art serve as marks of identity and thus of distinction; they are therefore coveted and imitated by others who aspire to a similar status, and hence lose their power of distinction through the imitation. There had been a modest market in art for the masses such as cheap woodcuts. Since Wedgwood's time there has been a general increase in prosperity. As more and more people attained a state of affluence in which they could start to think of luxuries, this market expanded to the variety of mass art today. The expansion was accelerated by the spread of literacy and the swelling stream of information. Literacy and the concomitant increase in newspapers, magazines and novelettes are of course themselves both the symptoms and the motors of a general rise in cultural capital.

Paradoxically, the increasing amount of information has disadvantages for the work of art. Its emotional impact derives from a certain freshness, a possibility of novelty and surprise. Not many people read the same story over and over again. A work of art can get too well known, like Mozart's 'Eine kleine Nachtmusik', Michelangelo's 'Christ in the last Judgment' or van Gogh's 'Sunflowers'. Pop fans are not particularly eager to hear once more the Beatles in 'All you need is love'. The emotional impact has worn off by too much publicity or playing. Which sightseer has never felt a slight pang of disappointment when the sights looked exactly like the photographs[30]?

The work of visual art is recognized at a glance. Walking in a museum, the connoisseur can spot the Lichtensteins, Wesselmanns or Nolands, the Rouaults, Soutines or Picassos from afar. We seem to be able to assimilate pictorial information in larger doses and more quickly than auditive information. This may be one reason why the speed of turnover seems to be greater in the visual than in the other arts. Another is that the visual arts are a favorite hunting ground for ad-men; they too contribute to the spread of information, and to the 'debasement' of art. Finally, works of visual art are unique objects of luxury, sold for fairly high prices. This makes them at once more atractive than books or music as marks of distinction to the rich and more quickly 'contaminated' for the cultural elite.

All artists themselves of necessity contribute to the speed of change. To be noticed at all, in a field so full of competition, they have got to express something new and different. They must establish their artistic identity by an original contribution. The art critic Harold Rosenberg wrote about *The Tradition of the New*:

In the arts an appetite for a new look is now a professional requirement, as in Russia to be accredited as a revolutionist is to qualify for privileges... Whoever undertakes to create soon finds himself engaged in creating himself. Self-transformation and the transformation of others have constituted the radical interest of our century...[31].

The same urge towards originality at all costs is signalized by the painter-critic Michel Tapié:

Today, art must stupefy to be art. At a time when, for the best reasons and the worst, everything is brought into play to explain art, to popularize and to vulgarize it, to get us to swallow it down as a normal complement to our everyday living, the true creators know that the only way for them to express the inevitability of their message is through the extraordinary — paroxysm, magic, total ecstasy.
... the Individuals mature whose work makes us see that a new world, another world exists, or perhaps is only made clearer by the passage from one potentiality to another, from a finite to an intuitive infinite and thence to a transfinite, a reality in whose realm man can at last risk everything. For some time now we have been hearing the so-called right-thinking people say that *this* time we have gone so far beyond the limits that at last no one could possibly be fooled..., that *until now* one might, just, strictly speaking, have agreed..., but that now... and all the rest. Unfortunately for them, *now* a new era *is* beginning, with sensibilities both free and pure enough to walk into it confidently, and heedless of any way out[32].

Tapié revels in the resistance provoked by a new art-form; it is a 'proof' that it is really new and effective. But complete freedom and absolute novelty are illusions. No one, least of all the professional artist, is a clean slate; even the most uneducated have seen countless works of art in schoolbooks, newspapers and magazines. Whatever artists may have learned during their period of training — and with a view to their claims for originality they are often prone to disclaim any debts — awareness of the 'scene', of what other artists were doing, was certainly among it. Absolute novelty, if it could be conceived and made, would be incomprehensible, like a foreign language one does not understand. Elaine de Kooning wrote on tradition:

Western art is built on the biographical passion of one artist for another: Michelangelo for Signorelli; Rubens for Michelangelo; Delacroix for Rubens; Cézanne for Poussin; the Cubists for Cézanne; and Picasso, the philanderer, for anyone he sees going down the street. That something new in art cannot come into existence despite influence is a ridiculous idea, and it goes hand in hand with an even more ridiculous idea: namely that something totally new, not subject to any influence, *can* be created[33].

Artists are usually keen to disclaim any influence from other artists, for it contradicts their claims to orginality. Yet some of them generously admit it. Tom Wesselmann said in an interview:

When I first came to painting there was only De Kooning — that was what I wanted to be, with all its self-dramatization... I got my subject matter from Hans Memling (I started with 'Portrait Collages') and De Kooning gave me content and motivation[34].

Or the Photorealists on Pop Art:

McLean: 'Sure, I owe a big debt to Pop'
Bechtle: 'Pop was the catalyst'
Eddy: 'Without Pop I don't think this would have happened'[35]

The freedom of the artist is rather negatively defined: if he wants to do something original he has to know and to avoid what the others are doing — and they are trying to do the same thing. The painter Ad Reinhardt has forcefully expressed this:

It's been said many times in world-art writing that one can find some of painting's meanings by looking not only at what painters do but at what they refuse to do. And today many artists like myself refuse to be involved in some ideas. In painting, for me — no fooling-the-eye, no window-hole-in-the-wall, no illusions, no representation, no associations, no distortions, no paint-caricaturing, no dream pictures or drippings, no delirium trimmings, no sadism or slashings, no therapy, no kicking-the-effigy, no guilt, no anguish, no supernaturalism or subhumanism, no divine inspiration or daily perspiration, no personality-picturesqueness, no romantic bait, no gallery gimmicks, no neo-religious or neo-architectural hocus-pocus, no poetry or drama or theatre, no entertainment business, no vested interests, no Sunday hobby, no drug-store-museums, no free-for-all-history, no art history in America of ashcan-regional-WPA-Pepsi-Cola styles, no professionalism, no equity, no cultural enterprises, no bargain-art-commodity, no juries, no contests, no masterpieces, no prizes, no mannerisms or techniques, no communication or information, no magic tools, no bag of tricks-of-the-trade, no structure, no paint qualities, no impasto, no plasticity, no relationships, no experiments, no rules, no coercion, no anarchy, no anti-intellectualism, no irresponsibility, no innocence, no irrationalism, no low level of consciousness, no nature-mending, no reality-reducing, no life-mirroring, no abstracting from anything, no nonsense, no involvement, no confusing painting with everything that is not painting[36].

There are two main categories in this list of noes: criticism of bourgeois taste (hole-in-the-wall, representation, entertainment, drug-store, etc.) and assaults on his contemporaries and recent predecessors (drippings — Pollock; slashings — Fontana; divine inspiration — Gottlieb and Newman; impasto — de Kooning).

Direct competition makes artists often rather aggressive to each other. It is rare to find artists speaking kindly about work of their contemporaries. Particularly those with a similar stance constitute a threat. Frank Stella on Victor Vasarély:

I think the obvious comparison with my work would be Vasarély, and I can't think of anything I like less... mine has less illusionism than Vasarély's, but the Groupe de Recherche d'Art Visuel actually painted all the patterns before I did — all the basic designs that are in my painting... I didn't even know about it, and in spite of the fact that they used those ideas, those basic schemes, it still doesn't have anything to do with my painting. I find all that European geometric painting — sort of post-Max Bill School — a kind of curiosity — very dreary[37].

There *is* of course a great deal of imitation. Once Abstract Expressionism was 'recognized' as an important contribution, it spread to the schools, partly helped by some of the Abstract Expressionists themselves who were teaching. And the schools went through phases of Pop, of Hard-Edge and Photorealism afterwards.

The ambition of every painter remains to make his own contribution, that may bring him hardship and ridicule but in the end, he hopes, will ensure him his niche in art history, in the legitimate culture of his age. The economic disadvantages are more than offset by the cultural glory.

But it remains a tough job. Knowing all that has been done — and that he therefore cannot do if he wants to realize this ambition — leaves many a painter in a quandary. He feels and hopes to be at the front of the cultural development, but it often looks like the edge of an abyss. Robert Motherwell on his work:

I find that I ask of the painting process one of two separate experiences. I call one the 'mode of discovery and invention', the other the 'mode of joy and variation'. The former represents my deepest painting problem, the bitterest struggle I have undertaken: to reject everything I do not feel and believe. The other experience is when I want to paint for the sheer joy of painting. These moments are few. The strain of dealing with the unknown, the absolute, is gone. When I need joy, I find it only in making free variations on what I have already discovered, what I know to be mine... The other mode is a voyaging into the night, one knows not where, on an unknown vessel, an absolute struggle with the elements of the real[38].

The one artist that the pioneer may imitate with impunity is himself. Many artists, once they have established their identity, stick to it. That is why all mature Rothkos, Newmans or Poons's resemble each other, and why we can recognize them so easily in a museum. It is the rare artist who, after having found his way, changes it to make another contribution. Mondrian and Picasso were such artists.

Repetition — Motherwell's 'mode of joy and variation' — is not only or even primarily practised because of its commercial advantages. The foregoing should make clear that it is pretty difficult for an artist today to find something personal and new to express about the visual world. His identity for outsiders hinges on his discovery; but as he is involved with his whole personality in the struggle for invention and subsequent recognition, it becomes also a mark of identity for himself.

His work embodies a new subjective interpretation of the visual world — even if it is such a 'cool' interpretation as in Photorealism. If he succeeds in getting recognition, his vision will be shared by many other people. They, too, will never see reality entirely in the same way as before. The Impressionists have changed our vision of light and shade, of the changing colors of light during the day, and of the variety of color in shades. Pop Artists changed our vision of commercial trivia, Photorealists our way of seeing photographs. If the artist is very successful, like Van Gogh, Mondrian or Pollock, his vision will be incorporated in ordinary home furnishings, printed textiles and jigsaw puzzles.

Religion and propaganda are also subjective interpretations of the world; they have several aspects in common with art. Artists have often worked as propagandists or been reproached for refusing to do so. The tie with religion is even closer. The first known works of art and the art of primitive tribes were always religious. Some artists are well aware of the proximity between the feelings engendered by their work and those of religion. Barnett Newman wrote in 1948:

We are reasserting man's natural desire for the exalted, for a concern with our relationship to the absolute emotions. We do not need the obsolete props of an outmoded and antiquated legend. We are creating images whose reality is self-evident and which are devoid of the props and crutches that evoke associations with outmoded images, both sublime and beautiful. We are freeing ourselves of the impediments of memory, association, nostalgia, legend, myth, or what have you, that have been the devices of Western European painting. Instead of making *cathedrals* out of Christ, man, or 'life', we are making it out of ourselves, out of our own feelings. The image we produce is the self-evident one of revelation, real and concrete, that can be understood by anyone who will look at it without the nostalgic glasses of history[39].

The last is of course the bid for general recognition that Newman craves for, and the outcome of his genuine conviction that he has discovered such a primeval, general form. In the light of what was written above, it seems unlikely that his claim could be substantiated. Indeed, in 1950 he had a one-man show at Betty Parsons Gallery which received a single favorable review. 'It was the only favorable review he would receive for years[40].'

For if Newman had freed himself from props and crutches and from the devices of European painting, the public had not.

But it was well aware that his utterly simple paintings were meant as a challenge to the 'outmoded images' to which it was used.

The whole development of modern art is accompanied by a stream of abuse, ranging from 'any child can do this better' to 'a scandalous hoax imposed by the art-mafia'. The new is not only exhilarating, it is also a threat to the already known. An artist may have found a way to 'revolutionize seeing', but many people dislike revolutions, even if they are 'only visual'. For our habits of perception are intimately tied up with our identities. The painting may express the artist's identity, but the spectators have their own identities to take care of and these are partly expressed in what they like in art.

Conservative attitudes find their natural mode of expression in conservative art: the art of the past, or of Andrew Wyeth today. The art-dealer Joseph Duveen succeeded almost single-handed in dislodging a number of American millionaires from their attachement to nineteenth-century French salon art and transferring it to old masters[41]. How much their paintings meant to them is evident from their insistence that the collections be kept together when they donated them to a museum. *That* particular collection was *his* (Kresge's, Altman's) personal contribution to American culture.

The only people who can really understand the contribution of the 'revolutionary' artist are those who share many of his experiences: his cronies, an occasional critic or curator who has followed him closely. The critic Clement Greenberg sat in for some time in the painting classes of Hans Hofmann:

The teachings of Hofmann on the pure plastic mechanics of painting gave him the tools for formal analysis of color, line, planes and their 'push and pull' of space in the art of Matisse and Kandinsky, and especially in Cubism — and a vision of artistic form as embodying its own relevance. And Hofmann students like Lee Krasner opened the way to Greenberg's acquaintances with young American artists like Pollock and De Kooning... But however indebted was Greenberg to Hofmann's formal vision and to Graham's artistic discoveries, it was Greenberg alone whose journalism championed Pollock, Gorky, De Kooning, Smith and Robert Motherwell to the public at large in the 1940's... He was asked to organize or write prefaces to exhibitions of the artists' work for academic and commercial galleries, both in America and abroad... His role easily shifted from the alienated critic writing art columns for intellectual magazines to an Impresario in the New York art world judged by his commitment to a specific type of art and respected for its ultimate (commercial and influential) success. As such he took on the character of a Prophet in the New York art world. Artists like Anthony Caro, Morris Louis and Kenneth Noland sought his criticism and advice, and gallery directors sought his predictions; when Greenberg selected the 'Emerging Talent' exhibition at Samuel Kootz Gallery in 1954, Louis and Noland were included[42].

Greenberg had been editor of the *Partisan Review* (1941–1943) and used *his* creative talent as a writer to further the cause of a group of artists, primarily the Abstract Expressionists. The very identification of a critic with a particular movement in art precludes a detached stance from which he can judge dispassionately some rival group. Greenberg disliked Pop Art, and said so repeatedly, but to no avail.

The goals of the artist are clear. He wants his 'self-evident image of revelation' to be seen and accepted by the people who count: his peers, his dealers, his critics, his collectors and above all museum curators. In the long run, he strives to leave his mark on the history of art, to be recognized as having 'deflected the course of art' or 'significantly contributed' to its development. 'Proof' of such a contribution is the literature devoted to his work: the page (or number of pages) in the respected trade journals (*Art Forum, Art News, Studio International, Art International, Cimaise*, etc.), the space in books reviewing a period, ultimately the monograph written by an eminent authority. He wants his work to hang or stand in major museums: the Museum of Modern Art, the Whitney, the Tate, the Stedelijk Museum in Amsterdam, the Centre Pompidou; perhaps even the Louvre or the Metropolitan. Henry Geldzahler, the Metropolitan's curator for twentieth-century art, wrote:

De Kooning has said that he never expected to see his work (*Easter Monday*) hanging forty feet from the Rembrandts against which he must finally measure himself. This kind of confrontation can only happen at the Metropolitan... The Museum should not attempt to survey the field but rather concentrate on key pictures that would continue the historical selection which is the strength of the Museum. Our Pollock, Gorky and De Kooning are excellent examples of what I mean by key pictures; high moments in the work of great artists[43].

Hanging in the Metropolitan means that you are up to par and have survived the severest tests.

Artistic recognition is usually accompanied by financial rewards, but the latter are not the major goal. Art is not a profession to get rich in quickly, neither for artists nor for dealers; it is too risky for that. The effort is to make a profit on cultural capital, not on economic capital (Figs. 12 and 13).

The road to recognition is fraught with difficulties. The first step for the artist is to have his work on view. Some galleries rent their space to artists; naturally, such galleries have a low standing with the 'informed public'. If he is noticed and gets some reviews, he may move up to a regular gallery, or to a 'better' one than the gallery that accepted him first. Galleries are not above bribing artists away from their competitors. At first, he gets often only included in group shows; the next rung is the one-man show. If he passes these tests he may be accepted in group shows in a museum; another step forward is the one-man show in a museum. At the early stages of his career, the judgment of the 'right' people in the art-world is crucial; if he fails their standards, he gets nowhere. Harold Rosenberg on exhibitions:

Figure 12
Lithograph to honor Brahms, by
Ludwig Michalek, on the occasion
of the unveiling of his statue in
Vienna in 1908

The turnout at a current art show, which consists almost exclusively of
artists and of practitioners of closely allied professions — art teachers,
museum employees, decorators, architects, designers, photographers
— is by comparison with the élites of other days a very odd group; not
only does it fail to represent social authority, it does not even represent
its own social function as a professional group, since other artists and
members of the same professions as those present, with an education,
income, prestige equivalent to theirs, despise this art or regard it as
irrelevant to their work; as a *New Yorker* novelist once said to me,
'Kafka is interesting, but of course he's not in my field'[44.]

The function of Rosenberg's 'odd group' is in my opinion
quite clear. If they like what they see, they can spread the word
and thereby promote the work of the artist. Self-praise (in
which all artists indulge, see for instance the quote by
Newman) is very ineffective; you need someone else to do the
selling.

Peggy Guggenheim, a collector and early promoter of the
abstract expressionists, has clearly described the process of
Jackson Pollock's 'breakthrough':

Figure 13
Le Corbusier and Henry Moore
after receiving honorary degrees in
Cambridge, England, 1959.
Though not so exuberantly as in
the past, cultural heroes still
receive their share of honors

In London, in 1939, Herbert Read had conceived the idea of holding a spring salon. In 1941, I decided to try it out in New York. I appointed a jury. The members were Barr, Sweeney, Soby, Mondrian, Duchamp, Putzel and myself. The first year it worked very well and out of the pickings we had a very fine show of about forty paintings. The stars who emerged were Jackson Pollock, Robert Motherwell and William Baziotes... This (i.e. Pollock's first one-man show) was held in November 1943. The introduction to the catalogue was written by James Johnson Sweeney, who helped a lot to further Pollock's career. In fact, I always referred to Pollock as our spiritual offspring. Clement Greenberg, the critic, also came to the fore and championed Pollock as the greatest painter of our time. Alfred Barr bought the *She Wolf*, one of the best paintings in the show, for the Museum of Modern Art. Dr. Morley asked for the show in her San Francisco Museum, and bought the *Guardians of the Secret*[45].

The Abstract Expresssionists had a harder time than most artists, because in the thirties and early forties modern art was seen by the small American art-establishment as almost an exclusively European affair (see chapter 7). And international recognition came for them only when the European dealers and critics, with the painter-critic Michel Tapié foremost among them, set their stamp of approval in the late fifties[46].

Art-dealers are cagey about committing themselves. They are aware that the Impressionists were not recognized in time, and that the dealer Durand-Ruel got rich in the end by stocking them. But they are *also* aware that the painters who *were* recognized in the Paris of 1870, Bouguereau and Meissonier, are nowadays considered of but little value (though they have come in for a reappraisal). By accepting an artist, they are themselves helping him to get recognition; will he turn out to be a Bouguereau or a Manet? Galleries are the financiers, the 'banks' of artists, and many of them have gone bankrupt by backing the wrong men, or backing them too early, etc.[47].

Museum curators are even more careful. They have trustees or board members breathing down their necks, and if they spend public money on an expensive modern work, they know that even outside the museum some tough questions may be raised. Their options are often more limited than a dealer's, because they cannot resell or exchange what they bought. Thus prospective purchases are very carefully screened. Even so, many directors are doubtful about their ability to spot genius. Norman Reid, director of the Tate Gallery, said in an interview in 1967:

We do have to accept the premise that not more than fifteen percent of our purchases *now* will have any significant value fifty years from today. We are buying today's painting at, I hope, reasonable prices so that we can make the Tate's modern collection as representative as possible, but we have no touchstone of flair which will ensure that our purchase choices will have a durability of fifty years. In this way, we do not differ from the great private collectors of today. We must face the fact that in the majority of cases both they and ourselves will be seen to have made wrong choices when we are examined through the wrong end of a culture telescope fifty years from now[48].

If this warning holds the curator back, his instincts propel him forward. The curator or director has also an ambition and a creative urge. He hopes to make art history by his acquisitions and his shows, by the artists he has discovered and the developments which he saw clearly before anyone else. Dore Ashton on the ambitions of the modern curator:

The average curator is beset with a number of conflicting ambitions. On the one hand, he fancies himself a reporter, bringing all the news to all the people all the time. On the other, he wishes to be registered in history himself as an interpreter and keen prophet. He goes about his business like a diviner, looking for signs.

His empirical research is conducted rapidly and the signs are collected with urgency. Armed with a few 'tendencies' he proceeds to make history ... Despite his basically empirical approach — what's going on in Chicago, New York or California — he longs to bring to bear the scholarly residue of his training. Consequently, trends and tendencies are merely interpreted; they are given generical titles and imposingly cloaked in professional jargon intended to lift them from the realm of the newsy chronicle into the august realm of permanent history.

In this process many arbitrary exhibitions are conceived and catalogued, with participating artists uncomfortably pegged, ready to be interred by the mayor with his silver spade in the space-capsule-of-our-culture-for-the-future. The package is always neatly labeled in the best advertising technique, and ready to be deposited forever. No sooner has the public been informed of a new 'historical' step, such as Primary Structure sculpture, or Systemic Painting or Eccentric Abstraction when these breathless history mongers are busy preparing still other brand names, viable, they believe, for future history[49].

The attitude is perfectly understandable. Barr in New York, Sandberg in Amsterdam and Pontus Hultén in Stockholm made their names with the exciting programs of exhibitions which they staged; on the strength of his work, Hultén became director of the foremost modern museum in France, the Centre Pompidou. Henry Geldzahler made the show 'New York Painting and Sculpture: 1940–1970' at the Metropolitan, but the show also 'made' Geldzahler[50].

The art world resembles a poker game. Artists, collectors, curators, dealers and critics all hold cards, but no one has a royal flush nor even a full house; yet, in true style, everyone bids as if he had. Some people are — or were — more influential than others: Barr, Duchamp, Sandberg and Greenberg were often mentioned as extremely influential for some time. Some art-dealers have strong cards: Castelli, Janis, Marlborough. But there is no multinational with absolute control of the market. It involves money and speculation, and therefore also some dirty tricks. Two studies in depth, one in the USA and the other in France, have failed to turn up a widespread corruption or a gigantic conspiracy[51]. Some of the ostensibly objective reviews are paid for by the gallery or the artist. Galleries and collectors have been known to bid high in auctions in order to raise the price of their own stock. But just as all the advertising of GM and Ford has not stopped the advance of Japanese and European automobiles, so all the tricks and sales talk will not decide the pecking-order in art. Bernard Buffet and Alfred Manessier are two artists who were launched in major campaigns; but their stars have gone down, not up. Peter Selz, curator at the Museum of Modern Art, America's foremost modern museum, organized in 1962 a panel discussion to stem the rising tide of Pop Art, with the well-known critics Kunitz, Kramer and Ashton, Professor Leo Steinberg and Henry Geldzahler. Only the last came out for Pop (and he was a young and relatively unknown assistant at the time); all the others were against. It was to no avail[52]. The art-world forms what the sociologist Norbert Elias has called a configuration[53]. Different groups of people have different interests; people in the same category, such as artists, dealers or collectors, often have opposed interests. Each tries to advance his own, each needs the others. Money, knowledge, talent and business acumen all play a part; but none plays a decisive part. It is an imbalanced network of forces in constant flux as new participants come into it and try to change it. One myth holds that it is *only* artistic talent that decides the issue; another myth that it is all a hoax and a game played by crooks. Neither is credible. The artistic aspect is probably the central and most important, but that does not make the social aspect disappear.

The most powerful in the configuration are probably the curators and directors of the prestige museums, such as the Tate Gallery, the Centre Pompidou, the Museum of Modern Art or the Stedelijk Museum in Amsterdam. Acceptance of an artist's work by them, particularly if it is exhibited in the permanent collection, means that the artist is in the antechamber to the hall of fame, that he has really left his mark on the art-scene. Yet these directors, too, often correct their original judgement, as the quotation of Norman Reid has shown. Then the Bernard Buffet, the Alfred Manessier discreetly disappears to the stockrooms to make way for a more likely candidate for eternal fame.

The power network in the art-world resembles those in the social sciences. In psychology, there are many conflicting theories: of personality, of emotion, of learning, of perception and of motivation (many of them covering only a single area), which are advocated side by side in the trade journals. As in art, the rival factions hate and despise each other, but they are usually unable to destroy each other. Yet the struggle for legitimacy is not wholly in vain; some theories, like behaviorism, are losing adherents. In psychology too, there are bigwigs with large laboratories and research staffs, who can exert more pull than the smaller fry, but who have no full control of the field. Elimination of some theories and acceptance of others arises by a sort of mutual and muted consent; the budding psychologist has to fight the skepticism of his peers and to wrestle for recognition. Sign of acceptance is publication of his work in a respected trade journal[54]. In sociology, the situation is similar and the disagreement is even greater.

The foregoing analysis gives some reasons why artists have to innovate and why the innovators are not united: Hard-Edge and Pop Art both took a stand against Abstract Expressionism, but also opposed each other. It shows why the changes, always proclaimed to be 'revolutionary' are in fact gradual: from Abstract Expressionism, over Rauschenberg and Johns to Pop Art, and from there to Photorealism.

'Legitimate' advanced art is only the top of the art-pyramid. The few American *avant-garde* galleries, mainly centered in New York for obvious reasons, are far outnumbered by the less experimental galleries and art-shops in other American cities (*and* in New York); their naturalistic landscapes and still-life studies adorn the walls of a large group of Americans who have learned to appreciate Impressionism and accept — but not yet like — Expressionism. This kind of art, found in an even more simplified form on Christmas cards and sold in Macy's, is usually completely ignored by the *avant-garde*; Ad Reinhardt's enumeration of things to avoid in painting is one of the few acknowledgements of its existence. Its ubiquity, in conjunction with Reinhardt's noes, can help to explain in part the choice of subject-matter by the Photorealists. John Kacere's female behinds show him to paint the nude — but with a difference. Ben Schonzeit's groceries and drugstores are also intended as another kind of still-life. By choosing the very material that up till then was considered the epitome of vulgarity and bad taste, the artist demonstrates his power; *he* decides what should be considered a proper subject for art.

And this power is indeed effective. The cafeterias of Richard Estes and the marquees of Robert Cottingham *have* created a new sensibility, another view of the too-familiar, for those in the know. No Airstream trailer looks quite the same, after you have learned to look at it through the eyes of Ralph Goings. The Impressionists have shown that a pier, a bridge, an old door or an office interior is worth looking at; Demuth extended it to factories and elevators, Davis to Odol bottles, John Salt and Don Eddy extended it again to wrecking-yards and parking-lots; they may have been sensitized by the photographs of Walker Evans.

A 'pyramid of taste' is a useful simile; the top is narrow, the base is wide, both in terms of products and of consumers. With Adorno, we ought to reject the idealistic view that the top hangs in thin air; it is understandable only in relation to the base. But his view that a sharp line divides the bottom from the top, and that everything below that line belongs to 'culture industry', is untenable, I believe. Below the top, in the appreciation of the consumers lies the advanced art of yesteryear, of Demuth, Hopper, Shahn, O'Keefe and Davis, nowadays appreciated by a large segment of the educated middle class. Below that again, the Ash Can School and the Impressionists and the innumerable vulgarizations. The experimentation of advanced art can be understood as an effort to create an exclusive preserve for connoisseurs, set apart from both the more accepted art of yesteryear *and* the conservative art preferred by the economic elite. But, just as Wells' systematic botanist, the connoisseur can still participate in larger circles. Appreciating Ralph Goings does not cut you off from Monet or Cézanne, any more than the seeing of art-house movies prevents the enjoyment of a western. But you get less of a kick out of a modern version of an Impressionistic landscape than you do out of Goings; the emotional impact has worn thin.

A rise in mathematical knowledge does not invalidate the tables of multiplication, but relates them to a larger structure. In the same sense does a rise in artistic knowledge increase your range of understanding and appreciation. The most personal and common themes have descended so far in the pyramid that many find them hard to appreciate; Gainsborough's 'Pinky' and Joshua Reynolds' 'Little Samuel' were high art two hundred years ago, but children's innocence is now only a subject for Halliday cards, even though children are as sweet now as they were then. Kacere and Wesselmann deserve admiration for bringing yet another meaning out of the nude, a subject which seemed photographed to death. Babies, nudes, loving mothers and sunsets have been overworked in art and advertising; consequently they are practically taboo in all levels of the pyramid but the lowest. Going down in the pyramid means enlarging the audience, for it potentially includes the higher levels as well. Intellectuals often indulge in reading a whodunit or seeing a B-picture. Hence the constant tug-of-war between directors and producers in Hollywood; but hence, too, the complaints of critics about the triteness of so many movies; they have seen the trick once too often.

For a member of the cultural elite, going down in the pyramid of products means meeting more and more familiar material in ever larger quantities produced under more visible economic conditions. This has probably induced Adorno and Horkheimer to lump it all together under the concept of 'culture industry'. It has led them to see quite sharply that highbrow artists react against their middle- and lowbrow competitors, but it has blurred their view on the points of similarity. There are different audiences and they have different tastes: 'Mary Hartman' addressed itself to a more restricted and sophisticated TV audience than 'Dallas' or 'The Jordaches'. Rockwell Kent worked for a smaller and culturally 'richer' audience than Norman Rockwell — without ever attaining the status of 'important artist'. The last two examples show with particular clarity that the idea 'that it is all a matter of talent' which distinguishes the *avant-garde* from the rest is wrong, and that the label of 'culture industry' is too easy. Both Kent and Rockwell were highly talented, versatile and inventive men. We get a better perspective if we see it as a different kind of specialization. Illustrators work of necessity for larger audiences than the *avant-garde*; consequently they have to adopt different strategies to get to the top of their particular area in the profession.

Awareness of the opportunities in the visual arts diverts a large proportion of art students from trying to reach the 'absolute' pinnacle of the *avant-garde*, into the much larger areas below the top: advertising, illustration, animation and layout work. Many continue for some time their 'free' work in their spare time; but when they are successful, the job absorbs these ambitions. To be good at it, you have to believe in the job you are doing; the material conditions of work affect your outlook. William H. Whyte has spelled out in detail the social and economic pressures which make young managers conform to the standards and beliefs of the company they are working for[55]. His analysis seems applicable to other jobs as well. The successful advertising artist may remember wistfully his youthful ambitions, he keeps an eye on what happens at the fine art front and uses it when the occasion arises, but he can put his soul into another ad for Nabisco. He remains still a member of the cultural elite; perceiving the different aims and audiences, he can maintain a divided loyalty. The situation of the 'practical architect' who regrets that he was not commissioned for the local theatre, but got only the police-station, is rather similar.

He, too, will try to turn out the best possible police-station.

The above analysis can help to explain the different reactions of the home-owners in Halen and Wertherberg, and also the reaction of the architects. The 'honesty' of exposed concrete and the 'simplicity' of painted cinderblocks looked cheap and shoddy to the lower middle class people in Wertherberg. So they hid the concrete behind rolled brick siding, which in turn looked 'cheap' and 'shoddy' to the architects. Each party made of course its appropriate value-judgements from its own position in the field. Exposed concrete may in Germany be interpreted as a saving on finishes, because the normal plaster finish has been omitted; hence its connotation of cheapness. Rolled brick siding is in keeping with many other materials used in lower middle class culture: imitation leather, imitation walnut, imitation antique, etc., and for that very reason anathema to an upper-class architect.

Taste depends on previous experience, sometimes on formal training; it is a part of our cultural capital and an important element in our social identity. Patterns of taste make sense, particularly when they are seen in relation to each other; they provide some of the reasons for the cultural lag, for the assimilation of the taste of one group by another and for the preeminent position of the cultural elite. This elite is no unified group with a common purpose; it is united only in its dislike of 'bourgeois' taste, but otherwise split up in factions struggling for leadership.

Division according to classes and fractions of classes is only part of the story (though an often neglected part, because it is thought to 'debase' art). The other part, mentioned here and analyzed further for architecture in Chapter 7, is the emotional orientation provided by art. Through art we may get a different view of who we are, what we are doing and whither we are going. It enriches our view of history, of our environment and of each other; it creates a fellowship across national boundaries and across the ages. It is this aspect which is behind the high regard and intense feelings which art evokes, and which partly explain why architects prefer to become known as 'artists' rather than as 'technicians'. The next chapter will deal more specifically with this predisposition.

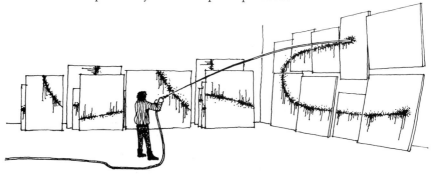

6 Architects and their Belief-systems

Architects share several of the characteristics and conditions of the visual artists. They, too, have a tradition, transmitted over the generations by a complex social system, and an 'avant-garde' consisting of warring factions, watched and followed at some distance by the ordinary practitioners.

But the differences are also considerable. Nearly all of their work is 'made to order'. A large and very heterogeneous group of people is involved in the execution of the architect's design: building inspectors, contractors, subcontractors and suppliers, construction workers, planners, realtors, lawyers, and structural and mechanical engineers. The only things that the architect (or his office) makes himself are the drawings, specifications and sometimes the contracts of the project; the actual building is done by others.

The Standard Form of Agreement between Owner and Architect (AIA Document B131) enumerates the following services performed by the architect:

.... ascertain the requirements of the Project
.... prepare schematic design studies
.... submit ... a statement of Probable Project Construction Cost
.... prepare ... Design Development Documents consisting of plans, elevations and other drawings and outline specifications
.... prepare ... Working Drawings and Specifications ... General Conditions of the Contract ... assist in the drafting of Proposal and Contract Forms
.... filing the required documents to secure approval of governmental authorities
.... assist in obtaining proposals from Contractors
.... make decisions on all claims of the Owner and the Contractor
.... make periodic visits to the site
.... issue Certificates for Payment[1]

Only the 'schematic design studies' and the 'Design Development Documents' engage the artistic talents of the architect; all the other activities have to do with practical matters. Inquiries held in the USA in 1950 showed that architects spent on the average 15.2% of their time on architectural design[2]; the same percentage was found in research in Holland. But nearly all of them want to spend *more* time on design, and less on meetings, supervision and administrative work[3].

Time spent on design may be severely limited by the demands of practice, but it is the part of the job that is most thoroughly enjoyed. Salaman questioned 52 London architects in 1970[4] and found that for 63% of them 'creativity, plus design enjoyment' gave the major work-satisfaction, and that 58% believed that architects differ from other people because of their 'artistic aesthetic awareness plus general consciousness of environment'. In an inquiry among 600 German architects[5], the statement: 'My chosen profession should give me the opportunity to do creative work' got by far the most adherence: 66%. Only 10% of the respondents agreed that the profession of their choice 'should offer them the opportunity to help other people'.

The primacy of the artistic task over the practical has often been stressed by architects in their writings. Paul Cret wrote in 1934:

All education in Fine Arts (and it is not out of place here to reaffirm one's belief that architecture is primarily a fine art, and not a branch of engineering, of real estate or of a more or less hazy sociology) has for its main object the development of the artist's personality[6].

Cret taught architecture in the Beaux Arts system at the University of Pennsylvania. Le Corbusier, that arch-enemy of Beaux Arts, agrees with Cret on the primacy of art over construction or practical usefulness:

Architecture is the masterly, correct and magnificent play of masses brought together in light.

Architecture has another meaning and other goals than to emphasize construction and to answer needs (needs in the sense, as here understood, of usefulness, comfort and practical disposition). ARCHITECTURE is above all the art which reaches the level of platonic grandeur, of mathematical order, of speculation, of the perception of harmony by moving relationships. That is the GOAL of architecture.

You use stone, wood, concrete: you build houses and palaces; that is construction. Ingenuity is at work. But suddenly, you touch my heart, you do me good, I am happy, and I say: 'this is beautiful. This is Architecture. Here is art'. My house is practical. Thanks, just as I thank the railway-engineers and the telephone company. You have not touched my heart. But (now) the walls stand out against the sky in such an order that I am moved. I feel your intentions. You were gentle, brutal, charming or dignified. Your stones tell me...[7].

The overevaluation of the art side of architecture is partly a defensive strategy. The scope of the profession has been — and still is — continuously reduced. Structural design, heating and ventilating and the design of sanitary installations were lost to specialists and outside firms. Programming and building process management are on their way out. It leads architects to claim superiority for the one domain that is still entirely theirs.

But there are also positive reasons. As artists and image-makers, architects believe that they are close to the central values in their society. The historical tourist sights, from Williamsburg to Monticello, from the Taj Mahal to Notre-Dame of Paris, visibly demonstrate to them that architects leave their mark on the image of a period, and that on a scale, a 'canvas', of which other artist are understandably jealous. 'Arts is a cousin to religion, and its priests owe their high status in society to the respect for its ideological function. The admiration for bridges, dams and spaceships is of another, less exalted kind. Walter Gropius wrote in 1919:

What is architecture? Indeed, the crystalline expression of the noblest thoughts of man, of his character, his humanity, his creed, his religion![8]

And Eliel Saarinen wrote in 1948:

The soul of the past is conveyed to posterity through the infallible language of art, the greatest treasure of human culture. When studying this language of art — rich and fecund — it is as if dwelling in a sacred grove of memories where the thoughts, feelings and aims of our forebears speak to us their silent tongue, through form. And one gets a deep veneration for the work done[9].

Only about 15% of the architect's time is spent on design; all the rest goes into the practical problems of running an office, meeting deadlines, solving problems of detail and finance, etc. Most architects would probably subscribe to the view in a RIBA publication:

The architect has to be conversant with constructional techniques, and know a great deal about building materials. When studying the purpose for which his building is intended, he must be able to envisage the many functional problems that will arise in use, and arrange his design so that these will be solved in the most efficient way possible always bearing in mind the ultimate cost of the project[10].

Many architects would maintain that 'good architecture' is more efficient and not more expensive than 'bad architecture'. But 'good architecture' refers primarily to aesthetic quality. For, as the economist Marion Bowley noted a little sadly:

... architects are apt to consider themselves primarily as artists and their work as dependent on individual creative inspiration. The discovery of the aesthetic solution to a particular problem thus occupies the centre of their endeavour. They may only grudgingly admit that design for building in modern society involves much more than the solution of an aesthetic problem, and that the basically appropriate aesthetic solution is not independent of costs, other branches of expert knowledge, and the conditions of the building process itself. The profession is organised in fact in terms of architecture as a fine art, and not in terms of architecture as the design element of the production process for buildings[11].

Architects rate their peers on their artistic achievements, and not on practicality, economics or their ingenuity in detailing. Exhibitions on architecture are nearly always staged in art-museums.

The authoritative magazines in architecture, such as *Architectural Design, Progressive Architecture, The Architectural Review, Architecture d'aujourd'hui, Domus, Architettura, Werk,* publish buildings selected with a view to their aesthetic interest and discuss them primarily in aesthetic terms.

The pecking-order in architecture becomes somewhat better visible if we measure the amount of print given to some well-known architects in handbooks:

The grading varies with the data and place of publication, the personal views of authors and editors and the complexities of the lives of their subjects; yet the overall correspondence between the different columns is striking. The 'Four Great Makers' at the top of each list are recognized by all editors to be in a class by themselves.

Table 3

	Knaur's Lexikon, 1963	Pevsner Dictionary, 1975	Richards' Who's Who, 1977
Le Corbusier	6	4	2
Wright	4.8	4	1.9
Gropius	4.4	4	1.5
Mies	8.1	2.4	2.5
Aalto	3	1.5	1.7
Eero Saarinen	1.7	2	0.4
Louis Kahn	2.1	0.6	0.6
SOM	1.6	—	0.3
Rietveld	1.1	0.6	0.7
Utzon	1.6	—	0.3
Rudolph	0.3	0.6	0.3

Measured length in number of printed columns, exclusive of illustration. Sources: N. Pevsner, J. Fleming and H. Honour, *A Dictionary of Architecture*; J.M. Richards, *Who's Who in Architecture*; Knaur's *Lexikon der modernen Architektur.*

There exists a 'legitimate' architecture, comparable to 'legitimate' music or literature. It is held up by critics to the general public for admiration. An architect who has succeeded in obtaining a place in that category of excellence stands a good chance to get into the history books and thus to go down to posterity as having 'significantly contributed to the culture of his time'. He is much in demand as a guest speaker and visiting critic in the architectural schools. His work is discussed in the popular press (*Time, Newsweek, Fortune, The New York*

Times) and sent along on travelling exhibitions. And, perhaps most gratifying of all, he stands a better chance to obtain one of those coveted commissions for 'a cultural monument' — an embassy, a city hall, a museum — than his equally well known but less highly regarded competitors. On such a commission, in which economics are not the prime consideration, he can once more demonstrate his virtuosity as a designer and perhaps? rise still further on the list.

To be well known is a necessary but not a sufficient condition, as the sociologist Judith Blau has demonstrated[12]. She asked 420 New York architects, working for 153 Manhattan firms, to check 50 architects on whether they knew their names and whether they liked their contributions to modern architecture (table 4).

Some of the better-known names (SOM, Venturi, Soleri, Yamasaki, Goff, Harrison and Lapidus) were not universally liked. I am inclined to attribute their lower scores to (at least) two different causes. It seems likely that SOM, Yamasaki and Lapidus were getting less sympathy because they were seen as giving in to 'the dictates of business' and 'slick commercial taste'. Venturi, Soleri and Goff can never be charged with such failings; their lower marks are probably due to their very special stances.

All architects have to spend some time on specifications, estimates, client contacts and organization, as well as on design. Circumstances force most of them to concentrate on one side rather than the other. The 'top-notch designers' can be viewed as specialists on the artistic side, and the partners of the streamlined office offering comprehensive architectural services as their opposite number, specialized in the practical aspects of the profession. But the latter often seem to believe that they are not living up to the standards of the profession:

In all the publicity, in the large number of feature stories about Welton Becket and his firm over the years — there were many, the magazines *Time, Saturday Evening Post, Newsweek, Fortune* to name a few — a goodly number of attempts were made by writers to pin labels on the man and on his firm. 'Businessman's Architect' was one he particularly disliked... Although Becket never said it, what he really wanted to be known as was an 'Architect's Architect'. Of course, that phrase, when it is used at all, is not applied to the kind of architect Becket was. Maybe to the solitary, or almost solitary artist-architect who takes one job, or at most a few jobs at a time, and then only from those clients he likes for projects that interest him. Or it might be applied to the great masters, the ones who are sometimes called 'form-makers' or something similar[13].

The belief that the artistic aspects of architecture are somehow superior to the practical — a belief apparently shared by Paul Cret, Le Corbusier and Welton Becket — is transmitted from one generation to the next in architectural school.

Table 4   Attitudes about individuals and their contributions

Name	Percent like	Percent know	Ratio of like to know
Le Corbusier	95	100	0.95
L. Kahn	95	99	0.96
F.L. Wright	93	99	0.94
E. Saarinen	92	99	0.93
A. Aalto	91	94	0.97
P. Nervi	91	97	0.93
Mies van der Rohe	83	96	0.87
W. Gropius	82	97	0.84
I.M. Pei	82	99	0.83
M. Breuer	78	98	0.79
R. Neutra	78	94	0.83
The Architects' Collaborative	78	90	0.86
K. Tange	78	86	0.91
C. & R. Eames	76	83	0.91
B. Fuller	72	92	0.79
P. Rudolph	72	99	0.73
J. Sert	67	82	0.81
O. Niemeyer	67	95	0.70
M. Safdie	66	87	0.76
The Cambridge 7	65	74	0.87
E.L. Barnes	65	86	0.76
P. Johnson	62	96	0.65
R. Giurgola	61	73	0.83
J. Johansen	60	83	0.73
R. Meier	60	80	0.75
C. Moore	56	72	0.78
Skidmore, Owings & Merrill	55	96	0.57
H. Stubbins	51	76	0.67
P. Soleri	50	86	0.58
J. Stirling	49	54	0.92
J. Jacobs	46	68	0.68
V. Lundy	44	72	0.62
M. Yamasaki	44	98	0.45
R. Venturi	42	86	0.49
H. Greene	39	49	0.78
B. Goff	38	66	0.57
P. & P. Goodman	36	61	0.59
G. Kallmann	33	44	0.75
A. van Eyck	32	36	0.88
M. Nowicki	28	36	0.78
Archigram	26	44	0.61
E. Ehrenkrantz	26	37	0.70
F. Kiesler	25	40	0.63
J. Esherick	23	30	0.77
W. Harrison	20	87	0.23
E. Stone	19	98	0.20
K. Wachsmann	18	27	0.66
M. Lapidus	17	88	0.20
Superstudio	7	15	0.49
A. Speer	4	47	0.09

$N = 520$
Source: J. Blau, A framework of meaning in architecture, 1980.

The orientation on the art side is of a venerable age. The Yale School of Architecture started as a department in the Yale School of Fine Arts in 1916. In the Harvard Bulletin we find a description of the history of the Harvard school:

Instruction in architecture at Harvard University was begun by Charles Eliot Norton, whose lectures as early as 1874 included a descriptive and critical account of history of architecture. In the winter of 1893–94 Professor H. Langford Warren, who was to become the first dean of the Faculty of Architecture, gave courses in the history of Greek and Roman architecture, the success of which was so immediate that in the following year courses in medieval architecture, architectural design and drawing were added.

In 1895 the curriculum was reorganized to include engineering, graphics, and various liberal arts, and the degree S.B. in Architecture was awarded to students who completed the program[14].

Almost all architectural schools have courses on the following subjects in their core curriculum:

practical	building materials
	strength of materials, structural design
	building physics (acoustics, heat, loss, environmental controls)
	construction, detailing
	economics, cost control
	professional practice, law
	programming, space requirements,
aesthetic	ARCHITECTURAL DESIGN
	visual studies, basic design
	communication (drawing, rendering, graphics, modelling)
	history of art, architecture and urban planning

Several schools require preliminary training in the arts from their applicants: for instance, Yale and MIT insist on three terms of Studio Art and three terms of History of Art completed during undergraduate studies.

It is not only the architect who sees his design as a work of art. His client often takes the same view, and expects him to present it as such, in attractive drawings, renderings and models. This forces the architect to cultivate his graphic technique, to be able to 'sell' his design. But he is eager to do so and is trained in presentation during the 'crits' at school. Most schools offer a large variety of elective courses in visual studies and communication techniques: Harvard 7, Yale 16, Columbia 4, Cornell 18, Princeton 7 and MIT 65 in 1979–1980.

The emphasis on art-work has turned many well-known architects into brilliant draftsmen and/or renderers, e.g. The New York Five, Rudolph and Venturi. The drawings and sketches of Wright, Le Corbusier, Mies, Mendelsohn, Aalto and Neutra have always been considered as works of art in their own right. Many architects sketch or paint in their spare time; the outstanding example was Le Corbusier. The architects

Henry van de Velde, Behrens, Chermayeff, Breuer and Eliel and Eero Saarinen were originally trained as artists.

The relation between architecture and art history is more ambiguous. Art history is the 'scientific' study of art; it 'explains' it, catalogues it and criticizes it. Art historians — or *some* art historians rather — hold the key to the paradise of eternal fame. Moreover, art historians turn fledgling architects into men of taste by supplying them with the necessary cultural capital: the perceptive eye, the complex vocabulary, and a map of the artistic world around them in which they have to chart their own course. The architectural schools offer a rich supply of electives: Harvard 5, Yale 14, Columbia 21 (exclusive of preservation), Princeton 5, Cornell 26 and MIT 21 in 1979. Most courses on architectural theory also deal with history and are often given by art historians.

As in the other visual arts, training in architectural design involves examples, preferably 'great' examples, and the architectural historian can put them in some kind of orderly pattern. And, again as in the other arts, a great deal of architectural design is a comment on these examples, and progress is measured from them.

The boundary between a straightforward description of current architecture and a history book is consequently not sharply demarcated. Books like Gropius' *Internationale Architektur* and *Die neue Architektur und das Bauhaus*, Alfred Roth's *Die neue Architektur* and *A Decade of Contemporary Architecture*, or Robert Stern's *New Directions in American Architecture* can be called 'instant histories', although the authors are architects rather than historians.

Several distinguished architectural historians studied architecture and some practised it: Conant, Furneaux Jordan, Goodhart-Rendel, Dennis Sharp, Carrol Meeks, Wayne Andrews, James Marston Fitch, Charles Jencks, Kenneth Frampton. One architectural historian, Philip Johnson, became a famous architect after a career in history, and some architects manage to do both at the same time: Paolo Portoghesi and Jürgen Joedicke.

Examples from recent and not so recent history are often used in the schools to illustrate a point in a design course. Several architects have continued this practice in their theoretical writings: Le Corbusier, Venturi, Charles Moore. This use of history has two advantages: first it 'proves', or at least legitimates the theory of the author, and secondly the designs of the author, by being juxtaposed with the venerable historical examples, get an aura of already being incorporated in the corpus of architectural history. This method of 'upgrading' your work by putting it cheek by jowl with historical examples is quite old: it was practised by Palladio, Fischer von Erlach, Pugin, Viollet-le-Duc and Muthesius.

But the major effort of the schools on the artistic front is spent on attracting architects of note as design teachers, visiting critics or lecturers. The Yale School of Architecture has two endowed chairs for visitors. For the benefit of future students, who could recognize the standing of Yale in the field of architectural education, the occupants between 1966 and 1979 were listed in the 1979 *Bulletin*: Stirling, Venturi, Safdie, Cesar Pelli, Davis, Brody, Cobb (Pei's office), Hugh Hardy, Giancarlo de Carlo, Stanley Tigerman, Sir Leslie Martin, Richard Meier, Donald Stull, Kallmann, McKinnell, Goff, Robert Stern, Mary Jane Long (Colin St John Wilson's office). With the large number of architectural schools in the world and the rapidly growing number of students, nearly all architects who are considered 'interesting' or 'promising' have been invited at one time or another for a lecture and/or as a visiting critic. Those whose reputation is more securely established have often been asked to accept more permanent appointments.

What is in this for a school is obvious. Its reputation depends largely on the fame of its teachers. But there are also considerable rewards for the teacher himself.

Architectural history is taught primarily as a succession of great names: who followed whom and how one generation learned from its predecessors — Wright from Sullivan, Gropius and Mies from Behrens, Johnson from Mies, Venturi and Moore from Kahn, etc. The personal contributions of those men are emphasized. In other disciplines, such as chemistry, physics, mathematics or psychology, the founding fathers and the outstanding practitioners are mentioned too, but the emphasis is on the gradual, logical development of knowledge. Differences of opinion or untenable older theories receive a passing mention or are disregarded. In art and in architecture-as-an-art this is impossible. Le Corbusier's 'solution' to the housing problem can be condemned, but not disproven, and his *'Unités d'habitation'* cannot be overlooked, they are too large for that. The seesaw from one 'solution' to the next is all that the architects have as a 'development' of their art. Consequently the emphasis on the personal, the original and the individual is much stronger, at the expense of a more general theory, in comparison with the other disciplines.

Speaking in public is, like writing a piece or giving an interview, a bit of free advertising. It gives the architect an opportunity in addition to his buildings to advance his ideas; by 'explaining' them, he can reinforce their impact. An appearance in the schools provides an architect with a platform: a very tiny one in the case of a lecture, a rather large one if he accepts a teaching commitment. From that platform he can proselytize and try to create his own school. The examples mentioned above, the visible impact of such famous teachers as Mies, Gropius or Kahn, and his knowledge of the lasting effects of the Bauhaus reinforce his inclination to have a try at influencing the next generation. Atelier 5 got its orientation on Le Corbusier from Hans Brechbühler, himself one of the '*anciens de la rue de Sèvres*'. To have been influenced by a great man or a great school confers status on an architect, who is easily tempted to show some sign of his belonging to the elect. In the School of Architecture at the University of Pennsylvania:

Beaux-Arts traditions were maintained ... by various means: anecdotes or fables, for instance, tossed out during criticism or at smokers and other informal functions where it was certain that at least one faculty member would reminisce about the glories of Paris or Rome[15].

Every form of training, be it learning to ride a bike or speaking a foreign language, aims at a permanent change in behavior. In the early stages, the trainee is painfully aware of the externally imposed patterns of behavior; once he has mastered ease or fluency, he tends to forget the artificial character of the learning process. It becomes 'second nature', a *habit*[16].

On this habit-formation depends our ability to learn and do something else in addition. If we were unable to internalize the motion-patterns of driving, we would never be able to react fast enough in an emergency. If we never got over the grammatical decoding of a foreign language, we could not hope to concentrate on the meaning of the text; this is what happens with most people who try to master Latin. But with easier languages, e.g. German or French, many people reach the stage where they can forget about grammer or idiom.

Learning architecture is similar in many respects to learning a language. The rules (e.g. 'grouping the sanitary spaces around a stack', 'structure should be articulated', etc.) are internalized in four or five years of training and end up by looking like the only possible rules. They are used as a design guide and as a yardstick to evaluate other architecture. They — and even more the theories on which they rest — tend also to fade with time.

This is even more true of the 'foundations' of the art of architecture, those presuppositions which permeate practically all architectural theorizing, but which are often not made explicit (doubtless because they are not perceived as such by teachers and students alike). Yet they are, in my opinion, prime determinants of the attitudes of architects in their theoretical discussions and in their design work.

Some of these presuppositions are:

— the primacy of art over practical considerations (e.g. usefulness, ease of construction and maintenance, cost) in 'good design'. Pithily expressed in the opening sentences of Pevsner's *Outline of European Architecture*:

A bicycle shed is a building; Lincoln Cathedral is a piece of architecture. Nearly everything that encloses space on a scale sufficient for a human being to move in is a building; the term architecture applies only to buildings designed with a view to aesthetic appeal[17].

— within the technical field, the primacy of load-bearing structures over other technical aspects, such as acoustics, heat loss, detailing or ease of construction.

— the belief: that the architect has a responsibility not only to his client, but also to society at large; that architecture has a pervasive influence on human behavior and that the architect has a social mission in using this influence for the common good. In its more extreme form, this belief holds that the architect should 'revolutionize society' by his work; in a more modest form, that the architect contributes to social change. The AIA gave it the following form:

The architect creates man's environment ... His deliberations determine how people will be placed in relationship to one another, how whole societies work, play, eat, sleep, travel, worship — how people live[18].

— the recognition of a canon of 'good architecture', as distinct from 'bad architecture'. The work of the 'Masters of World Architecture' (Aalto, Mies, Gropius, Le Corbusier, Wright, Kahn) belongs to 'good architecture', and so does that of their conservative opposite numbers (Tessenow, Bonatz, Piacentini, Lutyens, McKim, Mead and White, John Russell Pope). The latter were 'heading in the wrong direction', but they were 'true architects' all the same, i.e. artistic architects. Juan Bonta has traced the rise of this canon in his brilliant book *Architecture and its Interpretation*. Excluded from this category is, for instance, the work of Emery Roth, Smith, Hynchman and Grills and of Morris Lapidus. The recognition of the canon implies also an attitude towards its future: continuity with the 'tradition of modern architecture' or opposition to it. It is in keeping with the growing conservatism in architectural design that Tessenow, Piacentini and Lutyens and the Beaux Arts have come in for a reappraisal recently.

An interesting example of the effects of training on architectural students is provided by the School of Architecture at the Illinois Institute of Technology (IIT), with its program and philosophy set by Mies.

Mies took a very lofty view of his own profession:

I hope you will understand that architecture has nothing to do with the invention of forms. It is not a playground for children, young or old. Architecture is the real battleground of the spirit. Architecture wrote the history of the epochs and gave them their names. Architecture depends on its time. It is the crystallization of its inner structure, the slow unfolding of its form[19].

But it unfolds its essence only to the initiated. Discussing architect–client relations with a journalist, Mies said in 1959:

M.   'Never talk to a client about architecture. Talk to him about his children. That is simply good politics. He will not understand what you have to say about architecture most of the time. An architect of ability should be able to tell a client what he wants. He may, of course, have some very curious ideas and I do not mean to say that they are silly ideas. But being un-trained in architecture they just cannot know what is possible and what is not possible'.

Q. 'But perhaps he would not like the finished building'?

M. 'That would not matter at all, although I have never had this experience. I may have had many wrangles with clients while a building was being designed, and often while it is being built, but always, in the end, they have been satisfied with the way I did it'.

Q. 'Do you submit alternative schemes to a client'?

M. 'Only one. Always. And the best one that we can give. That is where you can fight for what you believe in. He doesn't have to choose. How can he choose? He hasn't the capacity to choose....'[20]

In 1944 Mies formulated five principles of architecture which served as a catechism for the last two years of undergraduate study:

1. The structure as an architectural factor: its possibilities and limitations
2. Space as an architectural problem
3. Proportion as a means of architectural expression
4. The expression value of materials
5. Painting and sculpture in their relationship to architecture[21].

These principles show that architecture was exclusively seen from an aesthetic viewpoint. George Danforth, director from 1959 to 1975, wrote about function:

Functionalism is not a goal in itself. It is rather a means to the attainment of the goal of a rational architecture. It is assumed, without question, that a building must function well, but this would not justify it as architecture. The student must learn how to interpret function just as he does construction, but he must interpret these essentials in terms of ultimate architectural expression[22].

The characteristic Miesian spareness was instilled from the beginning:

... Study projects are always of the greatest simplicity. At no phase of his development should the student be confused or misled by work made complicated arbitrarily. At this point we are not interested in the solution of specific problems, for in these there always resides the danger of working for specific rather than basic answers. Our prime concern is to direct the training towards general principles[22].

The 'general principles' of Miesian aesthetics were taught in a very direct way ('space as an architectural problem').

Each student constructs a model in which he first places one wall in the given space and then by gradually increasing the number of walls he experiences the reciprocal reaction of these several elements and the given space. Through this abstract exercise and its development into an open-plan house the student should begin to grasp the complex and intangible interrelationship of spaces. After this stage the problems advance to large buildings of more varied purpose[23].

But always of utterly simple form, of course. The open-plan house referred to above was the courthouse, a problem which Mies had already set his Bauhaus students in 1930 (Fig. 14 and 15).

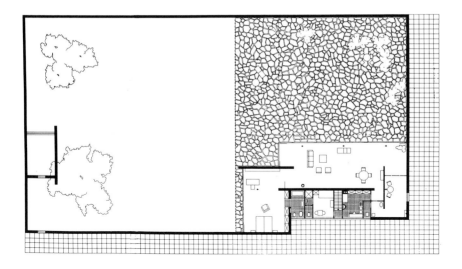

Precisely the example of the courtyard house has been applied with particular success by students in their studies at IIT down to the present day. Free as it is from excessively narrow functional constraints, it is an exercise in which the principles of systematic architecture can be studied clearly and concretely...[24].

Advantages of the courthouse as a problem are: (1) it is complexly isolated from its surroundings, so you can study your problem in a vacuum, disregarding adjacent buildings; (2) a patio-house is of necessity of a single story, so you have no 'excessively narrow constraints' in the form of a second story which has to fit into the first, a staircase, etc. Indeed, it comes as close as possible to the abstract exercise described before. It is a logical sequence; but it reinforces once more the view that architecture is an aesthetic exercise in which function comes in as an afterthought.

Figure 14
Courthouse plan by Howard Dearstyne, 1931. Student project on a problem set by Mies when he was director of the Bauhaus

Figure 15
Mies amidst his students at IIT, about 1950. And what are they working on? Indeed, the courthouse problem

Construction got more attention than function, but construction interpreted as load-bearing structure and seen from an aesthetic viewpoint again. Danforth wrote:

A great deal of emphasis is placed upon construction, for it is our objective, inculcated in the students from the beginning of their studies, to achieve a structural architecture, an architecture growing out of structure, but elevating structure to the level at which it transcends mere engineering and invites evaluation on an aesthetic basis[25].

It was a narrow and dogmatic program, but also a highly consistent one. The serene simplicity of Mies' buildings on the IIT campus still make a very effective contrast with the honky-tonk of the ordinary Chicago around them. His principles allowed students and staff to look at the normal commercial building, and even at the principles of other schools with aristocratic disdain. Danforth was well aware of the monastic atmosphere of his school:

In a program of education the objective of which is to establish order, method and clarity in every phase of the work a religious discipline is imposed upon both students and faculty. Such a discipline reflects an acceptance of the objectivity which is characteristic of this technological age and which the student must understand to enable him to function intelligently in his future practical work[26].

An occasional student wondered about the rigor of the program. Bertrand Goldberg said in an interview:

I once asked Mies, when I was a student of his, 'If the great architecture is to be a continuation of your rectilinear forms, why should there be another architect? Will our future consist only of copies of your work?' Mies's reply was, 'Na, Goldberg, genügt das nicht?' (Well, Goldberg, doesn't that satisfy?)[27]

But great care was taken that the community of true believers was not put in jeopardy by dissent. The journalist Madelyn Roesch wrote in 1979:

To the casual observer, then, IIT presents a model of homogeneity. The majority of faculty members attended the school (many of them studying with Mies), although the proportion is changing. George Danforth, a former head of the school, says that 'to a certain extent, the faculty is chosen for uniformity. There is a great deal of unanimity of thinking among them'[28].

'Outsiders' were accepted for teaching strength of materials or acoustics. But for years, the prerequisite for a member of the design staff was that he had himself been trained in the school. Consequently very little changed in the curriculum:

The elementary exercises in the curriculum of IIT as Mies and his team established it have remained basically unchanged down to the present day. To the outsider this education and its tendencies seem monotonous and sterile[29].

This was written in 1977. I can corroborate this view from personal experience. When I visited the school briefly in 1975, I was amazed to find nothing but highly finished models of

Miesian buildings and very precise drawings which looked as if they came straight from Mies' office. The only difference was that the customary Miesian black or dark brown on the exterior framing had been replaced in some models by red or green. Mies had died six years ago and resigned from the school 18 years ago, but his spirit continued to hover over students and faculty alike. Aptly, his bust in brass stood exactly in the center of the building (Crown Hall).

Outsiders might consider this all very monotonous or sterile, but insiders felt united in their common creed:

In the confusion of modern trends these examples have held their own for many years and have forfeited nothing of their basic thinking... Time and again it is said that the architecture of Mies is no longer relevant. However, it is not fashion that interests us but carefully thought out structural design. Architecture cannot be recreated every week. The 'novel' is an epiphenomenon — only the 'good' can be the aim[30].

This text contains paraphrases from utterings by Mies himself: 'Ich kann nicht jeden Montagmorgen eine neue Architektur erfinden', and: 'I do not want to be original, Philip, I want to be good'.

The success of the IIT curriculum in maintaining itself over the years can be partly understood from its inner consistency, its iron logic. But a major factor was also the charisma Mies radiated himself, and the ways he used that charisma. Kevin Roche has given an impression of it in an interview:

... he was a very formidable character, very formidable. Just being in his presence was a little terrifying, in a sense. When he said something about architecture, it had the ring of absolutism'.
J.C. 'It was the final word?'
K.R. 'It was the final word! Whatever it was, it was the final word. You wouldn't ever *dream* of questioning him. ... He wasn't playing a role. He was impenetrable. There was no let up of this quality in him. There was no informal discussion. Or, when an informal discussion was carried on, you were standing up and he was sitting down: you were never both sitting down.
... His habit, which was very disconcerting, was to come and sit down; this was in graduate school. Then he would light a cigar and then remain perfectly silent for about two hours'.
J.C. 'While you worked?'
K.R. 'No, while we all sat there'.
H.K. 'And who talked?'
K.R. 'No one talked. You sat there, and there was absolute silence. He smoked enormous green cigars. You watched, simply watched, as the cigar gradually disappeared. And there would be a few lame attempts at getting a conversation started through which he would sit impassively'.
H.K. 'Nothing to look at?'
K.R. 'Nothing to look at. You might be unfortunate enough to have him sit at your board; then everybody would stare bleakly at whatever little crummy thing you had at your board. By the time the two hours were up, you were nearly hysterical; you stared in fear at this stupid thing you had done, being stared at in this way. It was very disconcerting, but its effect was devasting: when he said something, you certainly listened!'

J.C. 'Then what happened?'
K.R. 'Well my only reaction after one of these sessions was to go out and get a very strong drink to try to recover.
... I had some friends whom I kept contact with, and it took them years to recover. Some of them never recovered from it, even twenty, twenty-five years later. They're still in that same post-war period and still think in the same way'[31].

A permanent change in behaviour if there ever was one.

The impact of Mies' school and his buildings on US architecture was rather large. Chicago is studded with buildings which have been obviously designed by former IIT students. A great many post-war skyscrapers in New York are consciously designed in the Miesian idiom. Mies certainly left his mark on the scene.

Today, the spell has lifted. Many architects would concur with Patrick Nuttgens' criticism.

The architecture whose value depends on words rather than intrinsic appearances is also at an end in Chicago; especially the architecture dominated by Mies van der Rohe.
The famous apartments on Lake Shore Drive look shoddy outside and are unremarkable inside. The Illinois Institute of Technology School of Architecture building is a bleak, insensitive nonentity. We would not know about its aesthetic qualities if we had not been told. It was an illusion whose single virtue was consistency and whose characteristic was elimination. Almost nothing, proclaimed Mies, and accidentally reached beyond it to the final goal[32].

The distance that separates us from the heyday of Miesianism allows us a more dispassionate look at his well-designed educational system. The extreme rigor and forcefulness of IIT show, more clearly than elsewhere, the mechanisms by which a belief-system is transferred: the religious overtones around 'ARCHITECTURE', the hallowing of principles of design, the interrelation of difference tenets. Other schools cannot enforce such dogmatic loyalty to a single view of architecture, because the prevailing body of doctrine is not so well thought out and so restrictive — it usually has a lot of loose ends — and also because the school cannot afford the luxury of hiring only its own alumni. Other great teachers have had a comparable, though perhaps smaller impact: e.g. Walter Gropius, Louis Kahn. And in all architectural schools something similar happens as in IIT, only in a more muted form: an architect collects a following of sorts and infuses the younger generation with his own preconceptions. Only, there are often competitors, with different visions; which makes it harder on the teacher and more confusing for the students.

The partners of Atelier 5 ascribed their unity of purpose and their cohesion as a group to the singlemindedness of their employer, in contrast to the multifarious influences at the university. The architectural office is the second important social organization for the transmission of beliefs. To work in the office of a well-known architect is one of the acknowledged

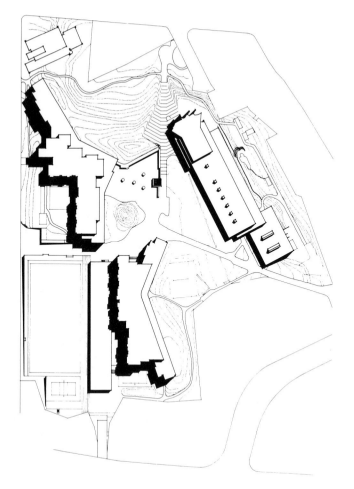

Figure 16
Ramibühl comprehensive high
school, Zurich, 1967–1970.
Architect Eduard
Neuenschwander worked
1950–1951 in Alvar Aalto's office,
and the influence of Aalto is
clearly visible in the project

ways of finding your bearings (Fig. 16). Kevin Roche said so in
an interview:

H.K. 'Where did you work in England?'
K.R. 'With Maxwell Fry'.
H.K. 'Gropius had already gone?'
K.R. 'Gropius had left. This was just after the war, and at that time,
Maxwell Fry was really the leading office in England. My ambition, of
course, like the young kids at that time, was to work with all the
leading architects in the world. I started off with Mies and went to
Chicago'.
H.K. 'From there to Saarinen'.
K.R. 'I had plans then to go to Aalto'.
H.K. 'Why did you select Aalto after Mies?'
K.R. 'It's another end of the scale, in a sense'[33].

Mies and Gropius acknowledged their debt to Peter Behrens,
for whom they worked for three years. Wright always
mentioned his *'lieber Meister'*, Louis Sullivan. Several of Le
Corbusier's collaborators made a name for themselves: Alfred

Roth, Maekawa, Sert, Brechbühler, Senn, Altherr, Braem, Wogenscky, Candilis, Woods[34].

Working in an office requires fairly rigid adherence of the employee to the belief-system of his boss. As most architects choose their employer, like Kevin Roche, and know what to expect in advance, this does not create a problem.

In IIT too, adherence to Miesian doctrine and canon of forms was more or less enforced — or shall we say: 'emphatically suggested'. Teachers in most schools however frown upon student designs which look like a copy of their own work. But they *also* frown upon designs which flout their own architectural principles: no ticky-tacky neo-vernacular for a teacher who believes in the grand manner; no pathos or bravura for Venturi, who believes in the ordinary and the understatement. By trial and error, students find the optimum between slavish following and rebellious originality. This technique of steering a middle course between dependence and independence is used again in their later careers, for there, too, they are recognized by their peers and critics as 'promising' if they neither stray too far from the herd nor remain an indistinct sheep in it.

Exactly like artists, architects have to be 'original' if they want to get into the *Who's Who in Architecture*, and for the same reasons. The emotional impact wears off, the architect has to stand out against the background of his competitors, and the power of distinction of legitimate architecture is gradually lost as *avant-garde* ideas are appropriated by others. 'Commercial architects' play the same role in architecture as advertising agencies do in the visual arts: they scan the field for usable examples. As in the arts, the role of middlemen and informers is played by the trade magazines: they alert the followers to what is new on the scene, and the *avant-garde* to the herd on their heels. The flood of publications has speeded up the rate of change.

The *avant-garde* is well aware that its privileged position depends on remaining ahead of the others. Jerzy Soltan, a Polish architect and member of 'Team X', wrote in 1960:

In fact, during the last four to six years, the approach to the modern movement has changed very much. Everybody everywhere expresses the wish to be modern. No more war between the new and the old! The old, as it seems, has ceased to exist!... But it is obvious that 'modern' does not mean the same to everybody. For CIAM, the notion 'modern' was backed and supported by a philosophy, a logic and economy, a reliability, a straightforwardness in function and structure, etc., etc., connected with poetic, emotional and plastic values. For CIAM aesthetic values did not exist *per se* in an autonomous way.

Not so with the 'new modern', where everything from town planning to building relies on applied decoration with modern elements. I have seen, in Lebanon, housing units designed very much under the influence of Le Corbusier, erected at a distance of some 6 ft. from each other and lined up four to six in a row. I have seen, in the USA, sunbreakers suspended on northern elevations. The list of such

examples from all over the world can be lengthened ad infinitum.

The reasons for this are certainly complex, but the main ones are that the 'new modernists' did not change their approach (it is not so easy), they changed only their manners — [35].

But too much originality does not pay off either. A design that is 'too far out' will be dismissed as 'whimsical', 'original at all costs', or 'googy-architecture' by the critics, for they lack the standards and categories by which they can judge it. Wright, Goff and Green were relegated to this limbo of incomprehension for years. The brake on originality operates of course as much on the architects as on the critics, for they, too, have difficulties in conceiving something outside the established categories, which is yet not completely arbitrary (Figs 17 and 18). In this reticence, the force of *habit*, formed during years of architectural training, becomes manifest. Even if the architect wants to be completely original, to 'start from scratch' — and many do want just that — he cannot really withdraw from the tenets and categories he learned in architectural school, which have become second nature to him.

Figure 17
La Tourette, convent near Lyon, 1957–1960. Architect: Le Corbusier

Figure 18
Boston City Hall, 1968.
Architects: Kallmann, McKinnell
and Knowles. The resemblance to
'La Tourette' is too strong to be
only a coincidence

The effort to be different, but not *too* different, a sort of originality-within-limits, goes a long way to explain the changes in architectural fashions, in 'styles'. By far the largest number of 'new designs' made and shown in the trade magazines consists of variations *within* an established idiom: e.g. Mies or late Corbu ('Brutalism') in the sixties, Kahn in the early seventies. These variations are *formal*, i.e. they recombine parts of the canonical works of the 'World Master(s)' in a new way. If two different 'idioms' are considered compatible, they can also be combined. The simple is made complex: it leads to *mannerist variations*.

The limits imposed by habit on the acceptance of the new can be demonstrated with some examples.

Henri Evers taught architectural design in the Technische Hogeschool at Delft from 1905 to 1926. His designs, such as the Rotterdam City Hall, show affinity to the work of Otto Wagner. In his teaching he tried to be up to date and introduced his students to the work of Wagner, Hoffmann and Frank Lloyd Wright (through the Wasmuth publication of Wright's work of 1910). Two of his promising pupils, Duiker and Bijvoet, started to work in his office on the Rotterdam City Hall in 1913. They won the competition for a new National

Figure 19
Competition project for the
National Academy of Fine Art,
Amsterdam, 1917–1919.
Architects: J. Duiker and B.
Bijvoet. In the interior of the main
auditorium, the influence of
Wright's Unity Temple is clearly
visible

Academy of Art in 1917 with a design that showed a strong
influence of Wright (Figs. 19 and 20). H.P. Berlage, the leading
Dutch architect of the beginning of the twentieth century, was
on the jury. Berlage too was very impressed by Wright's work
and had praised it abundantly in his *Amerikaansche Reisherinneringen* (American Travel Reminiscences) of 1913.

The Academy was never built. Berlage recommended Duiker and Bijvoet to one of his own clients, the General Union of
Diamond Workers, in 1924. The two young architects had read
Le Corbusier's *Vers une architecture* (1923) and had moved to a
functionalist idiom. They first built a washing plant for

GROOTE GEHOORZAAL   □   □   □   □   □   □   RIJKS-ACADEMIE

Figure 20
National Academy project,
interior of the main sculpture hall.
The detailing of spandrels and
beams resembles the interior of
the Larkin building

diamonds in this style, and thereafter (1926–1928) a health
resort, 'Zonnestraal' (Figs. 21 and 22). Though Duiker and
Bijvoet, and all Dutch functionalists architects of the twenties,
considered Berlage as their 'father', Berlage was highly critical
of their endeavors from the start. In an interview in 1924, he
said:

Figure 21
Laundry for diamond workers'
clothing, to recover the grindings,
at Diemerbrug, 1924–1925. The
first job Duiker and Bijvoet got,
through the recommendation of
Berlage

Figure 22
'Zonnestraal', health resort for
tubercular patients in Hilversum,
1926–1928. Architects: Duiker
and Bijvoet. This design shows
how far Duiker and Bijvoet had
gone beyond their original
Wrightian inspirations, after the
'industrial' experience of the
laundry and probably after
reading *Vers une architecture*

Figure 23
Sydney Opera House, 1956–1973.
Architect: Jørn Utzon. Saarinen
as a jury member recognized what
Utzon tried to do (even if it wasn't
as simple as Utzon or Saarinen
thought it was)

... The new objectivity, which has a rationalistic tendency, is determined, just as rationalized production, by the idea: as fast as possible and as cheap as possible. Architecture needs also the necessary completion with sentiment, which is lacking in the new objectivity. ... I consider the new objectivity as a transition, but in reality it is a symptom of the degeneration of bourgeois society[36].

Oviously, Berlage would never have recommended Bijvoet and Duiker if he had had an inkling of their change of heart; his recommendation rested squarely on their handling of the Wrightian idiom.

A second example is the competition for the Sydney Opera House (Fig. 23). The deliberations of the jury are secret, but it is generally agreed (and supported by some jury members[37]) that Eero Saarinen strongly favored the design of Jørn Utzon, and against some opposition finally convinced his fellow jurers to premiate that project, late in 1956.

Saarinen had designed in 1955 the Kresge Auditorium at MIT, covered by a concrete shell resting on three points, and the Yale Skating Rink in 1956, covered by an undulating roof hung over a large arch (Figs. 24 and 25). Utzon's shells with their minimal supports and their billowing surfaces fell in line with the kind of problem he had been working on. He

Figure 24
Kresge Auditorium, MIT,
Cambridge, Massachusetts, 1955.
Architect: Eero Saarinen. A thin
concrete domed triangular roof,
'floating' on three points of
support

'confirmed' his interest in this kind of form, and that he had
learned something from Utzon, by the design of the TWA
terminal at Kennedy (originally Idlewild) Airport (Fig. 26).

Competitions involve a considerable investment in time (and
money) by the participants. Yet they are rarely short of takers.
One reason is that the constraints which normally guide and

Figure 25
Ingalls Skating Rink, Yale
University, New Haven,
Connecticut, 1956–1958.
Architect: Eero Saarinen. Another
exercise in thin, curved roofs

Figure 26
TWA building, Idlewild, New York, 1956–1962. The daring of TWA may have been prompted by the Sydney example

mould an architectural design between its inception and final presentation are more restricted. The reactions of the client to the schematics or contact with building inspectors and the fire department may deflect a brilliant idea from its course and lead in the end to a compromise which hardly enhances the aesthetic reputation of its architect. In a competition there is no such chance of deflection, for contact with the client is forbidden. This raises the risk for the client that he gets some beautiful designs, but which are only partially adequate to his needs. Many clients are consequently wary of competitions, and when they decide to hold them, they often try to safeguard their interests by very detailed programs. Some juries scrupulously lay aside all projects which do not meet the program, but as the majority of the jury consists of architects — an AIA requirement, and a requirement in most countries — they are often tempted by 'brilliant ideas'. The Opera House in Sydney is a case in point; the winner 'broke most of the competition's rules'[38].

The major reason for the architects' interest in competitions is that they allow a short-cut on the road to fame. The competition usually gets a considerable amount of publicity. Normally, a young architect has to spend quite a bit of effort to draw the attention of the professional press; as a winner of a competition he gets it all thrown in his lap. He may become famous overnight. Utzon did, and so did Viljo Revell with the

Toronto City Hall or Wilhelm Holzbauer with the Amsterdam City Hall. Aalto built his career to a large extent on competitions, starting with the Paimio sanatorium, Eliel Saarinen made his name in Finland by winning the competition for the Helsinki railroad station, and founded his American career on his second prize in the Chicago Tribune Tower Competition. Le Corbusier moved forward from the ranks of promising young architects when he was one of the ten prizewinners for the League of Nations building (*and* when he made a lot of noise about it). Eero Saarinen came into his own by winning the Jefferson Memorial Competition in St Louis in 1948.

Similar to the competitions in many respects are the awards and prizes: Reynolds Awards, P/A Awards, and, with higher standing, AIA Merit and Honor Awards. The highest honors are the AIA and RIBA Gold Medals, a kind of Nobel prizes in architecture. The juries are made up exclusively or nearly exclusively of architects, which ensures their competence — read: the prevalence of the architectural belief-system.

A good standing with his peers is essential for an architect who wants to be an artistic rather than a financial success. The example of Duiker and Bijvoet showed that other commissions may come your way if you have made a favorable impression on an influential elder colleague. *Fortune* reported in 1966: 'Groups of architects are invited into government to advise, and to screen the assignment of tasks to other architects'[39]. One such group was the 'Architectural Advisory Panel' of private architects to advise on the designs and architects for new embassies. In Indiana:

... Roche has been cast in the 'patron' role in Columbus. For the last ten years, he has served on the architectural advisory committee, providing a list of architects to the school board (or to Miller) when a new building is discussed. Roche usually bases his recommendations on building type and job size. So far, Venturi and Rauch, Cesar Pelli of Gruen Associates, James Stewart Polshek, and Hardy Holzman Pfeiffer — all of whom have built in Columbus — were on that list[40].

To get on such a list, an architect has to be noticed by his colleagues, which is one good reason for submitting work for a P/A Award.

A favorable review in a trade journal can help too. Like their colleagues in literature and in the visual arts, architectural critics have a stake in the architects they promote. A new 'discovery' is a feather in their cap — but only if it is accepted by their fellow critics. Backing too many unrecognized and unrecognizable talents is bad for their standing — and for the circulation of the magazine as well. So the magazines often play it safe, and simply give their readers Richard Meier's or Stanley Tigerman's latest job.

The well-known architects are well aware of their attractiveness for the magazines. An editor of P/A once told me that architects play off the magazines against each other, granting now one, now the other, the 'first publication rights' on a new building. Small wonder that the review becomes rather flattering.

The fortunate individual inside the magic circle of fame comes in for a shower of praise.

Some samples:

The broad scope of Kurokawa's talent, ranging from the unrestrained futurism of his metabolism schemes, through a sensitive evocation of tradition in the two pavillions in the National Children's Land at Yokohama, to the disciplined eclecticism of the Yamagata Hawaii Dreamland, confirms a consummate mastery of architectural form[41].

It may ... be said of Mies that he is the architect *par excellence* of civilization, of law and order, of the great metropolis; in the poetic Spenglerian sense he is the architect of the Universal State, striving to preserve new and old values... His buildings achieve greatness when the 'as if' is so convincing that we believe in the reality of abstractions. ... If buildings may be judged as embodiments of a viable system of ideas, the buildings of Mies van der Rohe are among the most successful in history[42].

... Kahn's achievement of a single decade now places him unquestionably first in professional importance among living American architects. His theory like his practice, has been acclaimed as the most creative, no less than the most deeply felt, of any architect's today[43].

The last two quotations are from monographs on Mies and Kahn. To be the subject of a book (preferably not initiated by the subject himself) is the pinnacle of architectural fame. The most lavish example was Le Corbusier, whose work was published in seven volumes during his lifetime.

Just as the art critics, the architectural critics can try to bolster their discoveries by presenting them as a 'movement', which has to be highly praised of course, and presented as something new; e.g. C. Ray Smith on *Supermannerism*:

A new design movement in America is radically changing our vision — our way of seeing as well as what we see. It is revolutionizing our expectations of architecture, of design vocabulary and of the design professions themselves. It is altering our cultural consciousness and reshaping the country — in the houses of the adventurous, in the environments of our universities, in the commercial and business spaces of our cities[44].

Critics and architects have a symbiotic relationship with each other. The critic depends for *his* reputation partly on the quality of his material, on the architects he 'discovers'. But the architects also depend on the critic; the greater his talents, the higher his status, the more chance for the architects to rise (still) higher in fame. 'Functionalism' was a genuine movement, with a formal organization (CIAM), meetings and magazines; but it owes its fame to a considerable extent to the literary talents that Sigfried Giedion displayed in his *Space, Time and Architecture*, just as Giedion owes his reputation largely to his intimate knowledge (as secretary of CIAM) of the functionalist architects.

Critics can be a help, but a lot of the advertizing has to be done by the architects themselves. Frederick Gutheim on Dulles Airport in Washington:

Eero Saarinen did on that job something he never had to do on other jobs and something that other architects have not recognized needs to be done. He generated a tremendous amount of enthusiasm for the design itself. He convinced the Federal Aviation Authority that this was their great opportunity to raise the level of airport design all over the country. He was able to overcome the forces of indifference and inertia by personal appearance and by the most effective kind of selling; he was able to overcome the different processes of review by unremitting labor on his own part and by what I can only describe as a remarkable example of architectural leadership...[45].

The public relations work may range from interviews, lectures and papers to full-size books. Wright, Gropius, Neutra, Venturi and Charles Moore all wrote books to propagate both their ideas and their own buildings as embodying these ideas. The most prolific is of course Le Corbusier, who started a magazine two years after his arrival in Paris, wrote small monographs on several of his minor works and long tracts embodying his ideas and the major events in his life.

All the publicity — monographs, theories, histories, public lectures — helps to consecrate architecture as an art. It supports the idea that the cultural level of a nation is somehow 'reflected' in its buildings, that it is worthwhile to spend money on costly experiments in form and material to show that civilization is still alive and kicking. And it reinforces the belief of architects, acquired in architectural school, that to produce an artistic masterpiece is the ultimate goal of every self-respecting professional.

The exhortatory tone spills over in the popular press. In *Time* of January 8, 1979, we find a condensed version of some general beliefs held by architects:

... architecture is the social art: one looks at a painting or sculpture, but people live in a building. It is the most expensive art of all and therefore the slowest to change... Architecture is also the most visible of all arts. Buildings shape the environment; painting and sculpture only adorn it. All this has meant that though architecture changes more slowly than painting, its fluctuations mean more. When they occur, clearly something is up. What happened to architecture in the 1970's may turn out to be the largest revision of opinion about buildings — what they mean, what they do, how they should look — since the first third of our century, the 'heroic years' of Modernist architecture, when its terms were shaped by such men as Frank Lloyd Wright, Walter Gropius, Ludwig Mies van der Rohe and Le Corbusier.

The author accepts the prophecies of a 'radical change in vision', proclaimed by Jencks and Smith. Jencks is mentioned as the 'main definer, if not exactly its inventor' of the term 'Post-Modernism'. The cover story goes on to discuss the work of Johnson, Meier, Pelli, Moore, Venturi, Hardy, Tigerman, Gehry, Stern and Gwathmey. Architecture is kept in the public eye by *Time, Newsweek*, the *New York Times*; not as much as painting and sculpture (it is not as 'fine' an art), but still regularly enough. Under the headline 'The Architects: a Chance of Greatness', *Fortune* printed in 1966:

... In an age of affluence, the country has found a public passion for improving the physical environment, particularly in our cities. To pull them back from the edge of neon-lit decrepitude, the tweedy old profession of architecture is being summoned from the wings to stand as an oracle ... to an America seeking environmental beauty, design is the vital layer. The designer is the qualitative guide, the keyman of the profession of architecture. He must take the facts, the figures, the stresses, the charts, the cost data and frequently the client's quirks into the drafting room, and try to shape them into a building or an environment that is not a scramble of equivocations but a satisfying physical reality. Dulles Airport, the Seagram Building, the Guggenheim Museum, the Johnson Wax Plant, the Pepsi-Cola Building, CBS, Chicago's Lake Shore apartments, all these creations demonstrate what design can do[46].

And the quotation demonstrates what *Fortune* can do for architects: i.e. put their 'chances for greatness' before a public of potential clients.

'Greatness' may however not be the first item on the agenda of a corporate executive browsing through *Fortune*. Cost and fast efficient service may come before architectural merit. Not hampered by any misgivings about 'neon-lit decrepitude', and little interested in artistic experiments, he will look for a very different — and less tweedy — architect. And he will find him in one of the large architectural offices specialized in comprehensive service rather than in art.

Builder Erwin S. Wolfson of Diesel Construction Company concedes quite frankly that the reason most New York office buildings are designed by three or four firms is that these architects know exactly the sort of cost-saving structure that the owners want. 'And it's not the architect's fault that we don't get more distinguished buildings', Wolfson says, 'It's ours'.

Developer Raphael D. Silver, who has completed one renewal project in Cleveland and who hopes to start soon on others in Cincinnati, St. Paul, and Passaic, New Jersey, is even more candid about the role that costs play in the choice of an architect for a speculative project. Says Silver, who has retained Richard A. Keller on all his projects: 'My concern was to find some one who, in addition to solid understanding of aesthetics, had a real appreciation of the economics of construction of renewal projects and could take a low-cost approach to the work'[47].

The two tracks on which the production of buildings runs, the artistic and the practical, are very much in evidence here. A substantial group of architects has concentrated on the practical side of architectural production. Many of these firms were well known in the USA too, but not as artist-architects: Welton Becket, Leo A. Daly, Charles Luckman Associates, Fellheimer & Wagner, Perkins & Will, Heery & Heery.

Welton Becket had 500 employees in 1971, distributed over five offices (Los Angeles, Chicago, New York, Houston, San Francisco). Each office had separate departments for design, architectural production, mechanical and electrical production, structural production, production administration and services during construction. The main office in LA has in addition departments in business development and public relations.

Officially, the firm offers its clients services in architecture, engineering, programming, space studies, research, survey and analysis, site selection, master planning, zoning assistance, industrial design, furnishing and decorating, graphics, plan checking, cost control and analysis, and store planning and fixturing[48].

The large number of in-house specialists promotes a smooth and efficient dovetailing between architectural, structural and mechanical design. Welton Becket prides itself — and with justification, in my opinion — on such an accurate estimating and cost control that the jobs on the average stay 3% under their budgets. A large number of important repeat clients testifies to the satisfactory service that the firm provides: 25 department stores for Bullock's, six hotels for Hilton and 15 more feasibility studies, 22 projects for Emporium, 15 for Del E. Webb Corporation, 40 for UCLA[49].

They built offices for Alcoa, Anaconda, Bendix, Bethlehem Steel, Capitol Records, Dupont, Ford, General Electric, General Petroleum, Gulf Oil, Hallmark, Humble, Kaiser, Lever Bros. Lockheed, Philips Petroleum, Remington Rand, Scott Paper, Shell, Xerox. Many an architectural firm would be proud of such a record — and happy with this set of clients.

And yet, there is a nagging feeling of doubt. We have already read that the founder, Welton Becket, particularly disliked being called 'Businessman's Architect' — a label that would not seem inappropriate considering his clientele. The passages in Hunt's book on the firm relating to their design attitudes — undoubtedly reflecting the attitudes of the principals — are worth quoting at length, for they clearly reflect this ambivalence:

... The firm has been deeply interested in good design. Certainly, the people here might define that word somewhat differently from the way architectural critics define it. Here, the term means close attention to all the aspects of architecture to bring about a solution that hangs together well functionally, structurally, systematically, economically and aesthetically. For the most part, the word 'design' would not be used simply to describe appearance or aesthetics. Some architects have described the work of WB&A as 'good to competent'... a cool impersonal look at the work of this firm will reveal a number of things... Such a look will reveal that this firm never erects monuments to itself. The buildings are for the clients... And if the definition of design as used in this firm and in some others, be accepted — that of integrating structure, function, aesthetics, economics and all other aspects of architecture into a successful whole — the level of competence here is approached by almost no others. Of course, it must be admitted that this is not what brings prizes to architects from their peers. WB&A has won its share of all kinds of awards (well over a hundred); it has won national AIA Merit Awards but not an Honor Award. But WB&A wins prizes enough of another kind, the kind that brings in an increasing amount of work each year and the kind that has caused great numbers of clients to come back every time they have a new building to do...[50].

At this juncture, it should be pointed out that there is no Becket 'style' as such in the sense of Mies or TAC or SOM. The Becket Style consists of what might be called a multifaceted style... The designs of this firm are all attempts to fit the solution to the problems, to produce a building that reflects the needs and desires of the client to the extent that is possible without compromising the integrity of the firm as architects.

Thus the firm finds in itself no conflict — pehaps it would be more accurate to say little conflict — when faced with the prospects of doing five resort hotels in Walt Disney World. All utilize a very advanced solution in prefabrication and site assembly. One is strictly contemporary, but the others consciously styled to the escapism of vacationers into Polynesian, Asian, Venetian and Persian surroundings[51].

One looks in vain for the counterpart of this passage in any of the monographs on Wright, Le Corbusier, Mies, Gropius, Richard Meier, Gwathmey and Siegel or Michael Graves. They do not feel the need to emphasize that they give fast and efficient service, stay within the budget, finish the job on time, etc. The passage from Hunt's book shows very clearly that 'practical' architects acknowledge and make their bow to their 'artistic' colleagues. The art of architecture takes precedence over the practical aspects *also* in the eyes of its practitioners who find their major strength in the latter. This procedure is so self-evident that the artist-architects needs no 'defense' of their practical merits.

Emery Roth & Sons operate still further from the art-scene. They make no bid for artistic respectability, but only give the aesthetic side a perfunctory nod. Richard Roth wrote in 1957:

Is architecture an art? Is it a profession? Is it big business? Actually, good architecture, particularly in our particular field of the 'high-rise office building' has to be a combination of all three... Our particular field of practice is probably less understood than any other field of architecture. This is so, I believe, because it is almost inconceivable that one firm can turn out the number of buildings that we do and yet give each job sufficient study and accuracy to produce a relatively fine building. This can be done only because of our organization, our knowledge of our field, and the results we anticipate achieving. By the same token we are sometimes criticized unfairly, because of the basis on which we are judged: ours is not a field of architecture in which we create or try to create masterpieces. The entire endeavor in our office is to create the best that can be produced within the restrictions that are placed upon us; and these restrictions are seldom those of our client, but rather of lending institutions; economics; and municipal authorities' laws[52].

It should be evident by now what kind of service is given by the large 'practical' firms and what kind of clients they attract. These clients see aesthetics as only one of the elements of the brief among many others and certainly not at the top of the list. Yet they are aware that the building represents them and they usually feel they have a reputation to uphold. The General Manager of the Cooperative Insurance Society Ltd in Manchester has said:

If I may use a rather hackneyed phrase, we wanted to impress an 'image' on the people of Manchester and elsewhere of the strength and size of the CIS through the medium of a modern office building. Very few people see our balance sheet or read our chairman's report but this new building will be a constant reminder that CIS is a large and first class insurance office. We have already made use of the model in our advertising material and hope to extend this when the building is completed. We believe that these new premises will have an impact upon our staff, including the senior staff, by giving them a feeling of pride[53] (Fig. 27).

The advertising aspect of the company headquarters is also mentioned by Helmut Hentrich in his discussion of his design for the Thijssenhaus, the main office of Phoenix-Rheinrohr in Düsseldorf:

We have contracts which state that we are not allowed to copy this office building somewhere else. I think this is only fair. A company

Figure 27
The skyscraper in the background is the Cooperative Insurance Society's main office in Manchester, 1962. Architects: G.S. Hay, G. Tait. Intended, amongst other things, 'to impress an image on the people of Manchester'

Figure 28
Standard Bank, Johannesburg, South Africa. Architects: Hentrich and Petschnigg. 'For South Africa, this skyscraper has become the expression of novelty and progress'

must have some kind of face, not only in its products, but also in its office building. An office like Rank Xerox will be remembered. There are many boxes, and they are not remembered. Our office buildings have an individual character. Some firms have therefore turned these offices into their trademarks[54].

The singularity of the 'unique' work of architectural art is used for commercial purposes. Hentrich also discussed another one of his office designs, for the Standard Bank Centre in Johannesburg, South Africa (Fig. 28):

It is in any case a very lucrative building. In addition, this skyscraper has a stronger character. It impresses an image: everybody know that this is the Standard Bank, and the Bank has advertised a lot with this building, and advertised successfully.
For South Africa, this skyscraper has become the expression of novelty and progress[55].

Apparently, according to Hentrich, the building represents the modern western world, from which white South Africans feel cut off by a continent. And it shows at the same time the Standard Bank as a torchbearer of that modern western culture.

Architecture can *legitimate* power; and the 'better' the architecture, the stronger the legitimation. The jury of the Chicago Tribune Tower Competition ended its report as follows:

When the winning design is executed we feel that the judgement of the Jury will be more than justified and The Tribune amply compensated for what it has done to elevate Commercial Architecture into the realm of the Fine Arts and create for its own adminsitrative headquarters the most beautiful office building in the world to date, a fitting monument to the founders of the pioneer newspaper of the great middle west[56].

The distinction of the architecture reflects favorably on the client, who is seen as 'above' financial considerations.

The same sentiment is very much in evidence in the design of the Pan Am tower over Grand Central Station, New York (Fig. 29). *Architectural Forum* announced it in 1958 as follows:

'To make the world's largest commercial office building in the world', New York Builder Erwin Wolfson decided to enlist the services of 'the best architects' obtainable. Last month he announced that, from a list of 50 outstanding designers, he has selected Walter Gropius and Pietro Belluschi to serve with Richard Roth, of the office of Emery Roth & Sons as a three-man 'advisory panel of architects' for the $100 million, 3 million square foot, 50-story Grand Central City that will be erected over the back portion of New York's Grand Central Station starting late next year. An earlier announcement named the Roth office as the only architect[57].

Wolfson was the builder who said that it was his fault, not the architect's, that his buildings came out no better than they did. Nor was he really going to give Gropius and Belluschi much rope here:

Some changes will be made in the preliminary plans first issued by the Roth office but no change is contemplated in total size[57].

According to the Roths, it was their idea to invite the 'best architects':

A notable association in which the Roth organization was deeply involved was the Pan Am building in New York. There was reason to believe that any building of such a size and in such a location would inevitably be controversial in character, and further, Roth felt that many minds should be brought to bear on so prominent a building. The Roths decided to invite the participation of the best minds in the country. Pietro Belluschi and Walter Gropius both accepted the challenge of this controversial commission, and their work with the Roth organization is now history[58].

A few years later Marcel Breuer was invited for a similar role with *another* tower, over the front portion of Grand Central Station. But with the rise of the historic preservation movement — and the special qualities of the hall of the station, which would be lost — even his name could not carry this real-estate operation through.

Most sites in New York are less controversial and did not need the assistance of the 'best architects'. The developers could still give their buildings a contemporary look by simply

Figure 29
Pan Am building, New York, 1958–1963. Architects: Emery Roth and Sons. Consultants: Walter Gropius, Pietro Belluschi. Great names to legitimize a controversial real-estate operation. Commercial office buildings, in the style dubbed 'cheap Mies' by Philip Johnson, are visible on both sides of Park Avenue

imitating the work of the acknowledged 'masters'. Philip Johnson commented on it in an interview with *Time* in 1979 (Fig. 29):

'Every cheap architect could copy Mies', says Johnson. 'He could go to the client and say, I can do a building cheaper than I did it for you last year, because now I have a religion. We have a flat roof and simple factory-made curtain walls. It was a justification for cheapness that took over our cityscapes and that is what you see in New York today'. The universal glass box, cut-rate Mies (for real Mies was real architecture, and too expensively finished for most developers to tolerate), would cover any function: airport, bank, officeblock, church, club. It tended to be what the Germans label *Stempelarchitektur*; rubber-stamp building. Thus a debased form of Modernist dogmatism, what Charles Jencks called 'the rationalization of taste into clichés based on statistical averages of style and theme', turned out to be the official style of the 50's and 60's.

When repeated *ad nauseam* by architects all over the U.S. during the building boom of the 1950's, to the point where the curtain-wall grid had become the 'rational', cost-account face of capitalism itself, it was bound to provoke a reaction[59].

The whole mechanism of stylistic change in architecture becomes clearly visible from the foregoing string of quotations: the authoritative status of 'high art' and its 'acknowledged masters'; the resultant need for 'practical architects' to follow and copy them; the need for the 'masters' to outdistance the followers and change their style. *Both* parties, the 'artistic' and the 'practical' architects, are inextricably bound up in the same dynamic system. The practical architects are obliged to watch their colleagues and follow the trend, to produce 'contemporary design'. The artistic architects want and need the publicity, if they are ever to achieve some immortality in print. But that means also holding up the models for imitation; if they *do* collect a following, if they are really imitated on a large scale, like Mies was, they have lost their distinction. Their very success, the compliment that is paid through imitation, dislodges the *avant-garde*.

The *need* to be different, to have an architecture typical for your own group, your own kind or your own class (or faction of that class), is felt as much by users and patrons as by their architects. Edward Durrell Stone encased the US Embassy in New Delhi in a grille, a screen of pierced concrete blocks, a feature which became more or less his trademark in his later work.

Ambassador Ellsworth Bunker has sounded one note of warning however. He sees a resemblance between his headquarters and a subsequent Stone design for a pharmaceutical plant in the U.S., implying that this use of the New Delhi-type of pierced screen and other devices could debase the governmental character of his architectural currency[60].

The uniqueness that Phoenix-Rheinrohr required of Hentrich is extended here to the details.

The difference is the main thing; what that difference means is also important, but secondary to the identity that the difference affords. One of the many reasons why Americans prefer free-standing homes over townhouses or condominiums — even to the point of preferring mobile homes — is that they are identifiable as separate units. The developers obligingly tack 'marks of identity' on houses which are identical in plan and structure: a porch here, a dormer window there, a hipped roof on another (Fig. 30).

This form of 'individualization' is of course very transparent. For those patrons who want something 'really different' — and who are able to afford it — there are always architects around to supply it. The architectural historian Leonard Eaton compared

Figure 30
Developers' housing in Ann
Arbor, Michigan, 1975. At first
sight, the houses look all different;
but a closer look reveals that they
are all alike in size, location of
windows, doors, etc. The same
house design has been
personalized to please the
prospective buyers

the early clients of Frank Lloyd Wright in Oak Park, Chicago,
with contemporary clients of a more traditional Chicago
architect. The major difference was that the latter were firmly
entrenched in the North Shore Chicago elite, and the Wright
clients were not:

… most of these men were *not* affiliated with the large concerns which
dominated Chicago industry…
They tended to own or work for small or medium-sized companies…
None belonged to the aristocracy of the city business world. Among
them one searches in vain for Ryersons, Armours or McCormicks[61].

The implication is that they manifested their independence of
the North Shore establishment by settling in a new suburb and
choosing a young (Wright was then in his thirties) and
independent architect.

Architecture of 'quality', as discussed in the literature, and
also the main subject of this book, is only a tiny fragment of the
vast number of buildings produced each year. From the scant
data on architectural patronage, and against the background of
Bourdieu's research on taste[62], we can draw the following
hypothetical portraits of its patrons.

Patronage of advanced — nowadays 'Post-Modern' —
architecture correlates primarily with education. The economic elite, low on cultural capital, but aware of the authority of
'good modern architecture', plays it safe. They select 'recognized masters', particularly for building their place of work or

recreation: offices, theatres, clubs. These buildings should *affirm* their companies or associations, as well as their aware-ness of culture, so they like *monumentality* and the use of *expensive materials*. Many — perhaps most — of them have basically a conservative taste, because they had neither time nor interest to go beyond the objects 'of real beauty', i.e. antiques, ancient art, music and literature. Though they would consider it preposterous to build a Colonial Bank, or work in a fake Colonial interior, they have no objections against a Colonial home. Those with more cultural capital carry over their taste from the office to the home and buy Scandinavian or Herman Miller furniture, and live in a 'contemporary' house.

The cultural elite is the natural adversary of the economic, and preeminently the patron of 'advanced' architecture. Its members belong to the ruling class, some are called upon to serve as advisers to government, as ministers or secretaries of state departments, yet they know that the final, 'brutal' power of the economic elite eludes them. Therefore they accept with alacrity the challenge that 'advanced' architecture offers to 'established' architecture; it is a symbol of their own struggle. Against the overstatement and monumentality of the (finan-cially) rich they prefer understatement and anti-monu-mentality, and inexpensive rather than costly materials. They often cannot afford monumentality and expensive mater-ials anyway; their taste runs to the ascetic, both by necessity and by choice, as a mark of distinction from 'those bourgeois'.

There is some evidence for the last vignette. 'Cultural capitalists', i.e. artists and college graduates, predominated among the Halen home-owners, and the houses in Halen showed a lot of exposed concrete and cinderblock. The anger of the architects of Atelier 5 at the alterations made in Werth-erberg is understandable; the use of wrought-iron and expens-ive plywood is a denial of the value of their ascetism. They did not realize that, conversely, their use of exposed concrete is a denial of the (petty-bourgeois) evaluation of what is a 'proper' material for a home.

A (random) sample of the first tenants of the famous 'Weissenhofsiedlung' in Stuttgart shows the same preponder-ance of the culturally privileged: 3 architects, 2 artists, 7 academics, 1 lawyer, 1 medical doctor, 1 army officer, 4 businessmen, 1 bank employee, 1 railway employee[63].

The sociologist Irving Rosow tried in 1948 to identify the characteristics of patrons building modern homes ($n = 20$), by comparing them with people constructing (what architects called) 'semi-modern' houses ($n = 13$)[64]. Once again, it turned out that the 'moderns' had more education (80% college graduates, against 33% of s.m.), owned far more books, attended plays and concerts and visited museums in their spare time, whereas the 'semi-moderns' tended simply to relax.

If the portrait is correct, the advanced architects have a hard time finding work. Exactly like the *avant-garde* painters, they are often 'misunderstood' by their more successful and established colleagues, partly because their work challenges that of the influential elder architects. A painter can experiment all by himself, with a canvas and some tubes or can of paint, but an architect needs a client to realize his design.

The parallel to the studio painting made in 'splendid isolation' and regardless of its saleability is the *ideal project*. This needs no client, no compromise, no building permission. It is preeminently the object for the artistic experimentation, the 'visual laboratory' of architecture in which new ideas are tested out and shown to the architect's peers. Many have therefore tried their hand at it, particularly in times of slack. Well-known examples are: the sketches by Mendelsohn and Scharoun; the Rosenberg house by van Eesteren and van Doesburg; Gropius' Total Theatre; Le Corbusier's Plan Voisin, Radiant City and Museum of unlimited extension; Mies' glass skyscrapers; Wright's Broadacre City; Neutra's Rush City; and of more recent date: Hollein's Aircraft Carrier in the wheat fields; Tange's Tokyo Bay project; the Metabolists' city plans; Bakema's Pampus project; Erskine's sub-arctic village; and Tigerman's Instant City. Several of these examples were highly influential (Mendelsohn, Mies, Hollein, Tange, the Metabolists).

A number of architects are known *only* for their paper projects: Archigram, Superstudio, Friedman, Ragon, the Kriers, Koolhaas; and those of the twenties: Sant' Elia, Finsterlin, Scheerbart, the Vesnin brothers, Leonidov. Some come close to it: Hejduk, Rossi. As publication is the main vehicle of exerting architectural influence, and as a project is as easy to publish as a real building, it is quite natural that these visionary 'paper architects' are particularly esteemed by their peers. This phenomenon is far from new; Serlio and Vredeman de Vries were highly influential paper architects of the sixteenth century, Boullée and Ledoux of the eighteenth century, and Palladio was also for ages only known through his *Four Books on Architecture*.

The artistic architect has to be careful of his reputation. As he is often consulted by the authors of monographs on his work, he can influence his own *'catalogue raisonné'* (Fig. 31). Mies built at the start of his career two houses in eighteenth-century style and designed two more. He later discouraged their publication, as he considered them 'too untypical'[65]. Though Le Corbusier's *Oeuvre Complète* starts in 1910, and the houses for Jeanneret Sr, Favre-Jacot and Schwob were all designed and built after that year, he did not include them in his catalog (which is thus misnamed). The monographs on individual architects always give the impression that they proceed carefully from one well-designed job or project to the next. The odd jobs that nearly every architectural office has to do: altering a

Figure 31
Riehl house, Berlin, 1907.
Considered by the architect, Mies,
to be 'too untypical' to be
reproduced amongst his other
designs

flue, repairing a leakage, or adding a garage, often for former
clients, must come their way too; they are omitted from the
catalog as immaterial, and it is then easy to omit in addition a
few buildings that you no longer like.

The artistic architects may watch over their artistic reputation, but they may well be careless about their practical one,
because that is not their specialty.

Several years ago Progressive Architecture published a house designed
by Frank Lloyd Wright for the Affleck family. We wrote the Afflecks,
asking their opinion of the building after they had lived in it for some
years. Mrs. Affleck replied in great detail, recounting their experiences
with Wright, with sightseers, and with their neighbors, ending with
the remark (which we quoted) that 'I know the roof has leaked and the
the skylights leak, but I would rather live in this house than in any
other house in the world'.

A few months after the house was published, I met Wright at the
Princeton conference; he looked at me accusingly and said 'You're the
editor who published the Affleck house, and said the roof leaked' 'We
didn't say the roof leaked, Mr. Wright', I replied, 'Your client said
that'. Wright waved his hand in the air, and, as he walked away, said,
'Oh, the client — poor soul, poor soul'.

Not every architect can be so off-hand about his client's welfare and
few of them would consciously want to[66].

Technical teething troubles on cars can be cured in the
succeeding model. Buildings are often too dissimilar, too
unique for such simple types of correction, and architects are in
business to make new designs. All architects make mistakes,
but it seems possible to me that the artistic architects care
somewhat less than the practical architects, for their reputation
hinges on another aspect. They take often considerable risk to
get a certain visual effect: doors of story-height which might

Figure 32
Sydney Opera House, 1956–1973.
Main architect: Jørn Utzon. For
the interior: Hall, Todd and
Littlemore. Utzon gained
worldwide fame on this building
and the respect of his peers, even
though the budget was exceeded
by 700% and it took 17 years to
build

easily warp, exposed concrete in air-polluted areas, fixed and
unshaded glass in a southern orientation.

Proof of the hypothesis that an artistic architect can afford to
be negligent in practical matters and yet retain the respect of his
colleagues as a great architect is found in the drama of the
Sydney Opera House (Fig. 32). Utzon was unresponsive to
suggestions from his structural engineer, Ove Arup, that he
change the shape of the roofs (to the catenary, to facilitate
calculation) or their structural material to steel, he quarrelled
with Arup over decisions taken during a critical period when he
was on a three-months' holiday, there were frequent delays in
the delivery of architectural drawings, he insisted on building
the ceilings of his halls with a company in receivership, the
whole process of design and construction dragged on intermin-
ably, and when the New South Wales ministers began to
assume a firmer control and reduce his hitherto nearly unlimited power over the whole project, he resigned. True, the
client also made monumental mistakes, changing his mind

several times, getting work started on the foundations before the superstructure had been accurately designed, possibly abetting in the (too) low original cost estimate in order to get construction under way, and giving too much rope to the architect and so reinforcing Utzon's belief that he and only he could decide on every detail. But mistakes of the client do not excuse the mistakes of the architect. In particular the very slow rate of progress, which was bound to lead to soaring costs in this era of inflation, seems to be due in no small part to Utzon.

The whole affair was discussed extensively in the trade journals and in several books[67]. Architects all over the world watched with interest, and sometimes perhaps with apprehension, for the success or failure of Utzon with this building of worldwide renown would reflect on the profession at large. It certainly had an effect in Sydney.

Big Sydney clients are still saying to their architects: 'Now mind you keep within agreed costs! We don't want any Opera House stuff with this job of ours'[68].

But in 1966, Utzon received the prize of the BDA, the German counterpart of the AIA; his resignation is described as 'dismissal' and he is extensively praised for the Sydney Opera House, entirely in his own terms[69]. And in 1978 he received the RIBA Gold Medal; his sponsor, Denys Lasdun, refrained from mentioning the Sydney Opera House at all.

Utzon's design may have been based on a mistaken interpretation of the structure of shells, his handling of the project may be open to criticism; nonetheless he succeeded in putting Sydney on the architectural map. The striking image of the building found an echo all over the world, perhaps beginning with Saarinen's TWA building. That is no mean feat, and it is for this of course that Utzon got his awards.

Overaccenting the practical side of the Sydney Opera House brings out one of the main points of this chapter: the precedence of the 'art' of architecture over its more pragmatic and technical aspects. This chapter has tried to show that this precedence exists, that it is not self-evident, and how its support-system works. Teachers, critics and historians act in concert to keep the belief in architecture as an art alive. All this relates to the 'how' of the art of architecture, it does not touch upon the 'what'; that will be the subject of the next chapter.

Part II

7 Form and Content in Architecture

The home is our place, the one bit of space we can call truly our own. The office is a place to work in, the church a place to worship in, the pool a place to swim in[1]. Buildings are, in van Eyck's poetic description, 'bunches of places', all distinct, each with its own functions and consequently each with its own emotional significance. Constructing a building means setting apart a number of cubic feet for a specific kind of usage. Before construction, there was the vacant lot, empty, potentially full of different possibilities; afterwards it has been changed into a two-story house, a garage or a department store. Some of the possibilities have been realized and have solidified into rooms, driveways or loading docks; all the others have disappeared. We can no longer do everything with the site; the building allows some kinds of use but prevents many others. Different forms of behavior require different kinds of spaces; the adaptation of a room to a specific form precludes many other forms. Behavior is channelled and partially restricted by buildings. We shape our buildings and afterwards they shape us, as Churchill said; architecture has a strong influence on what we do and how we do it.

Different functions have different emotional connotations and they rub off on the buildings that house them. Expensive materials, like marble, walnut or stainless steel, are often used to distinguish the office from the factory, the boardroom from the typing pool or the banking hall from other bank offices. The surplus of height in churches or the towers on German city halls are expressions of the special character of these functions. From the hours spent on the selection of our own curtains or furniture, from our first appraisal of a bank, a dentist or a doctor on the basis of an impression of their interiors, and from our assessment of neighbors and acquaintances on first seeing their living-rooms, we are all well aware of the expressiveness of architecture and interior decoration. It is not enough that a chair is comfortable and lighting is adequate; chairs and lamps are also signs of a certain 'taste' and a particular station in life. They involve a choice and thereby embody an attitude, a vision, some kind of ideal.

Conversely, ideal worlds are nearly always envisaged in physical terms, and described as 'places', and not primarily as a state of mind. The Garden of Eden and Shangri-La, Cockaigne and Atlantis, Thomas More's *Utopia* and Samuel Butler's *Erewhon* all contain lengthy and detailed descriptions of their physical settings. The concreteness of the description makes the ideal seem more realistic: it is easier to think of an ideal world which you can somehow 'see' than of a set of abstract social relations.

Our own ideals are usually much more modest. They do not involve uninhabited islands, celestial cities or communitarian governments; they concentrate on our future and our life. But they share with the utopian visions the possibility of *symbolic realization*. A little boy cannot turn overnight into a space traveller or a baseball star; but he can decorate himself and his room 'as if' he had already done so. An admirer of the American pioneers cannot return to the rugged simplicity of an earlier age; but he can express his admiration in the decoration of his home, and this inevitably suggests — both to himself and to others — in its nostalgic image of the past a sort of partial return.

Always moving around in and between buildings, we are familiar with all kinds of space. A room or a building invites comparison in its elegance or simplicity, its informality or dignity, its gravity or lightheartedness. The room or the building projects an image. Owner or occupant are — even if only intuitively — well aware of this and strive to model this image in ways congenial to themselves and likely to produce a favorable impression on others. This can be criticized as 'pretense', but may be called with equal justice 'symbolized idealism'.

Perhaps because of the possibility of being criticized for 'shamming', the image-charager of architecture is but rarely recognized and admitted by architects. Morris Lapidus on his Fontainebleau Hotel:

... Mr and Mrs America have made up their minds that they are going to the most expensive hotel in Miami Beach. In their own minds they have already conjured up a picture of living the life of a millionaire. So I designed what I did for *them*; the immensity of a meaningless lobby, the overabundance of beautiful antiques, the feeling of great opulence. When they walk in, they do feel 'This is what we've dreamed of, this is what we saw in the movies, this is what we imagined it might be'[2].

The 'French Provincial' design of the Fontainebleau is obvious, blatant make-believe. An ordinary American Colonial interior with modern Windsor chairs, machine-made after the ancient model, is much less obvious, but it shares with the Fontainebleau the suggestive make-believe quality. And, as will soon be apparent, the modern interior, for all its 'honesty', works basically on the same principle.

It is inevitable that we form a judgement, and that this judgement is based on a comparison. Buildings and interiors are not perceived independently, but in relation to each other. Seeing some interior for the first time, we cannot help being reminded of other interiors which we know. These associations are constitutive for the meaning of what we see. This meaning embodies an attitude, a desirable form of behavior, even a way of life. In the movie-set and in the Fontainebleau, this meaning is itself a commercial commodity; in the neo-Colonial home, it is simply a modest statement of allegiance to traditional American values.

But at the same time, architecture *has* an influence on behavior. The walls of a room set very definite limits to what can be done with it; the arrangement of rooms in a building creates a pattern for the sequence of activities. So it is very natural for architects to conflate meaning and use, and to believe that the desirable way of life — as represented by the architectural image — is actually brought about by the building as a physical thing. It is this confusion between behavior as implied by the meaning of architectural forms and behavior as constrained by the concrete physical building which has led to the doctrine of architectural determinism: that architects are not only life's stage-designers but also its playwrights, that they can *enforce* new forms of behavior[3]. It was this belief which was behind the AIA statement quoted in the last chapter:

The architect creates man's environment... His deliberations determine how people will be placed in relationship to one another, how whole societies work, play, eat, sleep, travel, worship — how people live[4]

and behind the conviction of Atelier 5 that they had to 'educate' the people to live together.

The planner Charles Colbert expressed it thus:

If, as I believe, the essence of architecture is to change and improve lives, then the real shaping forces of architecture are a better understanding and some responsibility for the deeper motivations of man[5].

Colbert hinted already at the role of the architect as a sage, a prophet who has to 'lead' mankind. Harry Weese was more modest about it:

The minute the architect begins to study the human problem he is involved in, he writes a social program, which by his own prejudice and insight he can influence and advance. He aims high when he maintains that a given proposal is not only better from the point of view of land use but also of economics, health and privacy[6].

But architects have often been inclined to increase rather than minimize their claims. Particularly in Europe in the twenties, when the 'new architecture' was supposed to bring about a 'new man', some architects did not hesitate to lay down the law. Ferdinand Kramer advocated the use of communal kitchens in a low-cost housing project in 1929:

The cycle of everyday life is organized in such a way that it has in addition a great educational value. Collective living enforces a disposition for mutal help and discipline[7].

Beside the confusion between symbolic content and physical substance, there are several other reasons for architects to view themselves a obvious leaders and improvers of mankind.

First, they straddle two large and highly respected areas of cultural endeavor: they are both artists and technicians. Other artists may have visions of a better or a different world (and several of them did: Samuel Butler, William Morris, H.G. Wells, Piet Mondrian, Constant), but they get no further than a description, a picture or a model. And everybody *knows* that they cannot get beyond that point; whereas an architect is at least potentially able to realize the built shell around his vision. Against engineers, architects can appeal to their high status as artists. Besides, the engineering schools attract a more sober kind of student and do not encourage visionary design.

Second, the process of building involves the cooperation of a great many people from very different walks of life, and the architect has — or rather had, until recently — a rather prominent position amongst them. *He* advises the client, obtains the building permit and chairs the job meetings. *He* can allow or withhold a certificate of payment, order a contractor to demolish an inferior bit of work, and talk to the hard hats if he wants to discuss a point of detail. The fact that he is (or was) a central figure in the whole social network around the construction of a building may cause him to forget how temporary and flimsy this network is, and give him the illusion of a much larger social role.

Third (and probably the most important): the claim that town planning is a legitimate part of architecture. This claim, first laid — and with success — in fifteenth-century Italy, renewed in the following centuries and in all western countries, and only recently seriously contested, implies a vision of the future, of society as it is and as it ought to be. Architects, by the very nature of their work already involved in projecting ideals in their designs, were only too happy to provide such visions. Officially invited by rulers or municipal councils to forecast the future, they were easily led to believe that this role was also incumbent upon them in the design of the individual building.

Originally, architects were also capable of doing all the necessary work for a new town themselves: they could design and supervise the construction of canals, bridges and fortifications. These things have been taken away from them by engineers; yet the planning role remained, by and large, with the architects. A good case can be made for civil engineers or landscape architects as chief planners; though there are examples of planners from these disciplines, the architects have succeeded in maintaining their predominance in the field. Historical priority has contributed to this, but also the ability of architects to generate visions of the future. Some of the more well-known and influential futuristic plans were: Burnham's plan for Chicago, Wright's Broadacre City, Neutra's Rush City, Le Corbusier's Ville Radieuse, Rudolph's New York expressway, the plans of Tange and Bakema for suburbs on the water, Archigram's Plug-in-City.

This tendency of architects to aim at the large view, and to subsume their own activities in a general vision which involves politics, economics and social relations, was the motivation behind the manifestos of CIAM. CIAM was an association of architects with only a few professional planners amongst them. But they concerned themselves with much larger issues than aesthetics or new building materials. Already the opening sentences of the 'Declaration of La Sarraz' of 1928 raises the discussion to a plane of great generality:

The undersigned architects find themselves in fundamental agreement about their views on building and on their professional duty towards society, and emphasize in detail that they hold building to be a very elementary activity of man, which shares in its full scope and its full depth in the creative development of our life. The task of the architects is therefore to bring themselves into agreement with the great events of their time and the great goals of the society to which they belong, and design their jobs accordingly[8].

The Declaration contains paragraphs on economics, city and regional planning, architecture and public opinion and the relations with the state. A reduction of the number of building trades is predicted, land speculation is condemned, and changes are recommended in laws and in general education. The most famous statement of CIAM, the Athens Charter of 1933, was entirely concerned with city planning. The vision of a new framework for city planning was of necessity political and contained such statements as:

... the pressing need to establish the disposition of the land upon a basis that will satisfy the needs of the many as well as these of the individual. In case of conflict, private interest should be subordinated to public interest[9].

In line with these traditions, a group of eight West German architects claimed in 1963:

WE DEMAND

From the federal government: a new regulation on land, which ensures planning the legal right of disposition over landownership; changes in the laws of eminent domain.

From the state government: a decisive right for progressive planners and architects to partici- pate in decisions on a state building code[10].

Claims of this order of magnitude are seldom if ever made by other professional groups. They may be lyrical about their work, they may consider it vital for the welfare of society, but for all that, they do not believe that they have a more reliable view of the future and they do not set themselves up as legislators for others. Compare, for example, the general introduction of the School of Engineering in the *MIT Bulletin* of 1979–1980. The enthusiasm of the first paragraph is prob- ably intended as an antidote against the tendency to blame technology for many of today's problems and also against the waning interest in engineering. How natural would it have been to claim after that paragraph that only engineering could solve the technical problems of the present day! But this does not happen.

Never has the challenge of engineering been more exhilarating, the opportunities of engineering been more exciting than today, a time when resource limitations and environmental constraints are in conflict with the desire of society for an improved quality of life. Never has the role of the engineer been more exacting.
   Engineering is concerned with developing and using scientific knowledge and technology to meet the needs of a complex society in ways that are sensitive to the constraints imposed by that society.
   Shaping the physical and chemical behavior of materials into efficient systems providing energy, transport, communications, food, security, and the other needs of society is clearly the central activity of engineering, and that activity must be carried out within a social context, always subject to physical, economic, political and legal bounds, and to the cultural value structure of the society.

Overriding claims are seldom made by architects today[11]. After a period in which architects have been blamed for making our cities uninhabitable, and in which they lost ground again to other technicians, such claims would sound rather far-fetched. When the storm of criticism broke in the early sixties, the reaction of many architects was to step up rather than minimize their claims. The text 'WE DEMAND' stems from this period, and so does the following quote from Hans Hollein (the 'designer' of the aircraft carrier in the desert):

Architecture is not satisfaction of the needs of the mediocre, is not environment for the petty happiness of the masses. Architecture is made by those who stand on the highest level of culture and civilization, in the vanguard of the development of their era. Architecture is the concern of elites[12].

All this deals with the 'why' and 'if' of architectural visions and symbolism, but not with the 'how' and 'what'. The mechanics of symbolization are quite simple and can be shown with an example from the work of Le Corbusier.
   As a boy, Le Corbusier had wanted to become a painter. His most influential teacher, l'Eplattenier, made him change his

Figure 33
Le Corbusier surrounded by his
paintings

mind and choose architecture[13]. But he kept a lifelong leaning
towards painting and continued to paint right up to the end of
his career; did not see it as a hobby; he wanted recognition not
only as an architect but also as a painter, and in his later years a
museum could only exhibit his architectural work if it bought
one of his paintings[14] (Fig. 33).

His first commission in Paris was a studio-house (1922) for
his friend the painter Amédée Ozenfant, with whom he
exhibited and wrote a manifesto on painting, *Après le Cubisme*
(1919) (Fig. 34).

The main features of this house, a two-story living-room
with a fully glazed endwall and a sleeping balcony, were used

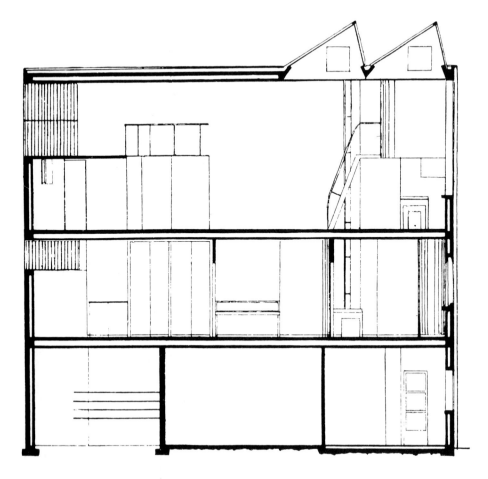

Figure 34
Section of Ozenfant house, Paris, 1922. Architect: Le Corbusier. The studio on the top floor shows the features which Corbu repeated again and again: double height, a mezzanine and a huge window-wall

by Le Corbusier again and again, even in housing projects which had nothing to do with artists and allowed a completely different solution, as Banham has noted[15]: on the Maison Citrohan (1920), the Pavillon de l'Esprit Nouveau (1923–1925), the Weissenhofsiedlung (1927) and the *Unité d'habitation* (1947–1952) (Figs. 35, 36 and 37).

The implication seems obvious. Le Corbusier considered the studio-house to be the ideal intellectual environment and transferred the forms of such a house to other projects in order to create the appropriate setting for spiritual development. Its meaning was clearly recognized by the (modern) architect Hans Schmidt, who wrote a slashing criticism of the Weissenhof house just after its completion in 1927:

Its author has intentionally designed it in such a way that it cannot be inhabited in the usual bourgeois manner. To have the living room, dining room, stairs, study, bedroom, bath and bidet gathered within four walls, as it were, without any insulation against noise and odours, hardly expresses the current concept of gracious living... Will this uninterrupted flow of space from one room to the next impose its own

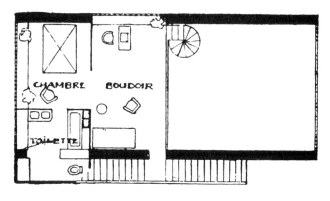

Entresol

Rez-de-chaussée

Figure 35
Plans of the Citrohan house, 1920,
by Le Corbusier and Pierre
Jeanneret. Though ostensibly
inspired by a Parisian restaurant,
it also shows the typical features
of the artist's studio: the
two-story living-room with
sleeping balcony and the huge
glass wall

pattern on the very life we lead? Or is it merely, as we suspect it is, a
harmless exaggeration, an extension of the life style of the artist's
studio, where an impromptu dinner is spread on a rickety table close to
the artist's easel, where the clatter of crockery and the tinkling of the
piano intrude agreeably on the writer's thoughts as he sits at his desk,
where the bed stands ready for models and lady friends alike, with
bath and bidet conveniently at hand[16]?

Le Corbusier's method of creating an ideal environment by
imitation is only a special case of a much more general principle.

For similar reasons have the Catholics of Montreal built their
cathedral as a faithful copy of St Peter's in Rome (down to such
details as Bernini's altar canopy (Fig. 38); or have some
Orthodox Greek parishes in the USA modelled their churches
on the Hagia Sophia in Constantinople[17]. The same mechanism
is behind the many US state capitol buildings in the form of the
Washington Capitol, behind the proposal of Stephen G. Porter
in 1920 to model all US embassies after the White House[18], and
behind the 1953 directive from the US State Department to
build all embassies henceforth in the 'Georgian and Renaiss-

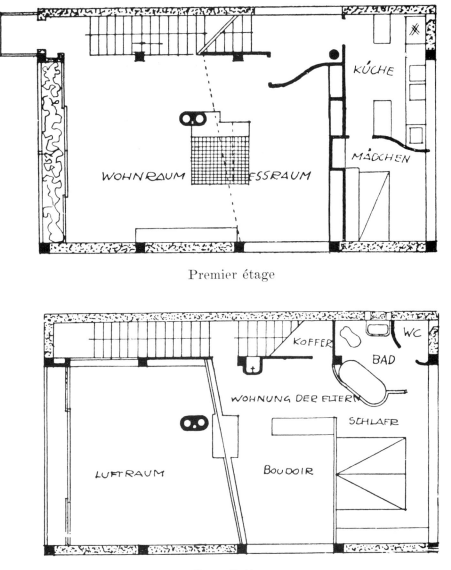

Premier étage

Second étage

ance neo-classical styles'[19]. It is the principle behind the windmill and drawbridge in Holland, Michigan (Fig. 39), and behind Colonial, Tudor and other 'neo-vernacular' architecture. *A meaning is transferred to a building by copying a form in which this meaning is clearly inherent.* The reason for it is obvious: it is hoped that the favorable connotations of the original will stick to the copy also. Domed Greek Orthodox churches or Colonial banks show that their owners uphold traditional values. A windmill and a drawbridge recreate something of the 'typical' Dutch atmosphere for the descen-

Figure 36
House in the Weissenhofsiedlung in Stuttgart, 1927, again with the two-story living-room and the glass wall. Architects: Le Corbusier and Pierre Jeanneret

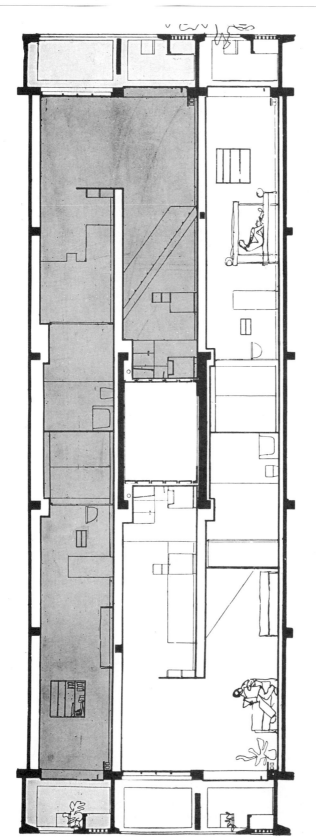

Figure 37
Section of the *Unité d'habitation*,
Marseilles, 1947–1952. Architect:
Le Corbusier. Once again, the
familiar features of the artist's
studio

Figure 38
Catholic cathedral of 'Mary, Queen of the World', 1870–1894, Montreal, Canada. Built as a 'faithful replica of St Peter's of Rome', in order to transfer the authority of the mother church to a Canadian building

dants of the Dutch settlers. The 'French Provincial' of the Fontainebleau Hotel suggests and old-world atmosphere and a refined *cuisine*. In semiotics, the discipline which studies signs and their meaning, this is called an *iconic symbol*.

It is usual among architects to hold architecture to be an 'abstract art', in contrast to 'naturalistic painting and sculpture'. With regard to the use of geometrical forms this is more or less correct; but it is wrong if 'abstract' is understood as the opposite of 'imitative'. Architecture can be as 'naturalistic' as photography in this respect: if you want to suggest a particular

Figure 39
Windmill Island, near Holland, Michigan. The recreation of a 'typical Dutch country-area' on American soil, for the benefit of the many people of Dutch origin in this area of Michigan. The tulips, the canal, the wooden drawbridge and the windmill are indeed 'typically Dutch'; but nowhere can you find a location in the Netherlands where all four can be taken in one shot

atmosphere, a certain life-style, what could be more ntural than choosing from the large available stock of building forms which are associated with it? The contempt of the architects of the modern movement for this method has made it all but disappear from consciousness. They claimed that they could do without it, a claim which can be disproven.

The effect of this principle on the beholder can be viewed with varying degrees of confidence. In its mildest form, it is seen as no more than a device to create an atmosphere. The inhabitants of Holland, Michigan, are perfectly well aware of what they have been doing, it is too obvious: Morris Lapidus was very conscious of the 'tricks' he played on his public. But values *do* inhere in forms, and buildings *do* have an effect on people. So it is tempting for architects to hope that the values they try to transmit with a specific set of forms will rub off on the clients; particularly when they believe passionately in these values themselves. And when you combine the symbolic meaning of architecture with the actual constraints which a building imposes on behavior, it is possible to hope that the building will 'really educate' people. In its extreme form, a building can be viewed as a utopian construction, an effective instrument to create a 'new man'. Modern architects in the twenties came close to this belief. Today, now that we know that the 'new man' has not arisen, this extreme confidence in the power of architecture has faded.

The method of copying forms in architectural design in order to transfer their favorable connotations is not a matter of choice but of sheer necessity. It is not the exception but the ubiquitous rule. The architectural student who uses the idioms he has learned from his teacher does so because he knows they will be favorably received. If architectural design was really 'free' — as the 'start-with-a-clean-slate' doctrine holds it to be — we would never have got a family resemblance among buildings of the same era. Architecture, just as the other arts, is a communication system. To be intelligible, even if it is only for himself, the designer has to use meaningful forms; but he cannot do otherwise, as all forms remind him of some other form and so are already meaningful.

Far and away the largest amount of copying is done within a 'school' or a 'tendency'. Architects show their sympathy with a certain current in architecture by using the forms of that current. This is after all what they have been taught to do in architectural school: to make variations within an existing idiom. It taxes only their powers of formal invention and does not require a reordering of their value-system. It is the architectural parallel of Thomas Kuhn's 'normal science'.

But it cannot be the whole story. The 'original models', which all the others copied more or less, must refer to something else, a meaning beyond the particular tendency itself. They must be connected with values outside.

A building which refers to one or more other buildings can do so in three fundamentally different directions:

      —in time: to the past
                    to the future
      —in space: to another place[20]

The first category is the most obvious one and the easiest to recognize. Renaissance and Neo-Classical architecture, all the eclectic architecture of the nineteenth and twentieth centuries, the 'Colonial' architecture still under construction in the USA today, all refer to the 'good old days of yore', when the world was a better place to live in, and man was happier, or more civilized, or more humane, or more religious, etc. For instance, Pugin advocated the use of Neo-Gothic architecture against the Neo-Classical still prevailing in his day (1843):

If we worshipped Jupiter, or were votaries of Juggernaut, we should raise a temple, or erect a pagoda. If we believed in Mahomet, we should mount the crescent, and raise a mosque. If we burnt our dead, and offered animals to gods, we should use cinerary urns, and carve sacrificial friezes of bulls and goats. If we denied Christ, we should reject his Cross. For all these would be natural consequences: but, in the name of common sense, whilst we glory in being Englishmen, let us have an architecture, the arrangement and details of which will alike remind us of our faith and our country, — an architecture whose beauties we may claim as our own, whose symbols have originated in our religion and our customs. Such an architecture is to be found in the works of our great ancestors, whose noble conceptions and mighty works were originated and perfected under a faith and a system, for the most part common with our own...[21].

Neo-Gothic was 'modern' in Pugin's time, which shows that the term has only a heuristic value. (In fifteenth-century Italy, 'modern architecture' stood for Gothic, Renaissance architecture being called 'ancient'; nowadays, we would label the first 'conservative', the second 'modern'.)

It is easy to refer to the past, but much harder to refer to the future. The founders of the Modern Movement tried to get around this difficulty by using the high-tech materials of their day: glass, steel, concrete and chromium; by referring to utilitarian buildings, such as grain-elevators, and in particular to factories, because they were believed to be recent and as yet 'uncontaminated'; and by borrowing freely from ocean liners, as the most 'advanced' constructions of their day. Archigram did the same in our time when they used forms borrowed from rockets, spaceships and moonlanders (Fig. 67).

The values associated with another place are the characteristics of the third category. US state capitols are not modelled on the Washington DC Capitol Building primarily for historic reasons, but with the purpose of transferring some of the authority of the federal government to that of the state. The windmill in Holland, Michigan, does not recall 'old' Holland, but what is seen as 'typical' Holland. St Peter's was imitated in Montreal because of the authority of the main church of

Figure 40
Housing in Andover, UK, 1972.
Architects: London County
Council. Garden-city
development, with detailing
intended to recall the old English
village (pitched roofs, brick and
stained clapboard, and many
projections and recesses to ensure
picturesqueness and small scale),
yet sufficiently different to show
that it is of this century

Catholicism, i.e as a place and not as a reminder of the past.

A large subgroup of this category is neo-vernacular architecture: the effort to transfer the homely virtues of the village to modern (sub)urbanized society. It is the youngest offshoot of the old bucolic or Arcadian ideal: a pastoral unpolluted world inhabited by simple innocent people, the habitat of natural man before the Fall. It is the root cause of the hamlet of Marie-Antoinette in the park of Versailles (1780) and of Ebenezer Howard's Garden-City movement (Fig. 40 and 41). The ubiquity of villages makes this one of the forms of

Figure 41
The 'farm' of Marie-Antoinette in
the park of Versailles, 1783–1785.
Architect: Richard Mique. A
building in 'rustic style' to allow
Marie-Antoinette and her
ladies-in-waiting to play the roles
of peasant women

architectural symbolism which is very easily and generally understood. The doctrines of the 'big bad city' and of healthy outdoor living support its positive connotations, and help to make it one of the most popular architectural idioms of today.

The three options for architectural symbolism (of the past, of the future and of place, for short) exist and have always existed side by side[22]. That of place, being neutral to time, can be combined with either the future or the past: e.g. the government of a developing country may require a ministry which is recognizably 'modern' and 'western'; the Getty museum in Malibu, California, a reconstruction of the Villa of the Papyri in Herculaneum, is intentionally both 'old' and 'Roman'. The symbolisms of the future and of the past are usually — and logically — seen as opposites (though in fact they are sometimes combined today, see chapter 9).

The symbolism of the future appealed strongly to a part of the European cultural elite of the twenties[23]. Many of them blamed the First World War on the older order and in particular on the economic elite. They cherished a hope for a better world in the future, with more social justice; often eking out a precarious existence, they did not consider themselves as belonging to the ruling class and hoped for a more important role for themselves too.

The spokesmen for the Modern Movement may have been encouraged to assume a leftist stance in Germany and Holland by a change in building practice. The First World War had led to a large housing shortage in both countries. Mass housing had aways been the nearly exclusive province of speculative builders and only rarely had architects been commissioned. This changed overnight in 1918. The newly formed housing cooperatives — many of socialist coloring — considered that the speculators had botched the job and turned to architects. Is it not possible that the change in attitude of architects towards housing, from disdain to genuine social concern, exemplified by the 2nd CIAM congress, is due in part to the change in the market for commissions?

A number of the artistically 'progressive' architects were also politically progressive: Ernst May, Hannes Meyer, Hans Schmidt, Mart Stam and Piet Zwart. Many more shared their social concerns without engaging in any overt political activity. But some of the artistically progressives only saw the new symbolism as another architectural idiom in which they might rebel against their teachers, for example. The 'Modern Movement' counted quite a few adherents without any interest in political reform: Oud, Mies, Breuer and Roth.

For if leftist leanings may be understandable in a member of the cultural elite, they are by no means a corollary. Even many people of the working class, who stand only to gain by social reform ('they have nothing to lose but their chains'), have staunchly conservative views ('lacking a proper class-consciousness'). The same applies to the cultural elite; many of its members have conservative convictions, either in politics, or in the arts or in both. An architectural student from a conservative background may well experience artistic radicalism as a threat to all that he holds sacred and beautiful, and therefore turn to conservatism in design. Abandoning the world of beauty that you know is not just a whim of fashion; it implies also a loss of social identity.

To classify all 'progressive' architects as 'Bolsheviks' (as the Nazis did) is far too simple. We have to be satisfied with the much weaker proposition that a leftist stance is found more frequently among 'progressive' architects, and right-wing leanings more frequently among artistically conservative architects.

The symbolism of the past is of course the natural mode of expression for conservatives. Thus it has often been used by conservative institutions, such as banks or the Catholic church. This may lead to a reaction from within those institutions, as not everyone needs to be consistently conservative in all areas. Some French Catholic priests, alarmed by the conservative image projected by their historicist art and architecture, tried to change it by inviting *avant-garde* artists and architects. Amongst the works produced through their efforts are the two religious buildings of Le Corbusier, Ronchamp and La Tourette[24].

The various forms of symbolism are clearly connected with different value-systems. Architects, once they have chosen a position and sorted out what they believe in and which design-principles they hold to be true, are extremely sensitive about them, far more than about practical arrangements in a plan or the use of certain materials or techniques. They try to push their design philosophy as the one and only answer to the problems of the day and are very critical even of slight deviations. The sensitivity of Wright or Le Corbusier to criticism was notorious. At the same time, they are prone to attack other architects in the most scathing terms, even if, to an outsider at least, they have quite a few points in common with the architect so criticized. This is because their whole artistic identity is tied up in their design philosophy and its symbolism; their struggle is an effort to establish *the legitimacy of their convictions*. Every new job is a 'proof' that they are right; every job by a competitor is a proof that he has succeeded in convincing some people, which is a challenge to all other positions.

Some examples. Mies in 1923 on his theoretical design for a concrete office building and on Mendelsohn's Einstein Tower:

Concrete buildings are essentially skeleton buildings. Neither vermicelli nor armored turrets. With load-bearing beam-construction: a non-bearing wall. Thus skin-and-bones structures[25].

Romualdo Giurgola on the book *Five Architects* (1973):

... this book is incomplete and inadequate. Its scope is devoted only to
the defining of a school or tendency in architecture; a tendency which
rests particularly on a slippery dialectic, learned citation, aesthetic
exclusivism and basic indifference[26].

Robert Stern on Eisenman:

What I do not believe is that so-called 'deep structure' contributes at all
to man's understanding of his place in relationship to the natural world
and other man-made objects — the essential purpose of architecture. I
do not believe that structure, no matter how 'deep' is a particularly
expressive tool in architecture. In fact, I think that all that superfluity
of walls, beams and columns which characterize his design contributes
to his claustrophobia[27].

and on Richard Meier's Saltzman house (Fig. 74):

Even as an object it disappoints and seems lumpish... I don't think I'm
carping to note that the bedrooms face west, with unshaded glass, a
good deal of which is fixed; that the house, generally short on operable
sash, is not adapted for air-conditioning; and that the three-storey
high diningroom, completely glazed along its southern end, is
spectacular and intimidating in equal measure, and virtually uninhabitable during the daytime[28].

Notwithstanding all the 'honor codes' and 'admonitions' of
architects' institutes, competition among architects is but little
restrained. this is reflected in the uninhibited attacks they make
on each other. Yet they are willing to collaborate, if their views
are sufficiently similar, and if they feel threatened by the
adherents of the opposite camp (see chapter 8). I have quoted
the derisive criticism of Hans Schmidt in 1927 of Le Corbusier
for one of his houses in the Weissenhofsiedlung, but a year later
they both became founder members of CIAM[29].

The struggle for the legitimacy of one's convictions, which is
in my opinion one of the root causes of the architects'
squabbles, can affect large groups of people over an extended
period. Thomas Jefferson wrote in 1782 about US architecture:

The genius of architecture seems to have shed its maledictions over this
land... the first principles of the art are unknown, and there exists
scarcely a model among us sufficiently chaste to give an idea of them[30].

The view that the USA had no culture of its own and needed
European models has persisted practically to this day. Henry
James described it in 1879:

One might enumerate the items of high civilization, as it exists in other
countries, which are absent from the texture of American life, until it
should be a wonder to know what was left. No State, in the European
sense of the word, and indeed barely a specific national name. No
sovereign, no court, no personal loyalty, no aristocracy, no church,
no clergy, no army, no diplomatic service, no country gentlemen, no
palaces, no castles, nor manors, nor old country houses, no parson-
ages, nor thatched cottages, nor ivied ruins; no great universities nor
public schools — no Oxford, nor Eton, nor Harrow; no literature, no
novels, no museums, no pictures, no political society, no sporting

class — no Epsom or Ascot! ...The natural remark, in the light of such an indictment, would be that if these things are left out, everything is left out[31].

An individual may derive his social standing from his past, and in particular from his ancestors. All western societies have their 'old families': the aristocrats and patricians in Europe, the DAR and the 'good old families' of New York or Boston in the USA. Just as an individual, a nation derives part of its feelings of national identity from its past and its ancestors. These were, for the white Americans, *not* the Sioux or the Apache and the American past, but their country of origin and European history. America is a 'new country'; this theme too was repeated over and over again; but for many educated Americans 'new' equalled 'parvenu'. The architect Joy Wheeler Dow expressed the hankering after a respectable past in 1904:

The home one builds must mean something besides artistic and engineering skill. It must presuppose, by subtle architectonic expression, both in itself and in its surroundings, that its owner possessed, once upon a time, two good parents, four grandparents, eight greatgrandparents, and so on; had, likely, brothers and sisters, uncles and aunts, all eminently respectable and endeared to him; that *bienséance* and family order have flourished in this line from time immemorial — there was no black sheep to make him ashamed — and that he has inherited heirlooms, plate, portraits, miniatures, pictures, rare volumes, diaries, letters and state archives to link him up properly in historical succession and progression. We are covetous of our niche in history. We want to belong somewhere and to something, not to be entirely cut off by ourselves as stray atoms in boundless space either geographical or chronological. The human mind is a dependent thing, and so is happiness. We may not, indeed, have inherited the house we live in; the chances are that we have not. We may not remember that either of our parents or any of our grandparents before use, ever gloried in the quiet possession of ... a homestead...; but for the sake of goodness — for the sake of making the world appear a more decent place to live in — let us pretend that they did, and that it is now ours[32].

The advocates changed, but the stereotypical image persisted. This is how the literary critic Malcolm Cowley remembers in 1951 the attitude right after the First World War:

Almost everywhere, after the war, one heard the intellectual life of America unfavorably compared with that of Europe. The critics often called for a great American novel or opera; they were doggedly enthusiastic, like cheer leaders urging Princeton to carry the ball over the line; but at heart they felt that Princeton was beaten, the game was in the bag for Oxford and the Sorbonne; at heart they were not convinced that even the subject matter of a great novel could be supplied by this country. American themes — so the older critics felt — were lacking in dignity. Art and ideas were products manufactured under a European patent; all we could furnish toward them was raw talent destined usually to be wasted. Everywhere, in every department of cultural life, Europe offered the models to imitate — in painting, composing, philosophy, folk music, folk drinking, the drama, sex, politics, national consciousness — indeed, some doubted that this country was even a nation; it has no traditions except the fatal tradition of the pioneer[33].

The same sentiment, but not as a reminiscence of the twenties, is echoed by the historian Daniel J. Boorstin in 1960:

Until now when we have started to talk about the uniqueness of America we have almost always ended by comparing ourselves to Europe. Toward her we have felt all the attractions and repulsions of Oedipus. Only by denying our parent can we become a truly independent New World; yet we cannot help feeling that the New World is the fulfilment of a European dream. We are both a happy non-Europe and a happy afterlife of Europe. Europe is both our beloved 'mother country' and the pernicious source of all 'alien ideologies'. We owe to her our religion, our common law, our ideal of constitutionalism; but also the ancient menaces of aristocracy, feudalism and monopoly, and the modern menace of communism... Most European nations do not even know from where their settlers came. We of all modern peoples are dominated by the specter of known foreign ancestors[34].

It is this specter that drives millions of Americans each year to board a plane for Europe — compared to this stream, the number of Europeans going to visit the USA is only a trickle. It is this specter that made the Michigan Dutch build their windmill and drawbridge, and made many famous Americans seek an exile, temporary or permanent, in Europe: Henry Adams, Henry James, Edith Wharton, Gertrude Stein, Ezra Pound. T.S. Eliot, Ernest Hemingway and the painters Mary Cassatt, James McNeill Whistler and John Singer Sargent. For some the mirage of cultured Europe as a contrast to uncivilized America faded away when they got a closer look. Malcolm Cowley, who went in 1921, could write two years later:

America is just as god-damned good as Europe — worse in some ways, better in others, just as appreciative ... As for its being the concentration point for all vices and vulgarities — nuts. New York is refinement itself beside Berlin. French taste in most details is unbearable. London is a huge Gopher Prairie... America shares an inferiority complex with Germany. Not about machinery or living standards, but about Art[35].

A man of letters might find it easy to reassess European culture; it was (and is) harder for visually minded people. One may find an American counterpart to the Oxford don; but there is no American counterpart to the medieval quadrangles of Oxford. Besides, architects cannot practise their craft from a distance, so many stayed not long enough to break the spell. The visual contrast between Europe and the USA remains, long after other contrasts are seen as relative. Edith Wharton has described it vividly in 1933:

One of the most depressing impressions of my childhood is my recollection of the intolerable ugliness of New York, of its untended streets and the narow houses so lacking in external dignity, so crammed with smug and suffocating upholstery. But how could I understand that people who had seen Rome and Seville, Paris and London, could come back to live contentedly between Washington Square and Central Park... This low-studded rectangular New York, cursed with its universal chocolate-coloured coating of the most hideous stone ever quarried, this cramped horizontal gridiron of a town without towers, porticoes, fountains or perspectives, hide-bound in its deadly uniformity of mean ugliness[36].

The admiration for Europe was bound to have a profound effect on architecture and express itself in a symbolism of place: a recreation of the beauties of the Old World on the soil of the New. Many architects crossed the Atlantic with the same feelings as Ralph Adams Cram in 1886:

Here were all the arts spread out, like a great tapestry by some magic struck into life: the pictures of a dozen galleries — five centuries of the primest achievement, not to speak of the Pre-Raphaelite collection in London; the sculpture of four thousand years; and the greater part of the noblest churches that Catholic Christianity had brought into being — from Ravenna and St. Mark's to Rouen and Westminster... At the age of twenty-three, with behind me only an America where the evidences of art and their manifestations were few, rudimentary, and, in addition, disappearing fast, such a journey was not only apprenticeship, but revelation[37].

The European architects themselves were at that time copying old masterpieces; so how could there be anything wrong with it?

This feeling of inferiority to 'old Europe', this passionate desire to copy and emulate it on American soil, is what motivated the architects of the Columbian Exhibition of 1894 in Chicago to design a 'White City' in Renaissance form, and nip the Chicago School of Sullivan and Root in the bud. It is the motivation behind the founding of the American Academy in Rome and behind the modelling of US architectural education on the example of the Ecole des Beaux Arts in Paris. Eclectic architecture persisted in Europe too, and even had a revival in fascist Germany and Italy; but architects of a different persuasion got more scope to display their talents in Europe than in the USA. Wright, Neutra, Schindler, Gill, Howe and Lescaze had a harder time finding clients, and got less spectacular ones than Gropius, Mendelsohn, Aalto, Le Corbusier, Duiker or Van der Vlugt. The latter also for years got far more publicity in their home countries than the former.

The effort of American architects to appropriate a geographically distinct culture is by no means unusual. Charlemagne tried to do it in ninth-century Germany[38]; Francis I tried to emulate Italian Renaissance culture in fifteenth-century France[39]; Inigo Jones made his name in a similar effort in seventeenth-century England[40]. All former colonies share the sentiments of cultural inferiority which have plagued the Americans for so long.

The architect Robin Boyd on the 'Australian ugliness' (1968):

... in England, unlike America and Australia, there is always something of genuine beauty around the corner, a medieval church or a glimpse of a field, hedge and honest stonework, even if it is hemmed in by rival service stations and haunted by the wiry ghosts of electricity and telephones… For years, Australians have been noted for seeking an answer from visitors 'What do you think of Australia?' 'How do our cultural achievements stand?' 'Is our work world class?' Amiable visitors respond by praising the high peaks of development. Less agreeable ones condemn the troughs, and the nation seethes with anger. For what was requested of the visitors was not criticism, favourable or unfavourable, of specific efforts, but something more fundamental: an assurance of how the averages stand, how the standards stand in the world scene. If one is not an initiator, if one lives by copying, it is essential to be reassured on such points at regular intervals[41].

But even countries with a long and venerable history and ancient monuments of worldwide reputation may want to transplant a set of values embodied in a foreign architectural form. Two incidents from the personal recollections of the architect Georges Candilis. The first happened when he worked in Morocco:

I stood before the leaders of the nationalist revolution…
'So it is you, Monsieur Candilis, who managed the construction of these houses?'
'Yes'
'Why do you make them so different from what is usual elsewhere'?
I moved closer to him.
'Because I look for solutions which are adapted to your conditions of life and the prevailing economic situation. And these situations require an architecture different from the one that is made today'.
'That is why we have called you. We know that you looked for something different'.
I thought happily that we had already found a common ground for our discussion, when he added icily and very clearly:
'Well, you are completely mistaken'.
I was speechless.
'I am mistaken?'
'Why don't you make the same houses for us as for the Europeans, the same houses as in France?'
'Because you do not live under the same circumstances as the people in France'.
And I, too, started to speak emphatically.
'I try to find your identity'.
The answer to that was implacable:
'That is neo-colonialism, a much more dangerous form of tutelage than all the threats from our declared enemies!'[42]

Candilis had a similar experience in Syria:

I was asked, not long ago, by the Syrian government to participate in a limited competition for the construction of a university in Lattaquié… Once again I was carried away by my great enthusiasm and I said: 'I am much obliged to you, gentlemen, because you have given me the opportunity to propose to you a university on the model of your admirable bazaars'.
The reaction was vehement. 'We want a university and no bazaar. We are just as far in our education as the Germans, the Italians or the French. And we want a university as they have in Europe, and no bazaar! We thank you for your trouble, sir'.
They decided for a *Herr Doktor* from Düsseldorf, who built them a germanic university[43].

It is this desire to be up-to-date, to appear as a fully fledged member of modern society, that probably induced the government of Pakistan to invite Louis Kahn to design the government buildings at Dacca.

For many European intellectuals of the early twentieth century, modernity was associated with the marvels of technology which had recently enriched their lives: trains, passenger liners, electric lighting, automobiles, electric streetcars, phonographs, movies and airplanes. The Futurists sang their praises:

We affirm that the world's magnificence has been enriched by a new beauty: the beauty of speed. A racing car whose hood is adorned with great pipes, like serpents of explosive breath — a roaring car that seems to ride on grapeshot is more beautiful than the *Victory of Samothrace*... we will sing of the nocturnal vibrance of arsenals and shipyards blazing with violent electric moons; greedy railway stations that devour smokeplumed serpents; factories hung on clouds by the crooked lines of their smoke; bridges that stride the rivers like giant gymnasts, flashing in the sun with a glitter of knives; adventurous steamers that sniff the horizon; deep-chested locomotives whose wheels paw the tracks like the hooves of enormous steel horses bridled by tubing; and the sleek flight of planes whose propellers chatter in the wind like banners and seem to cheer like an enthusiastic crowd[44].

An important part of these novelties came from America, the land of unlimited possibilities. American inventors like Bell or Edison had contributed largely to the 'First Machine Age', and, what impressed European visitors to the USA even more, the new technology was applied and exploited on an unprecedented scale. Though the Americans did not invent the assembly-line or the conveyor belt, they applied them more successfully than the Europeans and created mass production. Taylor and Gilbreth made production far more efficient by their time-and-motion studies. Henry Ford turned the automobile from a luxury article into a household commodity with the new methods.

The image of the USA as the land of the future, of technical prowess and Yankee knowhow, persists to this day. It has a long history, starting a century ago with, for example, regular reports on American building and production methods in European technical trade magazines: on district heating by steam, on cable cars and elevated railways, on Yale locks, on elevators and escalators, on mechanization of brick manufacture[45]. Erich Mendelsohn in 1928:

America assembles its building like a machine. Without scaffolding and everything thought out beforehand. The exhaust duct of the mechanical ventilation has already been erected and can start tomorrow.

... America manages construction with consummate skill, has calculated the structural possibilities of the new materials — but has not yet recognized their spirit, the boldness of their new design (-possibilities)[46].

The last part of the quotation refers to American Beaux Arts architecture, which — in the eyes of progressive European architects — did not live up to the promise of American technology. In the words of Le Corbusier of 1924:

Let us listen to the advice of the American engineers. But beware of the American *architects*[47].

In accordance with this vision of the USA — technically advanced, but culturally backward — the American buildings expressive of the future which were admired by architects were only utilitarian constructions: factories and grain elevators. Gropius wrote about them in 1913:

... in America, the motherland of industry, there are great industrial structures which, in their unconscious majesty, are superior even to our best German buildings of that type. The grain elevators of Canada and South America, the coal conveyors of great railways lines, and the more modern industrial plants of North America are almost as impressive in their monumental power as the buildings of ancient Egypt. They present an architectural composition of such exactness that to the observer their meaning is forcefully and unequivocally clear[48].

Figure 42
'Het Witte Huis' (the 'White House'), office building, Rotterdam, 1897–1898. Architect: W. Molenbroek. According to contemporary newspaper and trade journal accounts, built in 'the American manner'. Even the German Romanesque detailing of some contemporary American examples (by Root or Post) is faithfully imitated

Figure 43
Harry M. Pettit, King's Dream of
New York, illustration in *King's
Views of New York*, New York
1908. It was from this kind of
'vision' that European architects
like Sant' Elia derived their views
on the city of the future, as Cervin
Robinson has pointed out.

The preeminent symbol of American technical progressive-
ness was the skyscraper, a building type as firmly associated
with America as the windmill with the Netherlands. The Dutch
were the first to build one, complete with Richards-
onian Neo-Romanesque trappings and a roof terrace for
visitors, in 1898 (Fig. 42). Most European skyscraper projects
remained on paper, as symbols of the future: in Sant' Elia's
well-known designs, in Mies' glass towers, in Le Corbusier's
Ville Radieuse (Fig. 43) (the last even explicitly referred to the
skyscapers of New York; Figs. 44, 45, 46 and 47). These paper
skyscrapers were stripped of their American eclectic trimmings, for how could the architecture of the future be clothed
in the forms of the past?

Figure 44
Antonio Sant' Elia, 'The New City', 1914. The most influential of Sant' Elia's drawings and one of the more influential utopian paper projects of this century. In line with futurist tenets, the drawing emphasizes movement: elevator towers, traffic decks

The imagery of the symbolism of the future of the European functionalists was derived from disparate sources: from ocean liners, from materials considered high-tech (glass, steel, concrete) and from America. The USA contributed the factory aesthetic, high-rise building and the (steel) skeleton. The interest of functionalist architects in the skeleton, as evinced in the early work of Gropius, Le Corbusier and Mies, was caused primarily by its technical advantages, but can *also* be interpreted as a search for an adequate symbol of modernity, representative of the technical advances in building construction. In addition, it is probably also influenced by changes in

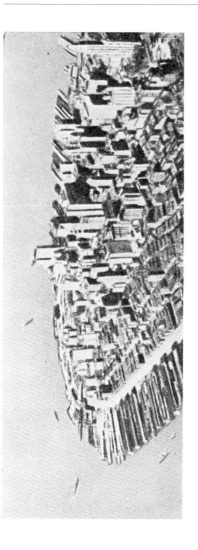

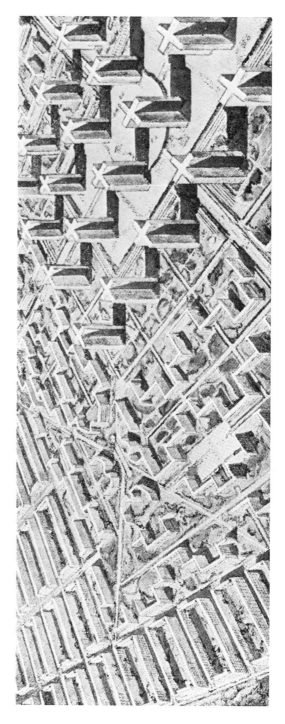

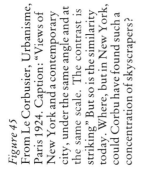

Figure 45
From Le Corbusier, *Urbanisme,* Paris 1924. Caption: "*Views of New York and a contemporary city,* under the same angle and at the same scale. The contrast is striking." But so is the similarity today. Where, but in New York, could Corbu have found such a concentration of skyscrapers?

Figure 46
Competition project of Mies van
der Rohe for a skyscraper in
Berlin, 1921. He wrote, when he
published the project (in *Frühlicht*
I, 1921/1922, 4): 'Only
skyscrapers under construction
show the bold structural thought,
and then the impression of the
high-rising steel skeleton is
overpowering. With the filling-in
of the facades with stone, this
impression is completely
destroyed... The novel structural
principle of these buildings
becomes clearly visible when one
uses glass for the now no longer
load-bearing exterior walls'. (Mies
van der Rohe, Friedrichstrasse
Office Building, 1919. Charcoal
and pencil on brown paper
mounted to board; 68¼ x 47.
Collection, the Museum of
Modern Art, New York. Gift of
Ludwig Mies van der Rohe)

architectural practice. All over the western world, the scale of
buildings was growing, the technology was changing and more
and more of these new buildings were designed by engineers.
By including pictures of bridges and grain-elevators, by
pointing to the examples of American engineers, by enthusiastic comments on the Fiat factory in Turin or Owen Williams'
factory in Beeston, and by the adoption of new materials, the
modern architects claimed a share of that growing market, and
tried to counteract the 'losses' to practical architects and
engineers. Sometimes they were successful, as for instance in
the case of the van Nelle factory in Rotterdam.

Most American architecture looked overly conservative to
progressive European architects, but a few architects seemed to

Figure 47
The Singer building under
construction. Illustration from:
O. Rappold, *Der Bau der
Wolkenkratzer*, Munich 1913.
Mies may have arrived at his view
by seeing a picture like this one

have slipped away from under the yoke of eclecticism: Sullivan
and in particular Wright. If Wright had a hard time getting
recognition in the USA, he was never short of European
admirers, particularly among his colleagues. Berlage wrote
about him in 1913:

Wright understands the effect of contrast, and himself gets thereby a
tremendous result; for whatever view one may hold in general, and
primarily in Europe about such questions, there is none here of such
monumental power. And when again power is the so very much
needed and to be regained characteristic of a work of art, well, then the
Larkin building is a great work of art.

I at least left it, in the conviction of having seen a truly modern
work, with respect for the master who made something that, as far as I
know, does not have its equal in Europe[49].

Wright's work was published in eight issues in the Dutch (expressionist) magazine *Wendingen* in the twenties, and exhibited in the Amsterdam Municipal Museum in 1931. It was closely imitated by the architects van 't Hoff, Wils, Duiker and Bijvoet. A modern architect from the land of the future was for them an irresistible example.

This last form of copying is different from the use of high-rise or skeleton. These last are — or can be — symbols of America, and by implication of the future. Wright was not copied for that reason, but because his architecture seemed free of all historic or local references.

But the other forms that were imitated, the American factories[50], the skyscraper and probably also the skeleton, were, I am inclined to believe, used as symbols of place. They referred to the future by using 'advanced' elements from American building art. American architects copied European buildings to upgrade the cultural level of their country, but the compliment was to some extent repaid by a number of their European colleagues.

Chapter 5 suggested that art is a symbolic language for emotional orientation in the world at large. This idea was applied here to architecture. If you want to live in the future, you can already surround yourself with an architecture of the future, using 'new' materials and constructions. If you identify with the past, you can build in the image of the past. Paradise may be far away, but the image of paradise may be just round the corner. This chapter mentioned only some of the more obvious elements and mechanisms. It is but one step from creating the image of the world of the future to enforcing the social life of the future. The 'utopian concepts' behind le Corbusier's *Unité d'habitation* and behind Halen are elaborations on the principles described in this chapter. The next two chapters will apply the two mechanisms described in this and all the earlier chapters (viz. a field of competing groups and a symbolic Utopia) to two coherent periods in architecture.

8 Case-Study: Dutch Architecture in the Twenties and Thirties

Changes in architectural design, though faster than in the past, and still accelerating, are slower than in fashion or music. Clients, and particularly those of the economic elite, are not inclined to experiment, offices which have found a personal style tend to stick to a success formula, and the architectural schools transmit the beliefs of one generation to the next. Most of the buildings of a certain period are therefore humdrum variations on the *avant-garde* of yesteryear. The majority of architects are primarily 'practical architects', limited by talent, by training and by economic circumstance in their freedom to create the unexpected. They expend their creative urge in the rearrangement of forms they know and believe in, occasionally enriched by novelties picked up from the trade magazines. Their job is more exciting than it sounds, for as no two briefs or two clients are alike, there is still ample scope for creative ingenuity in finding a satisfactory solution for a particular program within a limited budget.

But some architects set their sights higher. They are not satisfied with the state of architecture as they find it; they want to make it purer, or more modern, or less modern, or more logical, etc. So they start — or more often join — a campaign for a 'different', a 'new' architecture. For the reasons mentioned in Chapter 5 — the emotional impact has worn off, some clients demand a more distinguished architecture and the artistic architect has to distinguish himself — they try to alter the form, and sometimes also the content of the language of architecture. Innovations are often primarily a form of built criticism[1].

The changes are always partial. For the reasons outlined in chapters 5 and 6 — the interpretation of art in terms of a familiar frame of reference, the influence of previous training and experience — no architect is able to discard the work of his predecessors and contemporaries completely, even if he says he does. For instance, 'structural honesty', i.e. the articulation of the load-bearing system of the building, started with Neo-Gothic and the Arts and Crafts Movement in the 1860s and was carried over into Art Nouveau, Expressionism and the International Style. To emphasize the distinction between themselves and the common herd, innovative architects are wont to claim a greater originality than is warranted. This claim has led to the myths of the 'clean slate' and 'fresh start' which have so long bewitched architectural teachers and students.

To be really effective, the innovative work has to be seen not only as 'different', but also as 'better'; it has to gain acceptance. The verbal propaganda for a 'new' architecture is as much a part of the effort to change the course of design as the photographs and the buildings themselves. All are weapons in the struggle for legitimacy.

The Dutch Republic had known a period of glory in the seventeenth century. It had fought a successful war of independence (1568–1648), created colonies in the East Indies and in America (New Amsterdam), and Amsterdam had temporarily become the financial capital of the western world. Thereafter the economy began to decline and reached its lowest ebb in the nineteenth century. It only picked up after the unification of Germany (1870), when the rapid industrialization of that country stimulated the transit trade along the Rhine.

Hope for a new 'Golden Age' was expresssed in architecture by a symbolism of the past, referring to the typically Dutch early seventeenth-century architecture in red brick with white sandstone string-courses and keystones and stepped gables (Fig. 48). This was the dominant architectural vocabulary for

Figure 48
Competition project for the Amsterdam Exchange, 1885, by the architects Th. Sanders and H. P. Berlage. The tower in the middle of the side elevation is a copy of the tower of the Amsterdam Exchange of 1608. The seventeenth-century was the 'Golden Age' of Dutch trade, during which Amsterdam was the financial capital of the world; the seventeenth-century Exchange had been demolished in 1837

DE·NIEUWE·BEURS·OP·HET·DAMRAK·TE·AMSTERDAM·GEZIEN·KOMENDE·VAN·DEN·DAM·

Figure 49
Perspective drawing of Berlage's final design for the Amsterdam Exchange, showing the 'naked style' at which he had arrived in 1898

secular buildings at the end of the nineteenth century and it was against this ubiquitous style that innovative architects started to protest between 1890 and 1900. Convinced of the ineffectiveness of historic reference after a century of eclecticism, they wanted a 'new architecture' free from stylistic trappings. Berlage wrote about this 'naked style' (Fig. 49):

We thus want the essence of architecture, i.e. the truth and only the truth, because in art too, falsehood has become the rule and truth the exception... Natural, comprehensible things have to be made again, i.e. a thing without clothing covering the body. But even more: we architects have also to study the skeleton first, as a painter and sculptor does, to give the figure its proper form afterwards...
...Therefore, for the time being the study of the skeleton, i.e. the sober construction in all its roughness, to reach the full body afterwards, but without confusion by clothing. Even the last cover, even the fig-leaf has to go, for the truth we want is naked[2].

Though Berlage himself had designed in Neo-Renaissance — his project for the Exchange competition of 1884 had been in that style — he blamed commercialism for the artistic confusion:

And architecture itself? She, the grand mistress of all arts, is engaged in elevating itself from the morass of entirely faded convention on one side and subjectivism on the other, but above all in breaking away from the industrial rubbish, consequences of commercialism and capitalism, of which it had of all arts to suffer most[3].

Berlage was the spokesman and leader of the Dutch revolt against eclecticism, but he was not alone, nor did he create the 'new madness' singlehandedly. Another leading architect was K.P.C. de Bazel, whose simplifications in design temporarily helped Berlage to find his way[4]. Other participants were J.L.M. Lauweriks, H.J.M. Walenkamp and W. Kromhout.

The revolt against eclectic architecture was international. Wagner, Olbrich and Hoffman in Austria, Behrens in Germany, Mackintosh and Voysey in Great Britain, and Adler and Sullivan and the subsequent 'Prairie School' in Chicago, all strove towards a simpler architecture, free of stylistic references in the past. All were influenced by the similar efforts in the design of furniture and interior decoration of the Arts and Crafts Movement.

The rigorous and rationalistic approach of Berlage was not the only innovative movement. Rather than strip buildings of all decoration, Art Nouveau architects tried to supplant historic by naturalistic detailing. Of course Berlage was scornful about the competition:

...although there is, as far as I know, one principle that is honoured by all modern artists as true, i.e. the principle of simple honest construction, — one notices in studying the artistic expressions in various countries that with most of them this principle either only exists in words, or is badly applied. Is, to mention but one example, the whole so-called 'art nouveau'... not in reality the opposite of that healthy principle? But is therefore this same style not also already bankrupt, just because it applies that principle badly[5]?

By 1910 the rationalists had more or less won their case. Though older architects like van Nieukerken continued to design eclectic buildings, they simplified their details. Practical architects had started to follow the rationalists' example in growing numbers. The very success of the innovation produced a reaction from the next generation of architects. They considered Berlage's simplicity to be dull and monotonous. Michiel de Klerk, a rising 32-year-old architect, wrote in 1916 on the occasion of Berlage's sixtieth birthday:

What Berlage has done for the craft of building, namely to bring order into the existing chaos, will never be forgotten; yet he has never contributed to the art of building... It seems to me for the past decade Berlage has not been exemplary. He has not grasped what characterizes modern times: the titillating commanding aspects of mechanical technology which continuously surprise us today... Berlage's presence has certainly been of value in purifying the building crafts, yet he has not been able to influence architecture as a manifestation of style. His field was too narrowly bound, too exclusively technical and utilitarian, to have any bearing on our culture[6].

De Klerk retained from Berlage the articulation of interior subdivisions on the facade[7], the showing of the load-bearing structure and the preference for exposed brickwork. He created the 'titillating new' by freewheeling formal inventions in the rationalistic idiom of simplicity (which thereby lost its

Figure 50
Post office and housing blocks,
Spaarndammerplantsoen,
Amsterdam, 1918–1919.
Architect: Michiel de Klerk. From
Berlage, de Klerk adopted the
delight in the use of 'natural'
materials like brick and tiles (in
contrast to 'unnatural' stucco), the
avoidance of historicist references
and (less visible in this view) a
certain emphasis on constructional
elements like party walls or
chimneys. But the fanciful forms
and details were meant to contrast
with Berlage and provide the
'titillating new'

rationalistic justification), i.e. by mannerist variations (Fig. 50).

The new forms invented by de Klerk and his friends attracted many artistically ambitious young architects. It grew into a movement, the 'Amsterdam School', with its own publication, *Wendingen*. Architects of that persuasion joined the Public Works Office of Amsterdam and the State Building Service. In 1916 the board of the most important architects' association after the national association, Architectura et Amicitia, was taken over by architects of the Amsterdam School[8].

In the early twenties, the Dutch architectural scene comprised the following groups of architects. Pride of place went to the Amsterdam School, the more or less officially recognized *avant-garde*, which dominated the large housing program of Amsterdam.

The leaders of the earlier, 'rationalistic' revolution, Berlage, de Bazel and Kromhout, were still active, successful and highly respected. The 'practical' architects (as always in the majority), active in the smaller cities or designing the commercial and utilitarian buildings, followed them rather than the *avant-garde*; occasionally they added some frills taken from the Amsterdam School (Figs. 56 and 57). Eclectic architecture had all but disappeared.

A new group of artists, as yet rarely visible, was challenging the established *avant-garde*: 'de Stijl'. de Klerk's 'titillating new' was not new enough for them, and also too personal and idiosyncratic.

The rationalists' revolution had challenged the prevailing symbolism of the past by proposing an architecture stripped bare; a negation of the past but no positive reference to the future. And yet, it seemed in 1918 as if the world could and would be remade. A spate of inventions had dramatically changed the course of daily life: electric light, phonographs, telephones, autombiles and refrigerators. The Great War really seemed to have made a clean slate possible. Van Doesburg, the central figure in the de Stijl movement, remembered in 1919:

In that moment about 1916, in which nearly the whole world was still in the middle of the war, (and) perhaps because of that, there was that atmosphere in all of Europe which is the pre-condition for a collective, heroic act of creation. We all lived in the spirit of becoming. Though there was no war in the neutral Netherlands, it still affected contacts, tensions, and indeed spiritual ones, and nowhere was the soil more favorable to gather innovating forces[9].

Such forces were visible all over Europe. Russia had had a revolution in 1917, Germany in 1918–1919. The Dutch leader of the social democrats, Troelstra, proclaimed a revolution in 1918 which proved abortive but which frightened the ruling bourgeoisie into granting concessions to the social democrats. Many members of the cultural elite, and the artists foremost among them, felt that their hour had come. This was particularly so in Germany, which was disoriented by the lost war. The Spartacists tried to force a socialist revolution. Berlin artists formed the 'Arbeitsrat für Kunst' which adopted a socialist jargon. Dada proclaimed the end of all art. Hannah Höch, one of the members of Berlin-Dada, remembered the idealism of 1919 in an interview in 1978:

Young people cannot understand it because they remember the absolute prostration and crazy depression after the Second World War. But that did not exist after the First World War. We waited for a new beginning. We wanted to develop something new. We really had had the idea that there would never be another war. We were that naive. Our imagination and our intellectual capacity reacted against the chaos. That chaos became an impulse[10].

The confidence that a really new era was coming after the holocaust of the First World War is echoed in the opening passages of the first Stijl manifesto of 1918:

1. There is an old and new consciousness of time.
    The old is connected with the individual.
    The new is connected with the universal.
    The struggle of the individual against the universal is revealing itself
    in the world war as well as in the art of the present day.
2. The war is destroying the old world and its contents: individual
    domination in every state[11].

This vision embraced not only art, but 'life' and 'society' as well. Artists had to show other people the road towards a new, harmonious world:

Pure creative imagination has to build a new society, just as it has created a new expression in art — a society of the equivalent dualism of the material and spiritual, a society of equilibrated relations[12].

Mondrian saw this world of tomorrow very clearly:

... The dwelling must no longer be visually closed, separated. Nor the street. Though they have a different function, yet they must form a unity. To arrive at this, one must no longer consider the house as a 'box'. The idea home (Home, sweet home) must disappear. Likewise the conventional idea 'street'; one shall have to consider dwelling and street as a city, which is a unity, formed by planes composed in a neutralizing contrast, which abolishes all separation and exclusion. The same principle must rule the interior. This must no longer be a pile-up of rooms, created by four walls with nothing but holes for doors and windows, but a construction of planes in color and non-color, which go with the furniture and utensils, which must be nothing by themselves but contributing elements of the whole. And man? He must be nothing by himself and a part of the whole too. When he thus no longer feels his individuality, he will be happy in the earthly paradise created by himself[13].

Planes were in a 'neutralizing contrast' when they were perpendicular to each other. Orthogonal planes were the spatial corollary of Mondrian's and van Doesburg's horizontals and verticals in their paintings. They had arrived at these forms by carrying further the reduction of perceived natural forms to geometrical shapes started by Cézanne and continued by the Cubists. These lines therefore represented to them the ultimate reduction of the visual world, the 'equilibrium of the cosmos'[14], the opposition between the vertical and the horizontal signifying 'repose'[15]. Colors were reduced in the same way to the three primaries, red, yellow and blue, and two 'non-colors', black and white.

The effort of 'de Stijl' to penetrate to an ultimate reality by stripping perception of all that is accidental and anecdotal ('tragic' Modrian called it) is very similar to Berlage's thesis that architecture has to discard all ornament and stylistic decoration. But their geometry could also be interpreted in a positive sense. In its simplicity, regularity and precision it could be seen as resembling the products of mechanized production. It could be used as a symbolism of the future, because that future would be ever more influenced by technology. The architect J.J.P. Oud, a founder member of 'de Stijl' , described it thus in 1921:

... automobiles, steamers, yachts, men's wear, sports clothes, electrical and sanitary equipment, table-ware, etc., etc., possess within themselves, as the purest expression of their time, the elements of a new language of aesthetic form, and can be considered as the point of departure for a new art, through their restrained form, lack of ornament and plain colors, the comparative perfection of their materials and the purity of their proportions — largely due to their new, mechanical modes of production[16].

and more precisely in 1926:

The need for number and measure, for purity and order, for regularity and repetition, for perfection and closure: properties of the organs of human life, of technology, of traffic, of hygiene, inherent also in the nature of society, in economic conditions, in the methods of mass-production, found their precursors in Cubism[17].

If painting had reached the 'cosmic equilibrium' by pushing abstraction to its limit, architecture had to follow; as the quote from Mondrian already indicated. Such an architecture would contrast sharply with the work of Berlage and the Amsterdam School: no more pitched roofs or textured brick walls, no more arches or corbels. Oud sketched the differences:

All in all, it follows that an architecture rationally based on the circumstances of life today would be in every sense opposed to the sort of architecture that has existed up till now. Without falling into barren rationalism it would remain, above all, objective, but within this objectivity would experience higher things. In the sharpest contrast to the untechnically formed and colourless products of momentary inspiration as we know them, its ordained task will be, in perfect devotion to an almost impersonal method of technical creation, to shape organisms of clear form and pure proportions. In place of the natural attractions of uncultivated materials, the broken hues in glass, the irregularity of finishes, the paleness of colour, the clouding of glazes, the weathering of walls, etc. it would unfold the stimulating qualities of sophisticated materials, the limpidity of glass, the shine and roundness of finishes, lustrous and shining colours, the glitter of steel, and so forth.
Thus the development of the art of building goes toward an architecture more bound to matter than ever before in essence, but in appearance rising clear of material considerations; free from all Impressionistic creation of atmosphere, in the fullness of light, brought to purity of proportion and colour, organic clarity of form; an architecture that, in its freedom from inessentialism could surpass even Classical purity[18].

   This was easier said than done. For 'clear forms' and 'pure proportions' in black, white, red, blue or yellow would usually not show the materials they were made of, and so violate the dogma of Berlage about honest construction, a dogma in which many architects of de Stijl still believed. So most of them — including Oud — originally looked at Wright rather than Mondrian for examples (Fig. 51). Only van Eesteren, in collaboration with van Doesburg, produced architectural designs in 1923 which perfectly embodied de Stijl principles, followed a year later by the famous Schröder house by the cabinetmaker Rietveld and Mrs T. Schröder-Schräder (Fig. 52).

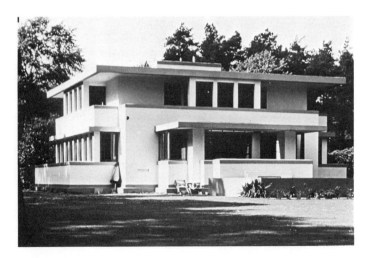

Figure 51
House, Huis ter Heide, 1915–1917. Architect: Robert van 't Hoff. Clearly a variation on Wright's Gale house.

Figure 52
Schröder house, Utrecht, 1924.
Architect: Gerrit Rietveld. A built
embodiment of de Stijl principles
developed in painting

There was also another aspect which the new architecture had to take into account. During the First World War an enormous backlog in housing had built up in the warring countries, and also in the neutral ones like the Netherlands, because of the shortage of building materials. The need was aggravated by the wave of marriages, postponed during the war, which now took place. In England, France, Germany and the Netherlands, the governments embarked on large subsidized housing programs.

As a consequence, the character of architectural practice changed. Before the war only a few architects had done low-cost housing; now it became a staple item in their portfolio, in some cases the only type of work they could find.

Eclectic and particularly Beaux Arts architecture had concentrated on the main type of job which was then considered worthy of an architect's attention: monumental public buildings. (It was of course also the main category in which architects found work). The new situation required an adjustment in the setting of goals. Low-cost housing did not allow too many frills; architects were allowed only a very narrow margin of freedom between minimum requirements and maximum costs. They now had to concentrate on the practical and strictly necessary. After the period of utopian daydreaming and paper projects (1918–1923) was over and the housing programs got under way, these new priorities had somehow to be incorporated in architectural theory.

Oud, serving as architect for housing projects in the public works department of Rotterdam since 1918, was very much aware of the constraints:

Carefully worked out plans, in the sense that maximum requirements are met by minimal spaces; systematic construction, as a result of economically effective placement of bearing walls (which initially influence the form of the plan); economic production of normal materials; practical construction management.

Certainly in architecture, means and ends mutually influence each other: clear apprehension of these conditions must lead to new methods and materials, and accordingly in pure expression, to new esthetic design[19].

Some of this concern for the practical demands of functional design rubbed off on the 'leader' of 'de Stijl', van Doesburg, either from his early contacts with Oud, or more probably from his collaboration with the architect van Eesteren. He wrote in 1924 in his 'Toward a plastic architecture':

3. The new architecture is *economical*, i.e. it organizes its elementary means as efficiently as possible without waste of either means or material
4. The new architecture is *functional*, i.e. it evolves from the accurate determination of practical demands which it establishes in a clear groundplan[20].

The demand for practical design dovetailed nicely with the admiration for high-tech machinery, for machines were not only regular, geometrically simple and smooth, they also *worked*. The futurists saw the essence of the machine age in the movements of cars, trains, ships and engines. Le Corbusier had also seen their adaptation to their function when he coined his much decried: 'A house is a machine for living... a chair is a machine for sitting'[21]. The same view, but now further articulated, is behind the polemic of Mart Stam, a young Dutch architect influenced by the Russian constructivists, against monumental architecture (1927):

The nut is angular, not round — we know why. The bath tub is smooth — we know why. The door is 2 meters high — we know why. Stones are sawn, cut, ground, polished; thereafter piled up, now in a rectangle, then in a hexagon, in an octagon or decagon, sometimes 1 meter, then again 20 meters high, *but nobody knows why. ...The building must be useful in the most extended sense (of the term)*[22].

The mechanical analogy, i.e. that a building has to be adapted to its purpose — and show it — in the same way as a machine, continued to grow in importance during the late twenties, until it furnished one of the terms by which this kind of architecture came to be labelled, functionalism.

It is this aspect which appealed primarily to a group of young Dutch architects, which published in 1927 a manifesto, *de 8*:

Figure 53
Housing block on the
Vrijheidslaan, Amsterdam,
1921–1922. Plans for these houses
were designed by the group of
speculative builders; the planning
review board obliged them to
engage a well-known architect —
in this case Michiel de Klerk — to
design the facade. It was the
practice of hiring the architect
only for the facade which the *de 8*
manifesto condemned specifically

What is DE 8?

DE 8 is	the critical reaction to the architectonic design of this day
DE 8 is	realist in its striving for immediate results
DE 8 is	idealist in its belief in international cultural cooperation
DE 8 is	opportunist because of social considerations
DE 8 is	neither for nor against groups or individuals, neither for nor against movements
DE 8 is	only for facts
DE 8 says	it is not impossible to build beautifully, but it would be better for the time being to build ugly and functionally, than to erect parade architecture on bad plans
DE 8 wants	to submit itself to its brief
DE 8 wants	no architecture of luxury arising from the voluptuous enjoyment of forms by talented individuals
DE 8 wants	to be rational in the true sense, i.e. that everything has to give way before the requirements of the brief
DE 8 wants	to strive for social foundation for the modern architect (The architect *à la mode* is well on the way to turn himself into a luxury and an expensive tradition)
DE 8 fights	only among professionals
DE 8 works	more for a building-SCIENCE than for a building-ART
DE 8 strives	for a place in society as

CREATIVE ORGANIZATION-MANAGER
DE 8 is ANTI-ESTHETIC
DE 8 is ANTI-DRAMATIC
DE 8 is ANTI-ROMANTIC
DE 8 IS RESULTANT   DE 8 is ANTI-CUBISTIC[23]

The manifesto is primarily a polemic against the Amsterdam
School architects. They are the 'talented individuals' wallowing
in 'voluptuous enjoyment of forms', the 'architects *à la mode*'
who designed 'parade architecture on bad plans', for they had
designed facades for speculative housing in Amsterdam the
plans of which had been designed by the contractor (Fig. 53).

The amount of space given above to architects of de Stijl and the functionalist movement may give the erroneous impression that they had won their battles by the end of the twenties. This is not the case. They *had* scored some important victories. They *were* well publicized (mainly by their own journalistic efforts), but they were only a vociferous small group, considered to be aberrant cranks by the majority of their colleagues, and probably by the majority of Dutchmen. Clients were few and far between, and their designs were turned down by the planning review boards which acted as watchdogs over the infringements upon town and countryside. Continuously under attack, they temporarily overlooked their internal differences and banded together, both nationally (in 'de 8', the Amsterdam group, and 'Opbouw', the Rotterdam group) and internationally, in CIAM. The attacks, and their firm conviction that they had the key to the future, made them double their efforts and try to create a consistent body of doctrine. After 60 years we can see now that it was an amalgam of different and not necessarily consistent elements:

— elementary geometric forms and primary colors from de Stijl

— horizontal strip-windows derived from steamers, high-rise buildings imitating American skyscrapers and the extensive use of glass, steel and concrete as a symbolism of the future

— emphasis on the utilitarian, practical aspects of architecture, partly induced by the machine analogy and partly by the changes in architectural practice.

Figure 54
Vreewijk garden city, Rotterdam, 1916–1934. Architects: Granpré Molière, Verhagen and Kok. A recognizable imitation of a Dutch village; the architecture of the houses in the Berlagian 'naked style'

Figure 55
Catholic church in Groesbeek, 1935. Architect: M.J. Granpré Molière. Though the Berlagian simplicity and structural honesty has been retained, the building clearly refers to early Christian and medieval examples

Their movement was a clean break with the past, and as such, a challenge to older architects and more traditional ideas; it was also intended as a challenge. Most of their older colleagues did not come round to their point of view — it would imply a denial of all they had hitherto believed in — but they *did* recognize the danger of the provocation. They found an eloquent spokesman for their point of view in Marinus Jan Granpré Molière, an architect of Berlagian convictions, a convert to Catholicism and a professor at the Delft School of architecture since 1924 (Figs. 54 and 55). From 1924 to 1950 he polemized against functionalism; thanks to this long drawn-out battle of words, we can now adequately set off the 'progressive' against the 'conservative' viewpoints on architecture and society. Some quotations can convey the flavor of the debate. Granpré Molière on functionalist architecture:

As soon as one begins to view technology as an asset by itself, as a being with a soul, as a principle creating a style, one has really sunk deeper than ever into superstition and idolatry... Sullen and puny, benumbed stand the fruits of rationalism and mechanization, our new architecture, in sweet gentle nature, below the high, wide sky, as witnesses of utter confusion and need[24].

Van Loghem (functionalist) on social change:

... The second group (does) not accept the permanent necessity for (social) subdivision... because this group sees the chaotic process of production everywhere as the motor of the destructive forces in

Table 5

FUNCTIONALISM	DELFT SCHOOL

Views on: SOCIETY

belief in the future —	idealizing of the past
for social changes —	for 'eternal truths'
leftist sympathies —	corporatism, 'restoration of the unity of society'

Views on: MAN

man should be 'liberated' —	man should be 'elevated'
for sports, hygiene —	for art, dance, music

Views on: ARCHITECTURE

knowledge = natural sciences —	knowledge = philosophy
accent on rationalism —	accent on emotions
analytic —	synthetic
function —	symbolism
new techniques —	old techniques
new materials —	'noble', natural materials
dematerialization —	emphasis on materiality
openness —	closure
temporary —	eternal
architecture is in principle the same everywhere —	architecture has local roots (regionalism)
building has practical relation to site —	building has aesthetic relation to site
preference for practical briefs —	preference for monumental briefs
ordinary building = grain-elevator, factory —	ordinary building = farm

society, its target is exclusively to make the obsolete and degenerated systems disappear, so as to arrive at an orderly and soundly organized world society...Though their struggle, from the nature of their job, is no political action, yet it cannot be otherwise than that their work is inspired by the new political, socio-economic and humanistic views[25].

Granpré Molière on social 'reconstruction':

On the road toward realization lies also the reconstruction of society, i.e. of the fraternal community of workers in the profession; in the Middle Ages it was ordered in the guilds, later totally demolished and abandoned to the rule of money[26].

...and on eternal values:

Invariably our spirit must be brought to bear upon the immutable values. Upon the eternal laws which determine life and work in the end. Thus we grow into bearers of culture, and thus we will once bear the fruits which are appropriate for us, nay, to which we are destined[27].

...and on the studio of the ideal artist:

No papers or magazines are lying around, for he is not curious; he reads little, because Truth itself teaches him. He also doesn't read the moderns, but the classics: Shakespeare, Dante, Homerus, for all who approach unborn beauty are new to him; or he reads the Scriptures, because he seeks Him who makes all things new[28].

Van Loghem on the artist:

The artist has to be ahead of his time and not lag behind the ideas of his time[29].

...and on openness:

When our housing blocks, resembling lumps of brick, will disappear to make way for purely proportioned glass towers, so that man's labor no longer has to take place in dark or electrically lit spaces, but is performed as it were in the open air, between plants, trees or in the clouds — in complete silence — then something will have changed for the better in city life and the image of the city[30].

Boeken (another functionalist) on openness:

Light and air! The closed walls open: gardens, parks and playing fields enlarge the living quarters with their air, light and sunlight[31].

Granpré Molière on closure:

A volume closed on all sides is the most perfect, therefore the most beautiful[32].

Enclosure is for us a sign of excluding all that is inferior or disturbing[33].

...and on craft techniques:

When we view, enter, go over and ascend the Gothic Cathedral from bottom to top, everywhere it vibrates with the marks of chisel and pick-axe, of hammer and brush, of the joy of work and the spontaneous creativity with which the craftsmen have handled these tools[34].

It is long ago that the carpenter sawed his own beams and the period that he made his own doors seems also to belong to the past: the period of home-made bread is past and the period that one cooks no longer one's own potatoes may perhaps be starting. But this slow development is no reason to overhaul all traditions and building methods[35].

The functionalist Stam on technology:

Modern building replaces:
1. The crafts by mechanized techniques
2. The capricious, individualistic by the collective, standardized,
3. The accidental by the exact[36].

The elements out of which Dutch funtionalist theory was fashioned may have been heterogeneous in origin, but came to be seen as coherent and consistent in the debate. On the opposite side, Granpré Molière was forced also to present a coherent viewpoint. Each side stimulated the other to reflection and clarification; functionalism and the Delft School developed in a dialectic relationship. The attacks of the other party closed the ranks and made the leaders enhance the differences with the 'enemy' and paper over any internal dissent.

De Stijl group and the functionalists believed in the radically new: a new art, a new architecture, a new man and a new society. They revelled in the battle; the very resistance of the others proved that they were on the right track. With Granpré Molière it was different. He was by nature a man of rather gentle disposition, which is the reason why he was loved by his students and could influence them so strongly. Harmony was his watchword, belligerence did not come naturally to him. The attacks of the reformers prodded him to action. The denial of harmony, their international contrast with all that he believed in, made him take up the cudgels for tradition and move gradually to a more and more consistent conservative position. He has given us a glimpse of this conflict from his own student days:

I associated most with my socialist fellow-students; I admired their certainty and their readiness to make sacrifices, and I could assent partly to their criticism of society. However, I came to resist the dogmas of my socialist friend; it was still in the beginning of getting acquainted with these circles that during a walk I talked with one of them about the separation between employer and employed; to contradict his expositions I described as an example how much the tie of love had effected in the factory of my father; he answered quietly: 'Yes, for such people we have as yet no use'. I fell silent, I was appalled; in the light of the pain I felt, I saw clearly that Europe would enter upon dark days in this way[37].

Molière's father was director of a sugar factory. Harmonious cooperation between employer and employed is a standard tenet of belief for the more enlightened members of the economic elite. I became one of the Molière students in 1945, and have no first-hand experience of his evolving attitudes before the war. From a study of his work and writings and a personal knowledge of the man, I believe that he would not have moved so far if he had lived in a more harmonious period; neither, of course, would the reformers have been inspired to go to extremes in such an age.

Molière made his name as an architect and planner with the garden-city suburb of Vreewijk in Rotterdam. In 1921 (he was then 38 years old) he was still well aware of its symbolism of 'somewhere else', i.e. that it represented a flight from modern society:

The garden-city can only be realized and perpetuated with the technical and organizational means of the age; as long and in so far as this movement rests on an aversion for culture, the contradiction exists that it uses that which it seeks to avoid. This contradiction will always appear; it is only necessary to point at the English garden-cities with the simulation of their schematic idyll, to show this in detail[38].

A complete explanation for the choice of position of each architect is hard to give; I can only adduce some elements which make the attitudes of a number of participants more understandable.

The founder members of 'de 8' had all studied together at the arts and crafts chool in Haarlem, under Vorkink and Blaauw, two architects of the Amsterdam School. The leader of the group, Ben Merkelbach, had worked for nine months in 1927 under Mart Stam on the functionalist housing projects in Frankfurt. Immediately after that period he got together with his former fellow-students and founded 'de 8'. It can probably be interpreted as partly due to a revolt by the young against the generation of their teachers, spurred on by the revolutionary ideas of Mart Stam and Ernst May, the chief architect of the Frankfurt municipal building office[39].

Architects belong to the cultural elite. A challenge to the 'establishment', i.e. to that architecture which is financed by and built for the economic elite, has a natural attraction for them, as was argued in chapter 6; it shows their independence, it marks them off as the pioneers of a new age, in which they will play a more prominent role. Many of the cultural elite are satisfied with an artistic revolution; if they can change the course of art they have shown their superiority. Some believe that the artistic revolution will of itself produce a changeover in all values, including the political, and produce a new society. And some go the whole way and become politically committed as a corollary to their creative work.

Van Loghem was a founder member of the League of Revolutionary-Socialist Intellectuals. In 1921 he changed the structure of his private architectural office by turning it into a cooperative with full profit-sharing for all his personnel. From 1923 to 1927 he worked in Russia on the design of a mining town in Siberia. The Soviet Union, based on Marxist principles and as yet untainted by the purges and trials of the early thirties, looked like the embodiment of the society of the future. Mart Stam went with the team of Ernst May to Russia from 1930 to 1934 and became a communist, going back and forth between Holland and the countries behind the Iron Curtain during his whole life. Many of the members of the Dutch functionalist groups were social democrats, some (like Zwart, Schuitema) with strong left-wing leanings. These political attitudes are not found among the adherents of Granpré Molière.

But if a leftist attitude is consistent with the symbolism of the future of the functionalists — and even alluded to in their manifestos — it is not an absolute necessity to believe in the one when you believe in the other. Stam and van Loghem dominated the 'Opbouw' group in Rotterdam in 1926–1928 and tried to radicalize it politically. Their activities alienated a number of members, who resigned. A speech of van Loghem as president of the group, given about 1932, reflects the internal conflicts:

If we focus now, with as a starting point the different items in the last meeting, we see a clear left-wing group, represented by members of

C.I.A.M., to which belong van der Vlugt, van Tijen and myself, whilst the group Schuitema, Zwart, Kiljan agrees as far as concerns the fundamental principles. The *right-wing* point of view has been defended in that meeting by Oud and Klijnen. Though Oud and Klijnen do not agree entirely, the difference in their attitudes is not important for us, because both do not take the stand of the social revolution and the spiritual struggle for it, by which the production for profit will be exchanged for socialist production and distribution. Though we as artists are no politicians, and would probably be bad politicians if we were called upon, this does not alter the fact that the entire content of our creative thinking is concentrated on the concept of social change[40].

The last sentence reflects the cagey attitudes of many *avant-garde* members towards politics. They thought politics to be 'dirty' and steered clear of it.

Entirely a-political was Group '32. Its core consisted again of former students of the Haarlem arts and crafts school. They shared an enthusiasm for functionalist architecture on artistic grounds, and had been particularly impressed by the buildings and writings of Le Corbusier; one of the members, Komter, had even worked for him. At first they tried to take over the board of Architectura et Amicitia, the architects' club. This was still, since 1916, a bulwark of the Amsterdam School, and architects of that persuasion had been able from this position to appoint members to crucial juries and committees, to advise on the choice of architects and to make propaganda through its magazine, *Wendingen*. The effort failed; thereafter, Group '32 joined 'de 8' in 1934[41].

In the early thirties, the following groups could be distinguished in Dutch architecture. The CIAM groups, 'de 8' and 'Opbouw', were generally recognized by their colleagues as the *avant-garde*, though their ideas were as generally rejected. They had not had the success that fell to the Amsterdam School a decade earlier, perhaps because the latter had not moved as far beyond Berlage as they had done. Next to them came a number of middle-of-the-road architects, like Wils and Dudok, who remained true to their example, Wright. A few members of the old Amsterdam School, Kramer, Greiner and van der Mey, were still active, but they had toned down their exuberance considerably, perhaps because complexities and formal fantasies were attacked both by the Delft School and by the functionalists. One talented member of the Amsterdam School, J.F. Staal, was moving towards the functionalist idiom. Berlage, now in his seventies, was working on his last project, the municipal museum in the Hague. The Delft School — Molière's first students finished around 1930 — was just appearing on the scene. Commercial architects like Warners, or industrial architects like van Rood, stuck, like all other practical architects (i.e. the majority in the profession), to a watered-down version of Berlage (Figs. 56, 57 and 58). In the twenties they had occasionally embellished their work with an

Figure 56
Catholic School, Oostzaan,
Amsterdam, 1928–1929.
Architect: W.H.M. Blaisse.
Typical of the simple and
straightforward traditional way of
building, derived from Berlage's
'naked style'

Amsterdam School detail; now sometimes an element derived from the functionalists appeared in their work.

Commissions became few and far between as the Great Depression deepened in the thirties. The image of the Soviet Union as the land of the future palled, when the Stalinist purges got under way. The whole idea of a rosy future in a peaceful world of tomorrow started to fade, as unemployment rose and

Figure 57
Board of Labor office building,
Rotterdam, 1934. Architects:
Lockhorst and Hooykaas.
Another example of this 'naked
style', the background for the
work of the artistically more
ambitious architects. The entrance
and the projecting lintel show
some influence of Wright,
probably mediated by Dudok

Figure 58
PNEM switching station of the
Provincial Power Company of
North Holland, Velsen, 1931. By
the 1930s, the Wrightian influence
had penetrated to the practical
architects

the slump grew from bad to worse. In politics this became
visible from the gains of right-wing parties, which preached a
return to the good old days. It had an effect too on the belief in
the symbolism of the future; some of its adherents started to
doubt the tenets of functionalism.

In particular the members of Group '32, who had joined 'de
8' for aesthetic reasons, were sensitive to the change in climate.
They started to praise the value of classical Greek art, and came
out in favor of ornament on buildings. In 1938 two of them,
Arthur Staal and van Woerden, made a plan for a town hall in
Huizen closely resembling an eighteenth-century Dutch country house (Fig. 59). This plan provoked a crisis; severe criticism
in 'de 8' caused all former members of Group '32 but one to
resign[42].

What the functionalists lost, the traditionalists gained. As the
future looked more and more grim, the past looked ever more
rosy by comparison. The Delft School scored an important
success when two of its young adherents won the national
competition for the city hall of Amsterdam in 1939 with a

Figure 59
Competition project for the city
hall of Huizen, 1938. Criticism of
this neo-baroque project caused
the architects, Arthur Staal and S.
van Woerden, and other members
of the original Group '32 to leave
'de 8'

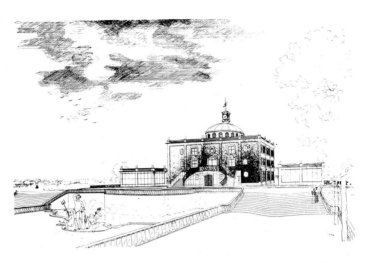

medieval-looking design. The functionalists saw clearly that
they had the tide running against them:

Were not all previous wars child's play compared to the world war of
1914, and what will be compared to that the war for which the whole
world now prepares itself on a scale and with technical means which
were inconceivable only ten years ago. Were not all depressions child's
play, compared to the depression with ravages the whole world since
1929? ... The fashionable flight towards the Middle Ages has to be seen
against this historical background. It is fear for today, and even more a
deep agony before the future... Granpré Molière and Zwiers...want to
return in the field of the arts towards the 'good old days'. Their
architecture is a flight from the present, which they do not understand
and despair of the future, which they do not see, and on which they do
not pin their faith in any case... This is how the fashion in gothic chairs
and medieval townhalls must be seen: *it is an anxiety neurosis*[43].

An absolute contrast with the hopeful years after 1918: then,
a future full of promise, a new world without war, a new social
order just around the corner; now, in 1939, nothing but despair
and the imminent threat of another world war. van Loghem has
described the intellectual climate of the early twenties in 1928:

So we stood in the postwar years, charged with new and beautiful
plans for the future, for which we had to find a form. Splendid,
impetuous years they were. The shining new cultural era which
dawned for us in the distance, and to which we might give our
energies, to contribute the material for the foundation. The buildings
of mankind, the creations in which the liberation of mankind would be
expressed, no longer seemed visions to us, but almost tangible
possibilities, which would be realized by the heads and hands of the
workers of the new era[44].

Every period has its progressives and conservatives. The
interbellum sharpened the contrast between the two: the end of
the First World War raised radical hopes to a fever pitch, the
Great Depression created widespread feelings of despondency.
The optimism of 1919 stirred some people to political revolutionary activity, and moved some artists and architects to

Figure 60
van Nelle tobacco, tea and coffee
plant, Rotterdam, 1926–1930.
Architects: Brinkman and van der
Vlugt. The main example of
functionalist architecture in the
Netherlands

extreme artistic positions. The Depression turned many people
to conservatism, to the right-wing parties, and promoted also
the conservative view in art and architecture. The political
turbulence of 1918–1923 and the slump and unemployment of
the thirties caused people to reflect on basic values and choose
sides. Economic, political and social issues forced themselves
on people's conscience, because of their urgency. Something
had to be done: either a new social order, or a return to an old
one; either for Keynes, or against. Architectural belief-
systems, which involved basic values, followed suit. The
variety in positions was thereby reduced to the basic opposition
between tradition and innovation.

Granpré Molière made his name as an architect with the
garden-city suburb Vreewijk in Rotterdam. The design, in line
with the English examples, was in neo-vernacular: it projected
the image of an ideal Dutch village. The client was a group of
businessmen who wanted a workers' housing project close to
their plants, shipyards and docks. The chairman of the
committee, K.P. van der Mandele, commissioned a house by
Molière when he had become a board member of the Rotterdam Bank. When Molière had become converted to Roman
Catholicism, he built several churches and a Catholic seminary.

The biggest and most conspicuous building of the functionalists was the van Nelle factory (Fig. 60). The director who
selected the architect, C.H. van der Leeuw, was a member of
the family who owned the company and belonged to the
established economic elite of Rotterdam. He had strong artistic
leanings. From 1907 to 1909 he tried to become a painter, but he
stopped when he considered himself 'not good enough'[45].
After building the factory (1926–1930), he moved to Vienna,
became a medical doctor and studied psychoanalysis with

Figure 61
Open Air School, Amsterdam,
1928–1930. Architect: J. Duiker.
The first plan was for a one-story
building, occupying the whole
block. The planning review board,
appointed to safeguard the
aesthetic quality of Berlage's plan
for the southern part of
Amsterdam (see Fig. 53), did not
allow a functionalistic building in
a homogeneous Amsterdam
school neighbourhood.
Consequently the architect had to
design a multistory building,
hidden inside a 'normal' housing
block

Sigmund Freud. From his days as an artist he retained a lifelong
interest in *avant-garde* art. In 1932 he commisioned Richard
Neutra to build him an experimental house in Los Angeles[46]. In
the 1950s he was president of the board of the Technical
University in Delft and commissioned van de Broek and
Bakema (the successors to Brinkman and van der Vlugt who
designed van Nelle) to design a large number of the new
buildings of that school. In 1954 he became a member of the
board of regents of the Kröller-Müller museum, the Dutch
national gallery of modern art. We may consider van der Leeuw
as a member of both the economic and the cultural elite, who
from that rather unique position could further the cause of the
avant-garde in a way which was beyond the means of most of
its supporters. The majority of briefs that the *avant-garde*
received were for houses for intellectuals, like the Schröder
house, commissioned by Mrs T. Schröder-Schräder, who had
herself studied architecture and collaborated with Rietveld on
the design.

A building which I would consider to be typical for the
functionalists, both in its purpose and in its client, is the
open-air school by Duiker (Fig. 61). Duiker got the job
through Dr Ben Sajet, a general practitioner of medicine and for
many years a member for the social democratic party of the
town council of Amsterdam. Duiker met Sajet when the latter
worked as a doctor in the tubercular sanatorium 'Zonnestraal'
in Hilversum, for which Duiker had become the architect, on
the recommendation of Berlage, as related in chapter 6.

The attitude of the economic elite towards architectural
design is shown in the story of the limited competition for the
'Bijenkorf' (beehive) in The Hague[47]. The Bijenkorf is a chain
of large prestige department stores, catering for the upper

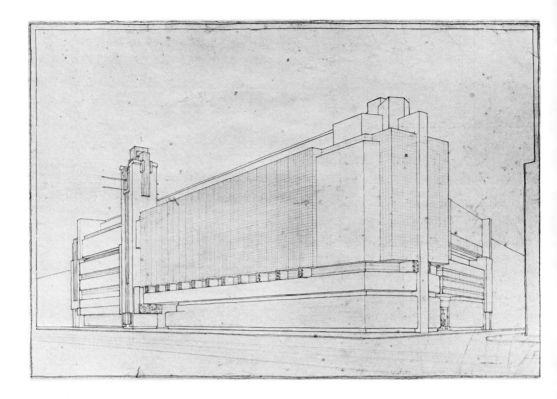

Figure 62
Competition project by Jan
Frederik Staal for the Bijenkorf
department store in The Hague,
1925. Selected by the jury, but
turned down by the client as too
modern

middle class. It carries fashionable clothes, modish apparel and
fairly modern furniture.

The directors invited seven architects to submit designs: the
van Gendt Brothers, J.M. Luthmann, M. de Klerk, P.L.
Kramer, J.F. Staal and A. Otten. The van Gendts and Otten
were practical architects, all the others belonged to the
Amsterdam School, then in 1923 at the zenith of its fame. The
board was advised by an Advisory Panel, consisting of two
architects, Gratama and Berlage, and a journalist, Steeman.
Gratama belonged to the Amsterdam School. The Panel
decided for the design of J.F. Staal (Fig. 62).

Staal was in 1923 in the process of shifting his allegiance from
the Amsterdam School to the Stijl. His design, with its
predominance of clear-cut rectangular volumes, looked more
abstract than the others; he had used a glass-brick wall, and, at
the ends, some *fenêtres-en-longueur*. The interpenetrating
volumes showed also an influence of Frank Lloyd Wright.

But if these limited references to the *avant-garde* were not
enough to frighten the Panel, they were too much for the
directors of the Bijenkorf. Gratama explained that they felt
Staal's design to go too far:

The Board of the Bijenkorf had a high esteem for the Staal project, and
it would also have willingly put it into execution, were it not that it
considered the general character of this architecture to be too strange

Figure 63
Bijenkorf department store, The Hague, 1926. Architect: P.L. Kramer. The 'last monument' of the Amsterdam School, and the competition design preferred by the management of the store

and too unsuitable for a department store and fashion shop in The Hague today[48] (Fig. 63).

The store stuck to this policy in its later choices of architects: Dudok in 1928, Breuer in 1946, Ponti in 1964. All of them architects of great repute, all of them having belonged once to the *avant-garde*, but by the time they were chosen definitely established, past middle age, and 'safe' choices. Modern architecture of recognized quality is what the Bijenkorf wanted, but it had no desire to get involved in the battles on the front. Which is entirely in keeping with the merchandise it carries and the public it caters for.

This chapter demonstrates how the principles elaborated in the preceding chapters can be applied to a limited period in architecture, coherent in time and space, but in little else. The young quarrelled with their teachers, the left with the right, etc. All against the background of the ordinary architecture of the day, an extended version of Berlage's 'naked style', itself once a revolutionary architecture before the First World War. The theory of competing factions in the cultural elite developed in chapter 5 offers a possible explanation.

Two groups stand out: the progressives and the conservatives. They developed their ideas in dialectical opposition to each other, and showed implicitly how much clarity of thought and extremity of position were themselves the products of the tussle.

Finally, the Great Depression of 1929 damaged the idealistic hope of a better world of tomorrow. A number of 'progressive' architects, primarily those who had joined the movement for exclusively aesthetic reasons, defected to the conservative camp.

It may seem peculiar to restrict this analysis to Dutch architecture. And why Dutch? Because the author is Dutch?

However, this examination of some of the 'origins of the Modern Movement' was possible for only a few cases and countries; or, more precisely, was easier with one country than with another. It required a country which had visibly and from an early date contributed to the Modern Movement; this eliminated not only the USA and the UK, but also all of Scandinavia. The firm hold of the Ecole des Beaux Arts on French architecture made France a less attractive candidate. Italy and, in particular, Germany would have satisfied the requirements, but it would have been difficult to disentangle architectural and political developments. This left Switzerland and Holland. By choosing one of them it would be possible to show that the 'swing to the right' occurred also in a country whose government stayed democratic and left architecture to its own devices. Being more familiar with the Dutch scene, I felt it was justified to opt for the Dutch as an example.

I needed this chapter to highlight in particular the opposition between conservatives and progressives and the effect of adverse circumstances on the view of some participants. All of this can be used to analyze the architectural scene of today, as will be attempted in the next chapter.

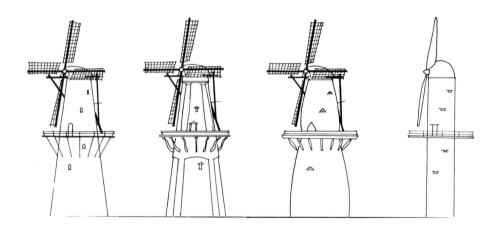

9 European and US Architecture Today

After the Second World War functionalism scored a decisive victory. In the USA, Gropius, Breuer and Mies had obtained influential teaching positions with the help of progressive members of the cultural elite; their assistants, like Stubbins, and their pupils, like Pei, Rudolph, Franzen, Barnes, Schipporeit and the members of TAC, soon started to spread the gospel (Fig. 64). The book of Sigfried Giedion, *Space, Time and Architecture*, an eloquent apology for functionalism by the secretary of CIAM, became a standard text in most American architectural schools.

In Holland, C.H. van der Leeuw was able, as president of the board of the Technical University, to get some functionalist architects nominated as professors in the department of architecture, to counteract the influence of Granpré Molière.

In Weimar Germany, functionalism had celebrated some of its earliest triumphs. Its leaders had fled the country after Hitler came into power, which gave them an aura of martyrdom. The obvious way to show yourself and the world that the cultural Germany was still alive and kicking was to pick up the thread where it had been broken and promote functionalist architecture. The city of Berlin staged an experimental housing development, the Hansa-viertel, in obvious parallel to the Weissenhofsiedlung (1926–1927) in Stuttgart, for which Aalto, Le Corbusier, Van den Broek and Bakema, Vago, Beaudoin, Gropius (with TAC) and a number of others were invited. Functionalistic architecture helped to demonstrate that the Hitler period was but an interlude.

As the gospel of functionalism spread, it was of course simplified — 'vulgarized' — to a standard set of stylistic markers: flat roofs, plain unadorned box-like buildings and a lot of glass. 'Every cheap architect could copy Mies,' Johnson said (p. 119), and this is what the practical architects did. Its

Figure 64
Lever House, New York, 1952.
Architects: Skidmore, Owings
and Merrill (photo: 1953). 'Many
in America can recall the delight
with which they greeted the first
few examples of functionalist
architecture, how happily they
contrasted with the ubiquitous
beaux arts buildings of the central
cities or the mock-Tudor or Cape
Cod of the suburbs. Yet gradually
delight turned to dismay as the
functional became the universal
style. The Lever Building on Park
Avenue still elicits a favourable
aesthetic response, but how much
less now than it did when it was
not yet surrounded by vulgar
imitations!' (D.J. Olsen, *The
Growth of Victorian London*,
London 1976, pp. 64–65)

acceptability after the Second World War hinged largely on its limited successes before that war and the concomitant aura of revolutionary novelty — an aura which wore thin as soon as every architect jumped the bandwagon. Its very success was the reason for its fall from grace today. Gropius, Mies and Breuer found in the USA the large jobs which they had always hoped for; the next generation of artistic architects had to design in a different way to show their relative independence from their teachers, but even more to stand out against a background of 'cheap Mies'.

One way to do this was to drop the apparent simplicity of the founding fathers. By underscoring the sculptural qualities of the building, by accenting the load-bearing structure of the interior volumes, they could step up the expression and yet stay within the confines of functionalism. Le Corbusier himself had shown the way with his Jaoul houses (1954) and the Ronchamp Chapel (1964). Bakema called it 'expressive functionalism', Banham and the Smithsons labelled it 'New Brutalism' (Figs. 72 and 73).

Changes in the building industry helped functionalism to come into its own. The backlog in new construction during the war and the destructions of that war had created a large demand. The demand increased the size of commissions, but there were often neither materials nor skilled labour enough for an adequate supply. Contractors turned to prefabrication and large-scale machinery: the mobile building crane made its entry on the site. The simple unadorned prismatic forms of functionalism were a boon for this new type of construction; they dovetailed neatly with the requirements of machine production and crane operation. Of course they also produced an architecture which is now decried as bland, sterile, monotonous and too large in scale.

Early protests against the new suburbs came from Aldo van Eyck:

Instead of the inconvenience of filth and confusion, we have now got the boredom of hygiene. The material slum has gone — in Holland for example it has — but what has replaced it? Just mile upon mile of organized nowhere, and nobody feeling he is 'somebody living somewhere'. No microbes left — yet each citizen a disinfected pawn on a chessboard, but no chessmen — hence no challenge, no duel and no dialogue... Architects left no cracks and crevices this time. They expelled all sense of place... They made a flat surface of everything so that no microbes can survive the civic vacuum cleaner; turned a building into an additive sequence of pretty surfaces... with nothing but emptiness on both sides[1].

He and his friend Herman Hertzberger looked for an architecture in which anonymity was to be replaced by intimate, direct relations between man and his buildings. Examples of such an architecture were found in the vernacular and in particular in the buildings of 'primitive' people:

'Primitive' architecture... has become a symbol reflecting directly a way of life which has come down to us through the ages, having its deep roots in the human and cosmic conditions[2].

Therefore they studied the Indian pueblos in New Mexico, the houses of the Dogon tribe in Central Africa and the Arabian Casbah. Architecture and urban planning had once more to be subsumed under a single discipline:

... it cannot but this will produce a humane Habitat. And that will more resemble an organized casbah than one is inclined to believe today[3].

Van Eyck covered his orphanage in Amsterdam with shallow domes (Figs. 65 and 66):

They provide coherence by their sameness, (they) differentiate because they slide along each continuously. It is as with old towns like Santorin, Mallorca, Assisi — at least, this was endeavored[4].

The idea that primitive and vernacular architecture are the 'true roots' of all building, to which we have to return again and again, is quite old. In the eighteenth century it finds expression in the praise of the 'primitive hut' by Laugier. It is of course related to the concept of the 'noble savage', portrayed by Daniel Defoe in Friday, a concept which found its most eloquent champion in Jean Jacques Rousseau, who sang the praises of the innate goodness of 'natural man'. The similarity with the rustic idyll of the garden-city movement is obvious.

Figure 65
Positano, Italy

There was however a small but important difference. The garden cities are meant to be seen as imitations of villages. Their inhabitants are supposed to recognize the symbolism-of-place, just as Americans were supposed to recognize old-world culture in Collegiate Gothic or in the classicist architecture of the Washington National Gallery. Architectural determinism may help in addition to recreate the desirable social qualities. The Amsterdam orphanage concentrated on the latter aspect only; it mattered little to van Eyck whether the users of the building recognized Santorin or Assisi. Essential were the small scale of the building blocks, the high density and the loving care bestowed on details like doorsteps, windowsills and retaining walls.

Moshe Safdie, the Israeli architect of Habitat at Montreal, took a similar position:

I came to the conclusion that one couldn't rehouse all the families living in slums in Chicago... in single-family housing — it wouldn't

Figure 66
Orphanage, Amsterdam, 1958–1960. Architect: Aldo van Eyck

work because of the numbers of people and areas of land you would need for it.

Yet high-rise wouldn't work either. We saw it in the most dramatic form, kids clinging to wire-mesh balcony railings on the thirtieth floor... people complaining about the horrible life. For the first time I experienced the life of a newly-built slum. It made you feel compassion for the people; it made you hate those buildings.

In retrospect, I had set out on this trip with preconceived ideas, feeling suburbia was bad — after all, the Mediterranean cities were my background. But my conclusion was new; I felt we had to find new forms of housing that would recreate, in a high density environment, the relationships and the amenities of the house and the village...[5].

Yet van Eyck and Hertzberger had no intention to join the traditionalist camp of the Delft School and Granpré Molière, even if their position showed some marked similarities. Time and again the reiterated their admiration for the functionalist pioneers. They used open plans, spatial partitions in counterpoint to the skeleton, articulated load-bearing structures, and their often preferred material was exposed concrete. Safdie too stuck to a number of functionalist traits. They saw their work as a continuation and extension of CIAM, and not as a rejection of its principles. I will come back to the reasons for this below.

Constructivism, de Stijl and functionalism had proclaimed a 'new architecture' for a 'new man'. These movements had started and been sustained by a wave of optimism after World War I. The era after the Second World War lacked this electrifying belief. Just after the first atomic bombs had exploded, and with the Cold War soon on its way, it was hard to believe that there would never be a Third, Fourth, etc., World War. Some artists still tried in the sixties to flog the dead horse of radical belief again. For instance, the architect Werner Ruhnau and the artist Yves Klein proclaimed 'Aerial Architecture' in 1960:

We propose to cover a city with a roof of moving air. A central motorway leads to the airport; it subdivides the city: a residential district and a district for work, industry and mechanical installations. The air-roof airconditions and at the same time protects the privileged space.
　Floors of transparent glass. Storage in the subsoil (kitchens, bathrooms, storage and mechanical equipment). The concept of the homely, which we still know, has disappeared in this city flooded with light and completely open to the outside. There is a new condition of human intimacy. The inhabitants live in the nude. The former patriarchal family system exits no more. Society is completely free, individual, impersonal. Main activity of the inhabitants: leisure[6].

This sounded quaint in 1960 and downright silly today.

Archigram revived the functionalist technique of symbolizing the future with advanced technology. The functionalists had used ships, skyscrapers and steel, glass and concrete as High-Tech; Archigram used details borrowed from rockets and moonlanders (Ron Herron's 'Walking Cities' Fig. 67), inflatable structures and plastics.

Our document is the space-comic; its reality is in the gesture, design and natural styling of hardware new to our decade — the capsule, the rocket, the bathyscope, the zidpark, the handy-pak... can the near-reality of the rocket-object and hovercraft-object, which are virtually ceasing to be cartoons, carry the dynamic... building with them into life as it is?... There is the same consistency in an 'Adventure-Comic' city of the 1962–63 period and in Bruno Taut's projects for Alpine Architecture of 1917, the same force of prediction and Style... It is significant that with this material there exists an inspirational bridge stretching both forty years into the past and perhaps forty years into the future, and perhaps the answer lies neither in heroics nor tragedy, but in a re-emergence of the courage of convictions in architecture[7].

The light vein of this quotation may be partly due to the youth of its author, who had not yet built anything, partly to the English upper-class attitude of never being caught out in a serious mood, but it is *also* due, I maintain, to a lack of conviction. Archigram does not believe in it. It toys with the idea of novelty and optimistic hope for the future. *Vide* the labelling of their work as 'cartoons' and in particular the two 'perhaps's' at the end. The 'new man' did not emerge in the twenties, and they do not expect him to turn up now. Archigram is only too aware that there is not much reason for

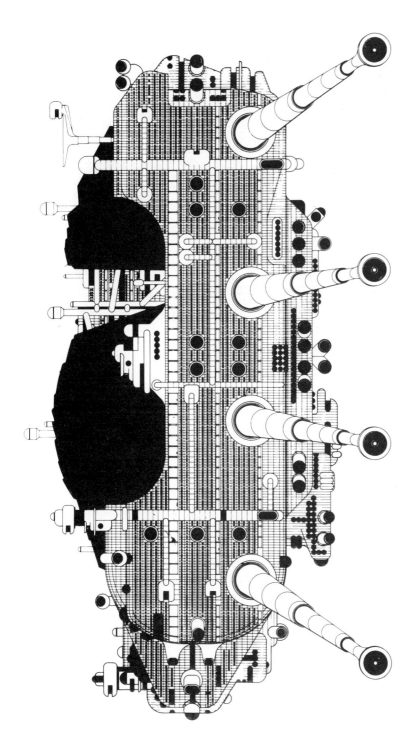

Figure 67
Walking Cities, project by Ron
Herron, 1964. Imagery derived
from the moonlanders

optimism. So they retreat into self-mockery. Warren Chalk wrote:

David Greene, Spider Webb and I clamoured ecstatically over the rocket support structures at Cape Kennedy. I visited the NASA control centre at Houston and later witnessed the second Surveyor-moonlanding on the monitors. But it was an omen. The technician assigned to me, sitting in front of a bank of 39 closed-circuit TV-monitors of the lunar operation, was in fact watching the Johnny Carson-show on the fortieth[8].

The Archigram impulse left at least one memorable building in Europe, the Centre Pompidou in Paris (Fig. 68), and several in Japan. But there is not much symbolism-of-the-future to be seen these days.

And with reason. If the future looked only moderately attractive in 1960, it looks gloomy today.

A world full of conflict, in which the West is losing its preeminence and is continuously challenged by the Third World, in which minorities clamor for a juster treatment, in which racial, religious and linguistic groups are continuously fighting each other even within the boundaries of a single nation — such a world induces a pessimistic outlook. Energy is getting scarce, but polluted water and air become daily more abundant. The arms race is going on at fever pitch.

There are quite a few parallels with the thirties. Business is in a slump, mass unemployment is increasing daily. The voters react also as in the thirties: conservatives have gained in England, Sweden and the Netherlands in the seventies, and the 1980 presidential election in the USA showed a Republican landslide.

I contend that voting behavior is indicative of the mental climate, and that this climate affects architects just as much as anybody else. The conservative viewpoint, having nearly become invisible during the sixties (it was always there, but got short thrift from the trade magazines for reasons mentioned below), reemerges triumphantly. Particularly in Europe, close to the Soviet Union and to the Middle East, less independent economically than the USA and still bickering over its own internal differences.

Léon Krier and Maurice Culot pleaded for a return to the old values in 1979 (Fig. 69):

Our proposal in terms of the European Urban tradition is to take up the discourse of the city where it was brutally interrupted by 'industrial civilization'... We must begin by rediscovering the forgotten language of the city that achieved its formal perfection in the eighteenth century.

... The symbolic and iconographic vacuity of 'modern' architecture can of course be explained by the fact that it has never been architecture but rather a form of packaging. And in its most ambitious examples, it can sometimes have been an 'art' of packaging. Certainly even the most ambitious will never succeed in constructing the city through packaging. Nor does 'modern' architecture derive from construction. The latter, with its roots in artisanal disciplines, was transmitted as a culture through history by the collective memory

Figure 69
Project for the Teerhof area to be reconstructed in the center of Bremen, Germany, 1978. Architect: Léon Krier. The buildings are *all* new; there are no historical buildings left on this island. Krier's style of drawing is copied from the work of the conservative German architect Heinrich Tessenow, who derived his drawing style from K.F. Schinkel

until its final destruction by the industrial division of labor and by an education based both on the alienation of knowing from doing and on the glorification of 'creativity'... There is thus nothing to be 'learned from Las Vegas', except that it constitutes a widespread operation of trivialization, a cynical attempt to recuperate and accommodate the leftovers of the greatest of all cannibalist feasts... We must forcefully reject the American city and become savagely European... Against the agglomeration of buildings and individuals we posit the city and its communities[9].

The favorite themes of the Delft School (and of other traditionalists) reappear: handicraft construction, regionalism, the value of tradition. And so the Krier brothers designed buildings in wood, brick and stone, with pitched tiled roofs, prostylar porticoes, streets lined by arcades, and city squares in the grand manner.

The Kriers are artistic architects. Behind them is a large array of practical architects doing neo-vernacular work, in the German 'Heimatstil', the English Neo-Georgian or the American Neo-Colonial (Fig. 40). Their work disappeared from the pages of the architectural trade magazines, but not from *House Beautiful* or *House and Garden*. With the resurrection of traditionalism as a 'viable alternative', even in professional circles, they return in the architectural press also. Here is a quote from Royal Barry Wills Associates, an architectural firm in the Colonial style since the twenties, on the everlasting value of the New England house and landscape:

... where could one ever behold a more sympatico melding of intimate landscape and simple, attractive houses than hereabouts — at least where industry hasn't cast its blight? The ancestral plowshares may have turned up a few stones and the climate may have had its harsh moments, but what an Eden of small green valleys, ponds and little streams, in which to build their trim, white domiciles, fronted in time by towering elms or maples! Here was a social continuity where families bred and succeeded one another, adding wings or barns as the need arose. Our assessment and use of this heritage is based on an appreciation of its physical charms and their adaptability to our present needs but, too, there is an inevitable residue of affection for the homes that sheltered our sturdy ancestors in the days before trailer living, fly-now-and-pay-later and the credit card[10].

The quotation is from 1976, but could be put side by side with the quote from J. Wheeler Dow of 1904 (p. 147) and one would not be able to guess that they came from books published 72 years apart.

The ubiquitous neo-vernacular suburban home — New England in the West and Mid-West, ranch house in Texas, Spanish Mission in California, Cotswold cottage or Neo-Georgian in England, etc. — is in fact conceived as an idyll in *contrast* to the place of work (where industry *has* cast its blight). Here the garden, the rustling brook, the old walnut tree full of squirrels and chirping birds, there the din, smoke and bustle of daily business. As Adrian Forty and Henry Moss wrote in a penetrating analysis:

The substance of this myth is that the village is the only setting in which authentic feelings, and intimate and meaningful social relations are possible, and the picturesqueness of traditional villages is a metaphor for these virtues; but excluded from the myth are all the negative aspects of village life, mud, isolation, bad public transport, no sub-postoffices, hostility between locals and commuters, mastery of landlord over tenant, farmer over labourer, and husband over wife...[11].

Forty and Moss point out that it gives an image of stability to essentially mobile middle-class families, and that neo-vernacular is also much more stylistically stable than the modern of whatever brand ('shrink-proof' they call it) because it will not so easily become obsolete. As already the Book of Genesis sang the praises of bucolic Eden, as Pliny recommended the virtues of country living, and country houses have been around since Roman antiquity, it seems that the myth is indestructible[12].

Neo-vernacular is recommended by the Essex County Council's *Design Guide for Residential Areas*; it is used with success by London County Council for its new estates, by developers in Port Grimaud, Reston, Viriginia and Levittown. Styles and fashions may come and go, but neo-vernacular is here to stay.

Yet the architectural trade magazines remain critical; *vide* Forty and Moss. Hertzberger has gone out of his way to dissociate his work from the neo-vernacular and trace his lineage to the functionalist pioneers[13]. The architects of La Tendenza, Aldo Rossi, Carlo Aymonino, Giorgio Grassi, Mario Botta, Aurelio Galfetti and Luigi Snozzi, though they have many points in common with the traditionalists (regionalism handicraft, timeless forms), are careful to attach themselves to the Italian *avant-garde* of the twenties and thirties, in particular to Giuseppe Terragni.

The cultural elite is in majority inclined to be progressive and oriented towards the future, according to Bourdieu; e.g. the characteristics of the Liberals quoted at the beginning of chapter 5. They still cherish hopes of a more equitable world in which their true role as spiritual leaders will be recognized. Yet these hopes are not strong enough to proclaim that world of the future brazenly; present conditions make such a stance look rather silly. So they do the next best thing, i.e. see themselves as the guardians of the *avant-garde* tradition. They attach themselves to the people who still *had* the courage of that conviction and flaunted it in the face of their contemporaries in the twenties.

But at the same time, largely thanks to their own efforts and those of the preceding generation, the modern 'International' style gained general acceptance (Figs. 70 and 71). The second generation of 'modernists' who were taught by Gropius or Mies is still around and reaping a harvest of large commissions; commissions from corporations and the super-rich, i.e. from

Figure 70
Health Association Center,
Minneapolis. Architects: Baker
Associates. Another ordinary
functionalistic building,
completed in 1981; this style was
the near background for the Late
Modern architects and the distant
background for the
Post-Modernists

the economic elite. They do not, they cannot identify with that, and besides they have to prove their creative leadership. The architectural *avant-garde* of today is hemmed in by a series of dont's, of noes, like Ad Reinhardt (p. 71). It is this, in my opinion, which explains their ambiguous position and to a large extent their 'Post-Modern' architecture.

The distant background is formed by the watered-down functionalism of practical architects: the large, simple, economic boxlike buildings which are still being built everywhere. Alll the rhetoric about the 'failure' or the 'death' of modern architecture is directed against that. The nearer background is that of the successful second generation of functionalist or modern architects, of what Charles Jencks has called appropriately 'Late Modernism'. These architects still believe (or sometimes, until recently believed — they often watch the younger generation closely) in the tenets of modern architecture. Philip Johnson said in 1955:

We have very fortunately the work of our spiritual fathers to build on. We hate them, of course, as all spiritual sons hate all spiritual fathers, but we can't ignore them, nor can we deny their greatness. The men, of course, that I refer to: Walter Gropius, Le Corbusier and Mies van der Rohe... Isn't it wonderful to have behind us the tradition, the work that those men have done? Can you imagine being alive at a more wonderful time? Never in history was the tradition so clearly demarked, never were the men so great, never could we learn so much from them...[14].

Paul Rudolph too acknowledged his debt:

... But let's face it. All this comes from Le Corbusier. He, of course, did it all much earlier and much better... I'm affected by everything I see. I make no bones about it. I haven't invented anything in my life[15].

Figure 71
John McCormack Building,
Boston, 1971–1975. Architects:
Hoyle, Doran and Berry. Another
example of an ordinary
functionalistic building

And a more practical architect like Helmut Hentrich voices
the same feelings:

Klotz — Mr. Hentrich, you belong to the second generation of the
moderns. The first generation was that of your teachers.
Hentrich — They were twenty or thirty years older than we. They
were the great innovators. From them we have everything. On their
foundations we sill continue to build today after fifty years. Not much
new has been added to it[16].

Figure 72
South Eastern Massachusetts
University, North Dartmouth,
1963–1966. Architects: Rudolph,
Desmond and Lord.
Monumentalization of supports
and cantilevers

The artistic architects of the second generation distinguished themselves from their more practical colleagues (such as Hentrich) by increasing the plastic effects, like Rudolph, Stirling and Johnson did, or by stepping up the High-Tech appearance (Norman Foster, Cesar Pelli) or by using more extravagant forms (Roche and Dinkeloo). All of those can be labelled 'mannerist variations' (Figs. 72 and 73). Their work is sufficiently close to 'standard functionalism' to be comprehensible and acceptable to the economic elite, yet sufficiently different to give a corporation a distinct look of cultural awareness. All 'deviations' allow a more monumental architecture; indeed, increased plasticity leads naturally to it.

Figure 73
College Park Insurance
Company, Indianapolis, 1965.
Architects: Roche and Dinkeloo.
Sloping facades dramatize the
Miesian box. The last three
examples of Late Modern
architecture are the *near*
background for Post-Modern
architecture, which has to differ
from these as well as from the
'ordinary' functionalistic
buildings

In their high seriousness, their monumentality and their permanence, these buildings affirm the values of their clients; Late Modernism is popular with corporations.

The position of the Post-Modern *avant-garde* can be seen, in my opinion, as a negation of both previous groups: of the run-of-the-mill functionalism of the practical architects, and also of the exaggerations of Late Modernism, yet (like both of these) still attached to the 'great traditions of the Modern Movement'. It is this last point which they have in common with Hertzberger, Safdie and Rossi. Historic references are possible, but they should be carefully balanced against 'modern' elements, to show that the architect knows which is which and that he is still on the right side of the boundary with the traditionalists. No Neo-Vernacular, no House-and-Garden Neo-Colonial for them. For that betokens middle-class values, *vide* Halen (chapter 4).

This kind of architecture is a critic's despair. The critic agrees that functionalist architecture is the 'Great Tradition'; as a member of the cultural elite he has helped to create that view. He *may* agree that it should perhaps be revised, but by this? Ada Louise Huxtable wrote recently:

I cannot think of better words for what is going on in architecture right now than ambiguous, strange and askew... Architects' writings today go beyond permissible ambiguity. They are being couched in the most obscure, arcane, and unclear terms, borrowing freely from poorly digested and often questionably applied philosophy or skimmings from other fashionable disciplines... Small ideas are delivered in large words and weighed down with exotic and private references. Intellectual trendiness is rampant[17].

Figure 74
Saltzman house, East Hampton, New York, 1967–1970. Architect: Richard Meier. A variation on the functionalism of the 'heroic period' of the twenties
(Ezra Stoller photo)

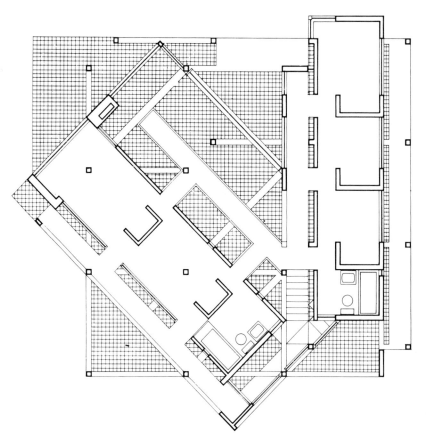

Figure 75
Plan of Miller house (House III),
Lakeville, Connecticut, 1971.
Architect: Peter Eisenman. A grid
of nine squares (Hejduk's
16-column problem) shifted and
partly rotated. Mannerist
operations on the basically
functionalist vocabulary

It is fairly clear who belong to the US group of 'Post-Modernists', but it is hard to find any common principles which unite them. I believe that the picture clears considerably if the *other* positions in the field are taken into account, if we look for what they are *against* rather than what they are for (Figs. 74, 75 and 76).

In a recent series of interviews, Barnes, Graves, Hardy, Meier and Stern all acknowledged that Post-Modernism is primarily a reaction against the architecture of the sixties[18]. Robert Stern said:

I think that the architecture of the fifties and sixties, so-called late modernism, was very limited and dull — focused as it was on a few very specific references that were usually utilitarian and technological, as opposed to cultural. Younger architects, starting with Venturi, and going forward for twenty years now, have challenged late modernism in many different ways. To say that the challenge isn't there, to say that the issues being raised are not real, is preposterous in my opinion. People who are heavily invested in late modernism see post-modernism as a threat because their view of architecture is so single-minded. If they bring in other meanings, look in other directions, they almost have to repudiate what they have stood for[19].

Which is obviously the reason why these people are against it. And conversely, this resistance bestows an aura of incom-

Figure 76
Les Arcades du Lac, St Quentin-en-Yvelines, near Paris, 1980. Architect: Taller de Arquitectura. Peter Hodgkinson of TA, in defense of their recent classicizing architecture, said: 'It's the vulgarisation of the (Modern) Movement that has so totally failed us, not the artists. The greatest masters of this last century (whether dead or alive) have reputations as firm as those of preceding ages. When the TA challenges the Modern Movement, it does so as the collective cause responsible for the catacopia constructed over the face of the world these last decades and the assassin of the people's patrimony. I must add that this lethal vulgarisation is mostly practised by the commercial architects who make up the body of the profession...' (Interview in *Architectural Review* **CLXXI** (1982), 1024, p. 31)

prehension and revolutionary independence on the Post-Modernists, in line with all *avant-garde* from the Impression-ists to Conceptual Art.

Knowing what to avoid is not much of a help at the drawing-board. What are the Post-Modernist architects to do? The simple boxlike modernism of the practical architects is out, obviously. Hugh Hardy spoke out against it:

If there's one thing people are doing now who are seriously interested in making bizarre shapes, it's not the bizarre shapes themselves, it's that this generation is trying to get out of boxes. The generation that preceded us stripped a lot away, which was a destruction of the box, but the limits with which they did it always included the floor and the ceiling. This generation is doing it much differently: the world now is made entirely of diagonals. What we're trying to do is bust out of the confinement of a static space — to go as far as we can to create spaces that are ambiguous, that don't end, that become something else. With the monumental — the static stuff — we're bored; it telegraphs to us, because when you come to the middle you can see the end. Here, we bent over backwards to exploit something that is constantly shifting and moving and changing[20].

Note the negation of both 'practical modernism' *and* Late-Modernism ('the monumental'), and the conscious effort to do something new and exciting. The last can be accomplished by diagonals and rotation and by complex spaces; this goes beyond the mannerisms which Johnson, Pei, Rudolph and Roche and Dinkeloo grafted onto the functionalist stem. An architecture of 'complexity and contradiction'; in the description of Robert Venturi:

Architects can no longer afford to be intimidated by the puritanically moral language of orthodox Modern architecture. I like elements which are hybrid rather than 'pure', compromising rather than 'clean', distorted rather than 'straightforward', ambiguous rather than 'articulated', perverse as well as impersonal, boring as well as 'interesting', conventional rather than 'designed', accommodating rather than excluding, redundant rather than simple, vestigial as well as innovating, inconsistent and equivocal rather than direct and clear. I am for messy vitality over obvious unity[21].

Rather similar is Charles Moore's doctrine of 'Immaculate Collision':

The idea is that if two or more plans or shapes or systems can crash into each other so as to achieve some serendipity, to gain energy from the collision, rather than to be maimed or destroyed by it, then a new device for designing would be at hand. My favorite images generally involve multiple layers of facade or of interior[22].

Each of the three previous quotations is a pleading for mannerism: turning the simple into the complex. Each leads to spatial complexity and ambiguity. A complexity which goes all over the range from the layered rooms of Richard Meier to the fragmented spaces of Frank Gehry and the Chinese puzzles of Peter Eisenman. And, most important, they are manneristic variations *different* from those of Johnson, Rudolph, Roche and Dinkeloo.

Historic and vernacular references are allowed, but should be distinguished from ordinary 'New Cape Cod'. Charles Moore:

I am especially interested in vernacular architecture. It is familiar to me, I enjoy it, and I believe it is proper for it to be the prime source for my own work. I think it is important to note that ours is not a peasant society; to see vernacular architecture as hooked to the land, free of exotic influences or of pretension, at some odds with an aristocratic 'high' architecture is, in the United States, altogether to miss the point[23].

So Moore uses it in a very freewheeling way, which always shows plainly that it is a *new* neo-vernacular. (In this it contrasts sharply with the work of Royal Barry Wills Associates.)

Robert Venturi went one step further in using the commercial vernacular of Las Vegas, a source previously untapped because of its supposed vulgarity. The last is in part its attraction. By using the vulgar and the cliché, the artist shows his power; he decides what is art and what is not (Rauschenberg: 'This is a portrait of Iris Clert if I say so'). A similar mechanism is partly beind the carwrecks of John Salt, the car accidents and electric chairs of Andy Warhol and the comics of Roy Lichtenstein. Venturi admitted that he got the idea from Pop Art.

Table 6
Robert Venturi contrasts his own apartment for the elderly, Guild House, with that by Paul Rudolph, Crawford Manor, to show the differences between his stance and that of the Late Modernists. Source: R. Venturi, D. Scott Brown and S. Izenour, *Learning from Las Vegas*, Cambridge 1977, p. 102.

Guild House	Crawford Manor
An architecture of meaning	An architecture of expression
Explicit 'denotative' symbolism	Implicit 'connotative' symbolism
Symbolic ornament	Expressive ornament
Applied ornament	Integral expressionism
Mixed media	Pure architecture
Decoration by the attaching of superficial elements	Unadmitted decoration by the articulation of integral elements
Symbolism	Abstraction
Representational art	'Abstract expressionism'
Evocative architecture	Innovative architecture
Societal messages	Architectural content
Propaganda	Architectural articulation
High *and* low art	High art
Evolutionary, using historical precedent	Revolutionary, progressive, anti-traditional
Conventional	Creative, unique, and original
Old words with new meanings	New words
Ordinary	Extraordinary
Expedient	Heroic
Pretty in front	Pretty (or at least unified) all around
Inconsistent	Consistent
Conventional technology	Advanced technology
Tendency towards urban sprawl	Tries to elevate client's value system and/or budget by reference to Art and Metaphysics
Looks cheap	Looks expensive
'Boring'	'Interesting'

It ties in nicely with his requirement that architecture should use conventions and be 'ordinary':

... Denise Scott Brown (Mrs Venturi) ...' we are taking a very broadly based thing, which is the popular culture and we're trying to make it acceptable to an elitist subculture, namely the architects and the corporate and governmental decision makers who hire architects[24]'.

Venturi again:

... learning from popular culture does not remove the architect from his or her status in high culture[25].

... We say our buildings are 'ordinary' — other people have said that they are ugly and ordinary. But, of course, our buildings in another sense, are extraordinary, *extra*-ordinary. Although they look ordinary, they are not ordinary at all, but are, we hope, very sophisticated architecture, designed very carefully from each square inch to the total proportions of the building.
John Cook — Why use the term ordinary at all?
Robert Venturi — It was partly a polemic, but also because on one level it *is* ordinary... It is a reaction to the heroic stance of architects like Paul Rudolph for example[26].

The same anti-monumental attitude is shown by Peter Eisenman, when he calls his own work 'cardboard architecture':

'Cardboard', usually a derogatory term in architectural discussion (as Baroque and Gothic were when first used), is used here deliberately as an ironic and pre-emptory symbol for my argument[27].

The reason is clear and indicated by Venturi: to put as much distance as possible between themselves and the Late Modernists.

From this anti-monumentalism stem the common characteristics of some of the work of the New York Five, Venturi, Moore, Hardy, Holzman, Pfeiffer and Gehry: a predilection for less permanent materials like wood, the use of screen walls (stylistically derived from Kahn's Luanda Consulate) and the use of paint to obtain architectural effects, sometimes with 'supergraphics'.

The reasons which make irony and less durable materials attractive to the American Post-Modern architects seem similar to those which made exposed concrete attractive to Atelier 5 and the inhabitants of Halen: the challenge to the affirmative values of the middle class and the economic elite, i.e. solidity, durability, and permanent, 'serious' beauty. The rising cost of labor may have added to the attractions of plywood and paint.

All the Post-Modern architects retain some kind of tie-up with the Modern Movement. Of Corbu's '5 points for a new architecture' (point-supports, roofgarden, free plan, *fenêtre-en-longueur*, free (i.e. non-loadbearing) facade), three are usually retained: the free plan, the free facade and the horizontal window. Accents on craft techniques, so typical of traditionalist architecture, are avoided. Forms are geometrical, and window reveals are very shallow, giving that 'unmistakable' modern look. Moore's Sea Ranch and Venturi's SUNY humanities building clearly use the forms of Modern architecture, the latter building with some reference to Aalto, as Robert Maxwell pointed out[28]. Venturi confessed his respect for the founding fathers:

Because we have criticized Modern architecture, it is proper here to state our intense admiration of its early period when its founders, sensitive to their own times, proclaimed the right revolution. Our argument lies mainly with the irrelevant and distorted prolongation of that old revolution today[29].

Meier, Gwathmey, Eisenman, Hejduk and Graves went considerably further. Their (early) work was all derived from early Corbu (late Corbu was preempted by the Late Modernists): the prismatic exteriors, the complex interiors, the strip-railings, the white color, the shallow curved wall (Fig. 74).

With these works the Post-Modern architects established themselves firmly in the 'Great Modern Tradition'. But historic and vernacular references have been increasing in their later work, in particular in that of Moore, Venturi and Graves. I would be inclined to ascribe this to the same mechanism as that which made the architects of Group '32 in the last chapter veer away from their original functionalistic stance. As social conditions look more threatening, the past starts to look more rosy by comparison. The upsurge of conservatism affects Post-Modern architects just like anybody else.

Both Late and Post-Modernists still live largely off the heritage of the functionalist movement. The Late Modernists still 'believe' in Modern architecture and design with a solemn seriousness. The Post-Modernists react against that with irony and wit. As sounding the trumpet for a 'radical break with the past' is Quixotic and not warranted by the times, as we all know how little came true of the high hopes of the twenties, the Post-Modern architects couch their theories in an ironic and casual language: 'Take it or leave it'. 'Functionalism' may have been a misnomer, but it did yeoman service as a battle-cry. 'Post-Modernism' is a nostalgic and wistful epithet, and for that, all the more appropriate.

The theory developed in this book does not explain everything about recent architecture, but I contend that is relevant to two important and related aspects. First the lack of coherence among the present-day *avant-garde* can be explained by postulating a pressure towards change without a belief in the future. Taken by themselves, only the disparity of various currents and individuals in recent architecture stands out. Once the background of 'ordinary' architecture is brought in, the different views start to make sense, because they can be interpreted as positions in a field. Various Post-Modern groups and individuals try to find a new position in this field — which means taking account of, but avoiding too much proximity to existing positions.

The second aspect is the growing nostalgia. The statements of the Kriers, Rossi, Grassi and — to some extent — Charles Moore are very similar to Molière's stance described in the last chapter: they too advocate a return to handicraft, to the true principles of vernacular architecture, and see architecture as eternal and autonomous. Meier's revival of early Corbu or Graves' leaning (imaginative, but leaning nonetheless) towards classical Beaux Arts architecture are also nostalgic signs on the wall. Such views are gaining influence today, as they did in the late thirties. But there is no corresponding rallying point for optimists about the future on the other side. Architects today are subjected to a string of contradictory impulses: the legacy of the 'true' original Modern Movement, which was committed to the future, yet is itself now a thing of the past; the tendency of the cultural elite to believe in another, better hereafter, in a world which hardly encourages such beliefs; the great many positions in the field of architecture which are already occupied and therefore out-of-bounds. Their combination leads to the lively, confusing and ambiguous scene of today.

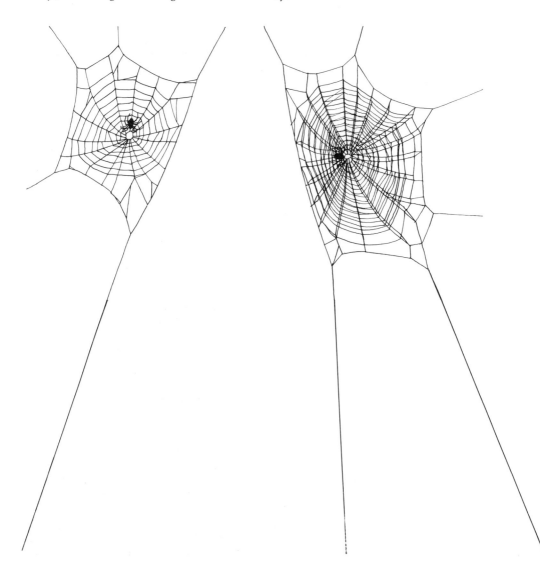

Appendix A
A Note on Methodology

The theory expounded in the foregoing pages is based on two major sets of data: the theory of Pierre Bourdieu and a number of quotations.

Bourdieu has built his theory on the replies to a number of questionnaires, reinforced by other statistical material, mainly from INSEE, the French National Bureau of Statistics. He has been criticized for his rather offhand treatment of statistical data, and also for the lack of precision in his own terminology and concepts: '... his theoretical stance is sufficiently ambiguous to excuse almost any inconsistency'[1]. For my purposes I interpreted his theory, which implies distortions, misreadings, and different accents. Inevitably, errors in Bourdieu's theory will be compounded here.

The use of quotations to make a point is a standard procedure in books about architectural history. Reyner Banham, in his *Theory and Design in the First Machine Age*, Vincent Scully, in his *The Shingle Style*, and Charles Jencks, in his *Modern Movements in Architecture*, all use it. Long arguments by the architects quoted are summarized in a capsule quotation; the method is open to the criticism that the quote is not sufficiently typical, or even that it can be contradicted by another — presumably more typical — quotation. This applies also, of course, to my text.

But there is also an intrinsic — and much more damaging — difference between the books just mentioned and mine. Art historians set out to prove a point about the behavior of an individual. What Berlage or Le Corbusier wrote or said is only supposed to involve himself in the context of Banham's book. In my book the pretensions are larger: the individual architect is supposed to be 'typical' for a whole group. To rest a case about for example 'practical architects' on a few quotations laid end to end is hazardous indeed. So it is easy to send the whole laboriously constructed edifice toppling by pulling out a few props.

For instance, in chapter 2 (p. 12) I argued that many architects could not keep up with the growing number of new techniques and specialists, and supported that by a quote from a 1971 report by Management Communications Services on the *Communication Needs of Ontario Architects*. A member of the allied trades in the building industry had said:

A great number of architects live on Cloud 9 so far as their idea of the future is concerned. They are not keeping up with such techniques as project management, prefabrication, systems building and the like[2].

Two other quotations from private owners in the *same* report contradict this:

In general, I've found architects very receptive to new ideas. Also I find that they communicate quite well in spoken and written word[3].

and:

On costing and delivery no complaints. The building was promised for a certain date and it was ready then and they estimated correctly too. But then it's in their own interest to be good[4].

Or, in chapter 8 (p. 165) I suggested that one of the attractions of geometrical shapes and smooth flat surfaces for 'de Stijl' artists was their affinity to machine production; they could serve as symbols for a High-Tech future. Van Doesburg and van Eesteren wrote in 1923:

Personal taste, including admiration for the machine (machinism in art) has no importance for the attainment of this unity of art and life. Machinism in art is an illusion like the others (naturalism, futurism, cubism, purism, etc.) and an even more dangerous illusion than any metaphysical speculation[5].

In chapter 8 I emphasized the optimism after the First World War, which led to revolutionary activity in politics and art and produced a spate of manifestos. In chapter 9 I suggested that such optimism was lacking after the Second World War, and that the manifestos of that period were lukewarm at best. To support this point of view I quoted Archigram and a manifesto by Werner Ruhnau and Yves Klein. I could have made out a case for a strong, yet realistic optimism after the Second World War, and a silly daydreaming after the First, by a different choice of quotations (e.g. from Bruno Taut's Frühlicht). Charles Moore is presented here as a Post-Modern architect; it is quite easily possible to introduce him as a traditionalist, bent on reviving the vernacular, by an appropriate choice of quotations.

Bourdieu has been criticized for his ambiguity and lack of precision. Similar imprecisions appear in my text. There is no sharp criterion of demarcation to separate the cultural from the economic elite. One of the influential clients in chapter 8, C.H. van der Leeuw, belongs to both. Nor are the practical architects clearly marked off from their artistic colleagues. In defense of this lack of precision I can point out that sharp boundaries between the 'practical' and 'artistic' architects do not occur in reality either, in my opinion. But if these categories shade into each other, what is then the sense of talking about conflicts between them and pitting them against each other, as was done here?

There are several loose ends. It is perhaps understandable how the majority of architects, contrary to their ambition, become 'practical' rather than 'artistic'. Many high-school teachers studied English in the hope of becoming writers; many professionally trained pianists have to make a living as music-teachers instead of appearing on the platform. In architecture, the first job one holds, the place of residence, talent, the first client, all exert an influence. Some of the social mechanisms of fame have been described in this book; but it is not clearly why *these* architects, rather than many other potential contenders, succeeded.

And why do some architects opt for the 'conservative' stance rather than the 'progressive', which is usually emphasized in the schools? The convictions of the Krier brothers or of Royal Barry Wills Associates are as deeply felt and as hotly defended as those of the opposite camp. It cannot be an urge to be 'original', to differ from the others, because that runs contrary to conservative beliefs.

The theory outlined here is most vulnerable from a methodological point of view where it uses quotations from many different sources, periods and countries of origin to bolster an argument, as in chapter 2, 5, 6 and 7. It is at its most convincing where the quotations make up a story and deal with a single subject or phenomenon: the baffling experiences of Atelier 5 in Halen and Wertherberg (chapter 4), the doctrinaire teaching of Mies at IIT (chapter 6). That is the reason why I focused on the New York School of painting in chapter 5; other groups and periods might have provided more apposite quotations, but the persuasive power of the whole would have diminished.

I also derive some comfort from the overall coherence[6] of this interpretation of architects' behavior. The different parts add up to a view which I believe to be consistent and able to explain some things which — at least to me — always appeared puzzling. But I am well aware that much more consistent and impressive theories have turned out to be figments of the mind, and that other interpretations are possible.

Bertrand Russell has coined the concept of 'degree of credibility':

I think… that everything we feel inclined to believe has a 'degree of doubtfulness', or, inversely, a 'degree of credibility'. Sometimes this is connected with mathematical probability, sometimes not; it is a wider and vaguer conception. It is not, however, purely subjective… 'credibility', as I mean it, is objective in the sense that it is the degree of credence that a *rational* man will give[7].

It is obvious that the 'degree of credibility' of the theory outlined in these pages is only fair at best. It rests on the coherence and consistency of the interpretation, and on the degree to which the readers are willing to accept the situations here described as 'typical' for the profession of the architect. It will convince primarily those who say: 'Something like this I have noticed too', i.e. those who are already half-convinced beforehand. To others it will appear incorrect, if not patently absurd.

Even if it clears up some points, it leaves may others in the dark. Is all the ingenuity spent on design reducible to a desire to be different? Can the thrill that any architect engaged in design physically experiences be explained by the mechanism here described? It is an essay, 'illustrated' rather than 'proved' by quotations; I hope that it helps to raise the awareness of the social constraints on design, but it shows even more clearly how little we know about what goes on below the surface.

Appendix B
Sources and
Acknowledgements

This book has its origin in a comment of one of my students, René Ackerstaff, on the disagreement among the leading architects of today about the future course of architecture. The main ideas were tested out in a lecture course in my school and in papers presented at the international conferences on architectural psychology in Louvain-la-Neuve, Belgium, and the University of Surrey, Guildford, in 1979.

The view that the varieties of taste make sense only when seen in relation to each other and connected to class positions is taken from Pierre Bourdieu's work. The concept of 'cultural capital', the conviction that the dichotomy between 'good art' and 'bad art' is itself a position *in* the field (and not 'above' it), and the dependence of all taste on 'legitimate' high culture are also due to Bourdieu. I differ from Bourdieu in seeing art-forms as more intelligible and less arbitrary. Suzanne Langer has shown that works of art can be seen as symbolic systems, connoting fairly well-defined concepts. The application of semiotics to architecture has been elaborated by Bonta, Broadbent, Eco, Hesselgren, Jencks, Koenig, Krampen, Norberg-Schulz and myself, among others.

Bourdieu's views have much in common with the theories developed by Norbert Elias. Elias too explains social phenomena with fields of interrelated positions ('configurations'); he sees social processes as more open-ended than Bourdieu and is more optimistic about the future. His account of how external pressures are transformed by the individual into internal constraints is more specific and convincing than Bourdieu's 'habitus'. From Elias I have adopted the view that many social processes are 'blind'. I disagree with his extreme emphasis on history and his distaste for statistics.

Important work on the sociology of art has been done by the Frankfurt School, in particular by Adorno and Horkheimer. They were the first to interpret the advance of the *avant-garde* as a flight from commercial vulgarization. I cannot follow them in their sharp dichotomy between high art and 'culture-industry'; I see these two areas connected by a range of intermediate forms.

I agree with the flourishing school of Marxist interpretation of art and architecture (e.g. Tafuri, dal Co, Castells, Harvey, Hadjinicolaou, Holz, Brake, Hauser) that art reflects class positions and that material conditions are too often underrated. I disagree with their traditional Marxist dichotomies and their chiliastic expectations.

Both Bourdieu and Elias can be interpreted as attempting to combine Marx with Freud; Bourdieu has also adopted elements from Durkheim and Weber. Suzanne Langer developed her semiotic theory of art from the philosophy of Ernst Cassirer; beyond him, it is connected with the work of Mead, Peirce and De Saussure. Simmel was, as far as I know, the first to suggest that material culture can be used as a means of identification.

I am indebted to Peter Gleichmann, Robert Gutman, Geoffrey Broadbent and Barry Russell for constructive comments on earlier drafts of the text.

Notes

2. Building

1. A. S. Eichner (ed.), *A Guide to Post-Keynesian Economics*, New York 1978.
2. J. Parry Lewis, *Building Cycles and Britain's Growth*, London 1965.
   H. W. Richardson and D. H. Aldcroft, *Building in the British Economy between the Wars*, London 1968.
3. Building and Civil Engineering Economic Development Committee, *The Public Client and the Construction Industries*, London (HMSO) 1975 (the Wood Report), quoted in: *The Architect's Journal* (14 May 1975), p. 1013.
4. W. R. Smolkin, The consumer demand for housing, in: K. Bernhardt (ed.), *Housing, New Trends and Concepts*, Ann Arbor 1972, p. 148. Smolkin is a marketing and feasibility consultant in New Orleans.
5. The best hospital money could buy, in: *The New York Times*, Wednesday, July 19th, 1978.
6. P. J. Meathe, Project delivery, in: R. A. Class and R. E. Koehler (eds.), *Current Techniques in Architectural Practice*, New York 1976, pp. 19–23.
7. P. J. Cassimatis, *Economics of the Construction Industry*, New York 1966, pp. 26f.
8. N. J. Demerath and G. W. Baker, The social organization of housebuilding, in: *Journal of Social Issues* 7 (1951), pp. 86–99.
9. A. Hendriks, *De prijsvorming in het bouwbedrijf*, Rotterdam 1957.
10. G. McCue and W. R. Ewald Jr., The Midwest Research Institute, *Creating the Human Environment*, Urbana 1970, Part II.
11. R. Gutman, Architecture: The entrepreneurial profession, in: *Progressive Architecture* (1977) 5, pp. 55–58.
    R. Gutman, B. Westergaard and D. Hicks, The structure of design firms in the construction industry, in: *Environment and Planning B* 4, (1977), pp. 3–29.
12. Architecture's biggest firms, in: *Arch. Forum* (Sept. 1958), pp. 112–114.
13. R. Gutman, Architecture, *op. cit.* (note 11).

14. Detailed discussion of the two principles (there called 'dispersed' and 'centralized') in: *The Architect and his Office*, Royal Institute of British Architects, London 1962.
15. Is architecture unfair to architects? in: *Progressive Architecture* (June 1972) No. 6, p. 101, The slump killed the union, in: *Progressive Architecture* (1976), No. 7, p. 31.
16. F. Marquart and C. de Montlibert, Division du travail et concurrence en architecture, in: *Revue française de Sociologie* **XI** (1970), pp. 368–389; p. 384.
17. A. Roth, *Begegnung mit Pionieren. Le Corbusier, Piet Mondrian, Adolf Loos, Josef Hoffmann, Auguste Perret, Henry van de Velde*, Basel 1973, pp. 27 f.
18. E. Tafel, *Apprentice to Genius; Years with Frank Lloyd Wright*, New York 1979.
19. R. A. Class, Trends in architectural practice, in: R. A. Class and R. E. Koehler (eds.) *Current Techniques in Architectural Practice*, Washington, New York 1976, p. 268.
20. Recorded statement of a member of the 'allied trades' (engineers, contractors, construction managers and developers) quoted in: Management Communications Services, *Communication Needs of Ontario Architects*, stencilled report to the Ontario Ass. of Architects, n.d., p. 56.
21. The need expert arrives on the scene, in: *Progressive Architecture* (June 1966), p. 169.
22. M. Lapidus, *Architecture: a Profession and a Business*, New York 1967, p. 201.
23. Die Stellung des Architekten in: *Werk* (1969) No. 10, pp. 675–679.
    P. Collins, *Changing Ideals in Modern Architecture*, London 1965, ch. 18.
24. Quoted in: F. Jenkins, *Architect and Patron. A survey of Professional Relations and Practice in England from the Sixteenth Century to the Present Day*, London 1961, p. 111.
25. Phyllis Lambert, How a building gets built, in: *Vassar Alumnae Magazine* (Feb. 1959), quoted in: P. Carter, *Mies van der Rohe at Work*, London 1974, p. 178.
26. M. Lapidus, in: J. W. Cook and H. Klotz, *Conversations with Architects*, London 1973, p. 173.
27. RIBA, *The Architect and his Office*, London 1962, p. 170.
28. *Ibidem*, p. 166.
29. *Ibidem*, p. 174.
30. *Ibidem*, p. 180.
31. G. T. Heery, *Time, Cost and Architecture*, New York 1975, p. 21.
32. W. McQuade, The architects: a chance for greatness, in: *Fortune* (Jan. 1966), p. 202.
33. How the Chase Bank was landed, in: *Fortune* (Jan. 1958), p. 140.
34. H. E. Phillips, Comprehensive architectural services for the large corporate client, in: *AIA Journal* (May 1964), p. 82.
35. The corporate clients: what are their attitudes? in: *Progressive Architecture* (June 1966), p. 158.
36. B. Perkins, Marketing architectural sevices, in: *Architectural Record* (April 1972), p. 66.
37. J. B. Halper, The influence of mortgage lenders on building design, in: *Law and Contemporary Problems* **32** (1967)2, p. 269.
38. F. Fogarty, How today's clients pick architects, in: *Architectural Forum* (Feb. 1959), p. 115.
39. J. B. Halper, *op. cit.* (note 37), pp. 270–271.
40. M. Pawley, *Mies van der Rohe*, London 1970, p. 17.
41. E. Larrabee, Summary of the proceedings, in: L. B. Holland

(ed.), *Who Designs America?* Garden City, New York 1966, pp. 338–339.

42. J. P. Bonny, Basics of contracting, in: J. P. Bonny and J. P. Frein (eds.), *Handbook of Construction Management and Organization*, New York 1973, p. 1.

43. E. J. Logue, The impact of political and social forces on design, in: L. B. Holland (ed.), *Who Designs America?* Garden City, 1966, p. 240.

44. J. B. Halper, *op. cit.* (note 37), p. 267.

45. P. R. Gleichmann, Ein Problem Kontrovers gesehen, Neue Wege der Architekturkritik, in: *Der Architekt* **6** (1977), pp. 239–242.

46. 'Blind' processes in history discussed in: N. Elias, *Was ist Soziologie?* Munich 1970.

47. W. McQuade, Why all those buildings are collapsing, in *Fortune* (Nov. 19, 1979), p. 62.

48. *Ibidem*, p. 58.

49. L. F. Salzman, *Building in England down to 1540,* Oxford 1952, p. 223.

50. J. Portman and J. Barnett, *The Architect as Developer*, New York 1976.

51. T. C. Bannister, *The Architect at Mid-Century*, New York 1952, p. 363.

52. Was wir wollen! Proklamation des BDA, reprinted in: B. Gaber, *Die Entwicklung des Berufsstandes der Freischaffenden Architekten*, Essen 1966, pp. 223–226.

53. W. R. Smolkin, *op. cit.* (note 4), pp. 149, 150.

54. C. Perin, *Everything in Its Place. Social Order and Land Use in America*, Princeton 1977, pp. 34, 35.

55. R. M. French and J. K. Hadden, An analysis of the distribution and characteristics of mobile homes in America, in: *Land Economics* **XLI** (May 1965)2, pp. 131–139; p. 138.

56. R. Cassidy, Home owners taken for a ride. A review of: *Mobile Homes. The Low-Cost Housing Hoax. A Report by the Center for Auto Safety.* New York 1974, in: *New York Times Review*, **VII**, (Jan. 12, 1975), p. 28.

57. P. Boudon, *Pessac de Le Corbusier*, Paris 1969.

58. B. Rudovsky, *Architecture without Architects*, New York 1964.
J. C. Depaule, *l'Architecture sauvage*, Paris 1970.
J. Wampler, *All their Own*, New York 1977.
A. Boericke and B. Shapiro, *Handmade Houses. A Guide to the Woodbutcher's Art*, San Francisco 1975.

59. L. Taylor, The meaning of the environment, in: C. Ward (ed.), *Vandalism*, London 1973, pp. 62, 58.

60. This paragraph is based on some first-hand experience, interviews with Dutchmen who practised in other countries and on the review: Le métier d'architecte, in: *Architecture d'aujourd'hui* **45**, (Nov./Dec. 1973)170, pp. 99–113.

3. The Evolution of the Profession

1. L. F. Salzman, *Building in England down to 1540,* Oxford 1952, pp. 187f.

2. *Ibidem*, pp. 33f.

3. *Ibidem*, p. 223.

4. R. Krautheimer, The Carolingian revival of Early Christian architecture, in: *Art Bulletin*, **24**, (1942), pp. 1–38.

5. A. Verbeek, Zentralbauten in der Nachfolge der Aachener Pfalzkapelle, in: V. H. Elbern (ed.), *Das erste Jahrtausend*, Vol 2, Düsseldorf 1964, pp. 898–947.

6. P. Booz, *Der Baumeister der Gotik*, Munich 1956.
   J. Harvey, *The Mediaeval Architect*, London 1972.
   P. Frankl, *The Gothic. Literary Sources and Interpretations through Eight Centuries*, Princeton 1960.
   Konrad Hecht has shown that Gothic architects drew to scale (K. Hecht, Zur Massstäblichkeit der mittelalterlichen Bauzeichnung, in: *Bonner Jahrbücher* **166** (1966), pp. 253–268) and that the idea that plans and elevations were based on geometrical schemes is a nineteenth-century myth: K. Hecht, Mass und Zahl in der gotischen Baukunst, in: *Abhandlungen der Braunschweigischen Wissenschaftlichen Gesellschaft* **XXI**, (1969), pp. 215–326; **XXII** (1970), pp. 105–263; **XXIII** (1971–1972), pp. 25–236. My own measurements of Amiens Cathedral, in: *Journal of the Society of Architectural Historians* **XXV**, (1966), pp. 209–212.

7. A. Erlande-Brandenbourg, La façade de la cathédrale d'Amiens, in: *Bulletin Monumental* **135** (1977), pp. 253–293.

8. L. F. Salzman, *op. cit.* (note 1), pp. 6–9, P. Booz, J. Harvey and P. Frankl, *op. cit.* (note 6).

9. L. B. Alberti, *De Re Aedificatoria*, Florence 1485, in the translation of J. Leoni, London 1726, repr. in: L. B. Alberti, *Ten Books on Architecture* (J. Rykwert, ed.) London 1955, pp. 1, 2, 206.

10. F. Borsi, *Leon Battista Alberti*, Milan 1975.

11. F. Jenkins, *Architect and Patron, A Survey of Professional Relations and Practice in England from the Sixteenth Century to the Present Day*, London 1961, ch. 6, 7.

12. J. Gibbs, *A Book of Architecture containing Designs of Buildings and Ornaments*, London 1728, pp. i, ii.

13. J. Summerson, *Architecture in Britain: 1530–1830*, Harmondsworth *op. cit.* 1953, pp. 210, 337f.

14. F. Jenkins, *op. cit.* (note 11), ch. 4, 5.

15. M. N. Rosenfeld, The Royal Building Administration in France from Charles V to Louis XIV, in: S. Kostof (ed.), *The Architect. Chapters in the History of the Profession*, New York 1977, pp. 173, 174.

16. F. Jenkins, *op. cit.* (note 11), ch. 7, and C. G. Powell, *An Economic History of the British Building Industry 1815–1979*, London 1980, pp. 28f.

17. J. Summerson, *Georgian London*, Harmondsworth 1969, pp. 69f.

18.. *Ibidem*, pp. 72f.

19. J. Soane, *Plans, Elevations and Sections of Buildings*, London 1788, p. 7, as quoted in: S. Kostof (ed.), *The Architect, op. cit.* (note 15), p. 194.

20. F. Jenkins, *op. cit.* (note 11), pp. 112f.

21. H. Ricken, *Der Architekt. Geschichte eines Berufs*, (East) Berlin 1977, p. 93.

22. M. S. Briggs, *The Architect in History*, New York 1974, p. 368.

23. B. M. Boyle, Architectural practice in America, 1865–1965 — ideal and reality, in: S. Kostof (ed.), *The Architect, op. cit.* (note 15), p. 315.

24. M. Greif, *The New Industrial Landscape. The Story of the Austin Company*, Clinton, NJ 1978.

4.   Case-Study: Halen

1. R. Perrinjaquet, *Eléments pour une sociologie de la production architecturale*, Paris 1978, p. 224.
2. *Ibidem*, From an interview with one of the partners, p. 213.
3. *Ibidem*, History of the project and the firm, and in: Zahlen Daten Fakten — Anhang zum Quadrat–Buch Wohnort Halen, in: E. Thormann-Wirz and F. Thormann, *Wohnort Halen*, St Gallen 1964.
4. N. Morgenthaler, *Atelier 5 — Terrace Houses: Flamatt, Halen and Brügg*, Tokyo 1973.
5. E. Thormann-Wirz and F. Thormann, Zahlen Daten Fakten, *op. cit.* (note 3).
6. R. Perrinjaquet, *op. cit.* (note 1), pp. 207–212.
7. R. Perrinjaquet, *op. cit.* (note 1), interview with a partner, p. 228.
8. R. Perrinjaquet, *op. cit.* (note 1) interview, p. 225.
9. E. Thormann-Wirz and F. Thormann, Zahlen Daten Fakten, *op. cit.* (note 3). The order of the professions listed there has been slightly changed.
10. *Berner Beiträge zur Stadt- und Regionalforschung*, Jhrg. 1974, pp. 52, 70.
11. Interviews with partners of Atelier 5, in: R. Perrinjaquet, *op. cit.* (note 1), pp. 228, 229.
12. E. Thormann-Wirz and F. Thormann, Zahlen Daten Fakten, *op. cit.* (note 3).
13. Atelier 5, Wertherberg 4 Jahre später, in: *Der Baumeister* **69** (1972), pp. 1409–1410.

5.   Society and Culture

1. Michael O'Donoghue, The Liberal Book, in: *Evergreen* **14** (Nov. 1970) 84, pp. 33–39.
2. P. Willis, L'école des ouvriérs, in: *Actes de la recherche en sciences sociales* (Nov. 1978) 24, pp. 50–62.
    F. Oeuvrard, Démocratisation ou élimination différée?, in: *Actes de la recherche en Sciences Sociales* (Nov. 1979) 30, pp. 87–97.
3. R. K. Merton, *Social Theory and Social Structure*, New York 1968, pp. 279f.
4. H. G. Wells, *A Modern Utopia*, London 1905, p. 322.
5. W. A. Stewart, Toward a history of American Negro dialects, in: F. Williams (ed.), *Language and Poverty: Perspectives on a Theme*, Chicago 1969.
6. A. Ross, U and non-U. An essay in sociological linguistics, in: N. Mitford (ed.), *Noblesse Oblige*, Harmondsworth 1963, pp. 9–32.
7. W. Labov, The logic of non-standard English, 1969, reprinted in: N. Keddie (ed.), *Tinker, Tailor...The Myth of Cultural Deprivation*, Harmondsworth 1973, pp. 21–66.
8. P. Bourdieu, *La distinction. Critique sociale du jugement*, Paris 1979. Specifically in music: N. Berthier, Melomanes et musique contemporaine, in: *Revue franc. de sociologie* **XVII** (1976), pp. 499–507.
9. L. Trilling, *The Liberal Imagination*, New York 1950, p. 222.
10. G. Crabbe, *The Library. A Poem.* London 1781, p. 5, line 41f
11. A. Copland, *What to Listen for in Music*, New York 1953, p. 15.

12. On brass bands: B. Jackson, *Working Class Community*, Harmondsworth 1972, ch. 3.
13. P. Bourdieu and M. de St. Martin, Anatomie du goût, in: *Actes de la recherche en sciences sociales* (Oct. 1976) 5.
14. P. Bourdieu and A. Darbel, *L'amour de l'art. Les musées et leur public*, Paris 1966.
15. P. Bourdieu, L. Boltanski, R. Castel and J.-C. Chamboredon, *Un art moyen. Essai sur les usages sociaux de la photographie*, Paris 1965.
16. *Webster's New Collegiate Dictionary*, Springfield 1976.
17. D. Ashton, *The Life and Times of the New York School*, Bath 1972.
18. P. Bourdieu, *op. cit.* (note 8).
19. First paragraph from the Preface to the Catalog of Wedgwood and Bentley, reprinted in: W. Mankowitz, *Wedgwood*, London 1953, p. 213. Second paragraph from a letter of Josiah Wedgwood to his partner Thomas Bentley, dated August 23, 1772, in: A. Finer and G. Savage, *The Selected Letters of Josiah Wedgwood*, London 1965, p. 131.
20. P. Bourdieu and A. Darbel, *op. cit.* (note 14).
21. *Ibidem*, appendix 5, table 4, p. 221.
22. B. Glaser (ed.), The changing role of the modern museum, a discussion with Lawrence Alloway and William C. Seitz, in: The Staff of *Arts Magazine* (ed.), *The Museum World*, New York 1967, pp. 16, 18.
23. P. Bourdieu, *op. cit.* (notes 8, 13, 14, 15).
    P. Bourdieu, Le marché des biens symboliques, in: *L'année sociologique*, Paris 1971, pp. 49–126.
    P. Bourdieu and Y. Delsaut, Le couturier et sa griffe: contribution à une théorie de la magie, in: *Actes de la recherche en sciences sociales* (1975) 21, pp. 7–36.
    See also: H. J. Gans, *The Levittowners*, New York 1967, pp. 24–41.
24. K. Mannheim, *Ideology and Utopia*, London 1976, pp. 137f.
25. Outlined in: M. Horkheimer and T. W. Adorno, *Dialektik der Aufklärung*, Hamburg 1947.
26. B. M. Berger, *Working-Class Suburb*, Berkeley 1968. In particular his conclusion (ch. VII) about the symbolism of cultural consumption is quite close to the position outlined here.
27. H. Gans, *Popular Culture and High Culture*, New York 1974.
28. P. Bourdieu and Y. Delsaut, *op. cit.* (note 23).
29. J. Duncan, Landscape taste as a symbol of group identity, in: *Geographical Review* (1973), pp. 334–355.
30. A. Moles, *Théorie de l'information et perception esthétique*, Paris 1973.
31. H. Rosenberg, *The Tradition of The New*, London 1970, pp. 23, 24.
32. M. Tapié, *Un art autre*, Paris 1952; translated excerpt in: H. B. Chipp (ed.), *Theories of Modern Art*, Berkeley 1969, pp. 603–605.
33. E. de Kooning, Subject: what, how or who?, in: *Art News* (New York) **LIV** (April 1955) 4, pp. 26–29, reprinted in: H. B. Chipp, *op. cit.* (note 32), p. 571.
34. Interview of G. R. Swenson with Tom Wesselmann, in: *Art news* (New York) (Feb. 1964), pp. 41, 64.
35. In: *Art in America* **60** (Nov.–Dec. 1972)6, quoted in: L. Alloway, *Topics in American Art since 1945*, New York 1975, p. 191.
36. A. Reinhardt, in: *Contemporary American Painting*, Urbana 1972, in: *New York School. The First Generation*, Greenwich, Conn. 1965, pp. 131–133.

37. L. R. Lippard (ed.), Questions to Stella and Judd. Interview by Bruce Glaser, 1964, in: G. Battcock (ed.), *Minimal Art. A Critical Anthology*, New York 1968, p. 149.
38. Group Statement, 'Artists' Sessions at Studio 35 (1950), in: *Modern Artists in America*, New York 1951, reprinted in: *New York School op. cit.* (note 36), p. 34.
39. B. Newman, in: *Tiger's Eye* I (March 1948) 3, p. 111, reprinted in: *New York School, op. cit.* (note 36), p. 110.
40. T. B. Hess, *Barnett Newman* (catalog of an exhibition in the Tate Gallery), London 1972, p. 54.
41. S. N. Behrman, *Duveen*, New York 1952.
42. B. Reise, Greenberg and The Group: a retrospective view, in: *Studio International* **175** (May 1968) 900, p. 254.
43. H. Geldzahler, Art at the Metropolitan (Modern, too), in: *The Museum World, op. cit.* (note 22), pp. 42, 43.
44. H. Rosenberg, *op. cit.* (note 31), p. 65.
45. P. Guggenheim, *Confessions of an Art Addict*, London 1960, pp. 104, 105.
46. W. Bongard, *Is de moderne kunst corrupt?*, The Hague, n.d., pp. 94f, (original: *Kunst und Kommerz*, Oldenburg 1968).
47. *Ibidem*.
48. S. Williams, New look at the Tate, in: *The Museum World, op. cit.* (note 22), p. 48.
49. D. Ashton, Curating instant art history, in *The Museum World, op. cit.* (note 22), p. 20.
50. C. Tomkins, *The Scene. Reports on Post-Modern Art*, New York 1976, ch. 1.
51. R. Moulin, *Le marché de la peinture en France*, Paris 1967, and W. Bongard, *op. cit.* (note 46). However, for a description of how the Marlborough Art Gallery once played the art-market, see: L. Seldes, *The Legacy of Mark Rothko*, New York 1978.
52. C. Tomkins, *op. cit.* (note 50), ch. 1.
    W. Bongard, *op. cit.* (note 46).
53. N. Elias, *Was ist Soziologie?* Munich 1970.
54. One psychologist has described this board of examiners which never meets as the 'forum' which decides on the ultimate value of every psychologist's contribution: A. D. de Groot, *Methodologie*, The Hague 1961.
55. W. H. Whyte, *The Organization Man*, New York 1956.

6.   Architects and their Belief-systems

1. AIA Document B131, Sept. 1963 edition.
2. T. C. Bannister (ed.), *The Architect at Mid-Century*, New York 1952, table 28.
3. *Ibidem*, table 27.
4. G. Salaman, Architects and their work, in: *Architect's Journal* **21** (1970) 1, pp. 188–190.
5. K. M. Bolte and H. J. Richter, Der Architekt; sein Beruf und seine Arbeit, in: *Detail* **8**, (1965) 5, pp. 885f.
6. P. Cret, *The Book of the School*, University of Pennsylvania Press, Philadephia 1934, p. 31, quoted in: J. Esherick, Architectural education in the thirties and seventies; a personal view, in: S. Kostof (ed.), *The Architect*, New York 1977, p. 274.
7. Le Corbusier, *Vers une architecture*, Paris 1923, pp. 16, 165.
8. W. Gropius, contribution to the exhibition pamphlet 'Ausstellung für unbekannte Architekten', Berlin 1919, quoted in: U. Conrads, *Programme und Manifeste zur Architektur des 20. Jahrhunderts*, Berlin, Frankfurt 1964, p. 43.

9. E. Saarinen, *Search for Form*, New York 1948, p. 1.
10. RIBA, *A Future in Architecture*, leaflet, London, n.d.
11. M. Bowley, *The British Building Industry*, Cambridge 1966, p. 437.
12. J. Blau, A framework of meaning in architecture, in: G. Broadbent, R. Bunt and C. Jencks, *Signs, Symbols and Architecture*, Chichester 1980, pp. 333–369.
13. W. D. Hunt Jr, *Total Design. Architecture of Welton Becket and Associates*, New York 1975, p. X.
14. *Official Register of Harvard University* 1 (September 5, 1979) 7, p. 13.
15. J. Esherick, in S. Kostof (ed.), *The Architect*, New York 1977, p. 240.
16. On habit formation as a motor of culture, see: P. Bourdieu, *Esquisse d'une théorie de la pratique, précédé de trois études d'ethnologie Kabyle,* Geneva 1972.
17. N. Pevsner, *An Outline of European Architecture*, Harmondsworth 1945, p. XVI.
18. *AIA Architect's Handbook of Professional Practice*, Washington 1963, ch. 4, p. 1. On this belief, see also: A. Lipman, The architectural belief-system and social behaviour, in: *The British Journal of Sociology* **XX** (June 1969) 2, pp. 190–204.
19. L. Mies van der Rohe, Address to the Illinois Institute of Technology, 1950, printed in: *RIBA Journal* (February 1959), p. 113.
20. Interview on May 29, 1959, in: *Interbuild* **6** (1959) 6, pp. 9–11.
21. From the IIT Bulletin 1944–1945, quoted in W. Blaser, *Mies van der Rohe – Principles and School*, Basle, Stuttgart 1977, p. 10.
22. G. E. Danforth, Architecture and planning at the Illinois Institute of Technology, 1959–75, in: W. Blaser, *op. cit.* (note 21), p. 99.
23. *Ibidem*, p. 100.
24. W. Blaser, *op. cit.* (note 21), p. 112.
25. G. E. Danforth, *op. cit.* (note 21), pp. 98, 99.
26. *Ibidem*, p. 100.
27. B. Goldberg, interview in: J. W. Cook and H. Klotz, *Conversations with Architects*, London 1973, p. 131.
28. M. Roesch, The making of an architect. A look at architectural education in Chicago, in: *Inland Architect* (September 1979), p. 7.
29. W. Blaser, *op. cit.* (note 21), p. 104.
30. *Ibidem*, p. 112.
31. K. Roche, in: J. W. Cook and H. Klotz, *op. cit.* (note 27), pp. 73, 74.
32. P. Nuttgens, Towards the future, in: B. Goldstein (ed.), *Architecture: Opportunities, Achievements*, London 1977, p. 98.
33. J. W. Cook and H. Klotz, *op. cit.* (note 27), p. 73.
34. W. Boesiger and H. Girsberger, *Le Corbusier 1910–65*, Zurich 1967, p. 8.
35. J. Soltan, in: *Architectural Design* (May 1960), quoted in: A. Smithson (ed.), *Team 10 Primer*, London, n.d., p. 14.
36. H. P. Berlage, in an interview with *Vooruit*, quoted in: *8 en Opbouw* (1932), pp. 43, 44.
37. J. Yeomans, *The Other Taj Mahal. What Happened to the Sydney Opera House*, London 1968, p. 34.
38. According to M. Baume, *The Sydney Opera House Affair*, Melbourne 1967, pp. 17f, there were six clauses for disqualification for an entry; Utzon's broke four of them.
39. W. McQuade, The architects: a chance for greatness, in: *Fortune* (Jan. 1966), p. 151.
    See also: R. Williamson, An architectural family tree that traces the paths to fame, in *AIA Journal* (Jan. 1978), pp. 46–54.

40. *Architectural Forum* (March 1974), p. 47.
41. P. Drew, *Third Generation. The Changing Meaning of Architecture*, London 1972, p. 70.
42. A. Drexler, *Ludwig Mies van der Rohe*, New York 1960, pp. 9, 10.
43. V. Scully, *Louis Kahn*, New York 1962, p. 10.
44. C. Ray Smith, *Supermannerism*, New York 1977, p. XXIII.
45. F. Gutheim in *AIA Journal* (June 1963), quoted in: L. Craig (ed.), *The Federal Presence*, Cambridge, Mass., London 1978.
46. W. McQuade, *op. cit.* (note 39).
47. F. Fogarty, How today's clients pick architects, in: *Architectural Forum* (Feb. 1959), p. 115.
48. W. D. Hunt Jr, *Total Design. Architecture of Welton Becket and Associates*, New York 1972, p. 21.
49. *Ibidem*, p. 25.
50. *Ibidem*, pp. 22, 23.
51. *Ibidem*, p. 130.
52. R. Roth, High rise down to earth, in: *Progressive Architecture* (June 1957), p. 196.
53. P. Manning, *Office Design: A Study of Environment*, Liverpool 1965, quoted in: H. Proshansky, W. H. Ittelson and L. G. Rivlin, *Environmental Psychology*, New York 1970, p. 473.
54. H. Klotz, *Architektur in der Bundesrepublik*, Frankfurt 1977, p. 121.
55. *Ibidem*, p. 136.
56. The International Competition for a New Administration Building for the Chicago Tribune MCMXXII, Chicago 1923, p. 47.
57. *Architectural Forum* (Sept. 1958), p. 47.
58. W. B. Foxhall (ed.), *Techniques of Successful Practice for Architects and Engineers*, New York 1975, p. 44.
59. *Time* (Jan. 8, 1979), p. 37.
60. *Architectural Forum* (Jan. 1959), p. 86.
61. L. K. Eaton, *Two Chicago Architects and Their Clients. Frank Lloyd Wright and Howard van Doren Shaw*, Cambridge, Mass. 1969, p. 41.
62. P. Bourdieu, *La distinction. Critique sociale du jugement*, Paris 1979.
63. Reichsforschungsgesellschaft für Wirtschaftlichkeit im Bau und Wohnungswesen E. V., *Bericht über die Siedlung in Stuttgart am Weissenhof*, Sonderhelft No 6, April 1929.
64. I. Rosow, *Modern Architecture and Social Change*, unpubl. MA thesis, Univ. of Michigan, 1948.
65. P. C. Johnson, *Mies van der Rohe*, New York 1953.
66. T. H. Creighton, The client, poor soul, in: *RIBA Journal* **56** (Sept. 1959), pp. 502, 503.
67. M. Baume, *The Sydney Opera House Affair*, Melbourne, Sydney 1967.
    J. Yeomans, *op. cit.* (note 37).
68. J. Yeomans, *op. cit* (note 37), quoting a Sydney architect, p. 160.
69. *Bauen and Wohnen* **20** (Sept. 1966) 9, pp. IX–10, 12, 14.

7. Form and Content in Architecture

1. See also the discussion in N. L. Prak, *The Language of Architecture*, The Hague, Paris 1968, ch. 3.
2. Morris Lapidus, in: J. W. Cook and H. Klotz, *Conversations with Architects*, London 1973, pp. 173–174.

3. The doctrines of the social commitment of architects and of architectural determinism are analyzed and criticized in two excellent papers by the architect-sociologist Alan Lipman: Architectural education and the social commitment of contemporary British architecture, in: *The sociological Review* **18** (1970), pp. 5–27; and The architectural belief system and social behaviour, in: *The British Journal of Sociology* **XX** (June 1969) 2, pp. 190–204. A very reasonable criticism is also found in: H. J. Gans, *People and Plans*, London 1968, ch. 1.

4. *AIA Architects Handbook of Professional Practice*, Washington 1963, ch. 4, p.1.

5. C. Colbert, Naked utility and visual chorea, in: L. B. Holland (ed.), *Who Designs America?* Garden City 1966, p. 229.

6. H. Weese, in: P. Heyer, *Architects on Architecture*, New York 1978, p. 44.

7. F. Kramer, Die Wohnung für das Existenzminimum, in: *Die Form* (1929) 24, reprinted in: *'Die Form' Stimme des Deutschen Werkbundes 1925–1934*, Gütersloh 1969, p. 151.

8. After the German version of the text, in: M. Steinmann (ed.), *CIAM. Dokumente 1928–1934*, Basel, Stuttgart 1979. There are considerable differences between the German and the French versions. The German text is the original, according to Steinmann.

9. Town Planning Chart CIAM, in: C. Benton (ed.), *Documents. A Collection of Source Material on the Modern Movement*, Milton Keynes 1975, p. 52.

10. 'Wir fordern', on the occasion of the exhibition 'Heimat, Deine Häuser', in Stuttgart, June 1963, in: U. Conrads (ed.), *Programme und Manifeste zur Architektur des 20. Jahrhunderts*, Frankfurt 1964, p. 177.

11. Exceptions are the texts by the Krier brothers, and, to a lesser extent, by Aldo Rossi.

12. Walter Pichler/Hans Hollein, Absolute Architektur, 1962, in: U. Conrads (ed.), *op. cit.* (note 10), p. 175.

13. S. von Moos, *Le Corbusier. Elemente einer Synthese*, Frauenfeld, Zurich 1968, pp. 21f.

14. Oral communication by R. Oxenaar, curator of the Municipal Museum at The Hague.

15. R. Banham, *Theory and Design in the First Machine Age*, London 1960, p. 217.

16. H. Schmidt, Die Wohnung, in: *Das Werk* **XN** (1927), reprinted and translated in C. Benton (ed.), *op. cit.* (note 9), p. 20. Schmidt was probably angered by the claims that the Weissenhofsiedlung contributed to the solution of the problems of low-cost housing. Schmidt was himself a leftist architect, who emigrated to the Soviet Union in 1930.

17. A. Cutler, The tyranny of Hagia Sophia: notes on Greek Orthodox church design in the United States, in: *Journal of the Society of Architectural Historians* **XXXI** (March 1972) 1, pp. 38–50.

18. S. G. Porter, White House for Tokio, in: *American Architect* **CXVIII** (13 Oct. 1920), p. 484, quoted in: W. H. Rhoads, The Colonial revival and American nationalism, in: *JSAH* **XXXV** (1976), pp. 239–254.

19. L. Craig (ed.), *The Federal Presence*, Cambridge, Mass. 1978, p. 442.

20. In a trivial sense, a building which refers to another building always refers to a thing of the past (the model exists already) and in another place. This is of course not what is meant here.

21. A. W. Pugin, *An Apology for the Revival of Christian Architecture in England*, London 1843, p. 6.
22. Charles Jencks has exploded the myth of a simple rectilinear historical development of architecture in his 'History as myth', in: C. L. Baird and C. Jencks, *Meaning in Architecture*, London 1969, pp. 245, 265.
23. See D. D. Egbert, *Social Radicalism and the Arts. Western Europe*, New York 1970.
24. These efforts are discussed in R. Moulin, *Le marché de la peinture en France*, Paris 1967, pp. 288f.
25. L. Mies van der Rohe, Arbeitsthesen, in G, 1923; reprinted in: U. Conrads (ed.), *op. cit.* (note 10), p. 70.
    Mendelsohn's Einstein Tower was conceived as a concrete structure, but for reasons of economy built in brick with an exterior coat of plaster.
26. R. Giurgola, The discreet charm of the bourgeoisie, in: *Architectural Forum* (May 1973), p. 57.
27. R. Stern, Stompin' at the Savoye, in: *Architectural Forum* (May 1973), p. 47.
28. *Ibidem*, p. 48.
29. See M. Steinmann, *op. cit.* (note 8). Schmidt and Le Corbusier both tried to impose their own views on the participants of the first meeting; it seems that Schmidt was more successful.
30. T. Jefferson, Notes on the State of Virginia/Query XV, 1782, in: D. Gifford (ed.), *The Literature of Architecture*, New York 1966, p. 77.
31. H. James, *Hawthorne*, London 1879, p. 43. James's book has been reprinted in: E. Wilson (ed.), *The Shock of Recognition*, Garden City 1947.
32. J. Wheeler Dow, *American Renaissance. A Review of Domestic Architecture*, New York 1904, pp. 18, 19.
33. M. Cowley, *Exile's Return*, Harmondsworth 1976, p. 94.
34. D. J. Boorstin, *America and the Image of Europe*, New York 1960, pp. 11, 12. See also: M. Mead, *And Keep Your Powder Dry*, New York 1942, ch. V.
35. M. Cowley, *op. cit.* (note 33), p. 107.
36. E. Wharton, *A Backward Glance*, New York 1964, pp. 54, 55.
37. R. A. Cram, *My Life in Architecture*, Boston 1936, p. 52.
38. R. Krautheimer, The Carolingian revival of early Christian architecture, in: *Art Bulletin* **XXIV**, (1942).
    G. Bandmann, *Mittelalterliche Architektur als Bedeutungsträger*, Berling 1951.
39. A. Blunt, *Art and Architecture in France: 1500–1700*, Harmondsworth 1953.
40. J. Summerson, *Inigo Jones*, Harmondsworth 1966.
41. R. Boyd, *The Australian Ugliness*, Victoria 1968, pp. 16, 73.
42. G. Candilis, *Bâtir la vie*, Paris 1977, pp. 190, 191.
43. *Ibidem*, pp. 192, 193.
44. F. T. Marineti, Foundation and Manifesto of Futurism, in: *Poesia* (Milan) (Feb.–March 1909) 1–2, and reprinted in French in: *Le Figaro* (Feb. 20 1909).
45. R. Tolzmann, *Objective Architecture: American Influences in the Development of Modern German Architecture*, unpubl. PhD thesis Univ. of Michigan, Ann Arbor 1975.
46. E. Mendelsohn, *Russland Europa Amerika*, Berlin 1929, p. 160.
47. Le Corbusier, *Vers une architecture*, Paris 1924, p. 29.
48. W. Gropius, Die Kunst in Industrie und Handel, in: *Jahrbuch des Deutschen Werkbundes*, Jena 1913, pp. 21, 22, quoted and translated in: S. Giedion, *Space, Time and Architecture*, Cambridge, Mass. 1967, p. 343.

49. H. P. Berlage, *Amerikaansche reisherinneringen*, Rotterdam 1913, p. 44. Discussion of the influence of Wright on Dutch architecture in: R. Banham, *Theory and Design in the First Machine Age*, London 1960, ch. 11, and in: A. van der Woud, Variaties op een thema, in: *Nederlandse architectuur 1880–1930. Americana*, catalog of an exhibition in the Kröller-Müller Museum, 1975.

50. A relatively early book on factory architecture is: M. Kahn, *The Design and Construction of Industrial Buildings*, London 1917, with mainly American examples.

8.   Case-study: Dutch Architecture in the Twenties and Thirties

1. P. R. Gleichmann, Ein Problem kontrovers gesehen. Neue Wege der Architekturkritik, in: *Der Architekt* **6** (1977), pp. 239–242.
2. H. P. Berlage, *Gedanken über Stil in der Baukunst*, Leipzig 1905, pp. 23, 24.
3. H. P. Berlage, *Studies over Bouwkunst, stijl en samenleving*, Rotterdam 1910, pp. 40, 41.
4. A. W. Reinink, *K. P. C. de Bazel — architect*, Leiden 1965.
5. H. P. Berlage, *op. cit.* (note 3), p. 68.
6. M. de Klerk, in: *Bouwkundig Weekblad* **36** (1916) 46, pp. 331–332 (translation by S. S. Frank).
7. S. S. Frank, Michel de Klerk's designs for Amsterdam's Spaarndammerbuurt, in: *Nederlands Kunsthistorisch Jaarboek* **22** (1971), p. 198.
8. *Nederlandse architectuur 1910–1930. Amsterdamse School.* Exhibition catalog of the Stedlijk Museum, Amsterdam, 1975, pp. 63, 64.
9. Th. van Doesburg, in *Neue Schweizer Rundschau* (1929), p. 41, quoted in: H. L. C. Jaffé, *De Stijl 1917–1931*, Berlin 1965, pp. 84, 85.
10. H. Höch in an interview with B. van Garrel, in: *N. R. C.-Handelsblad*, (July 21, 1978), p. CS 2.
11. *De Stijl* II, 1918; translation from S. Bann (ed.), *The Tradition of Constructivism*, London 1974, p. 65.
12. P. Mondriaan, Natuurlijke en abstracte realiteit, in *de stijl* II, p. 137.
13. P. Mondriaan, Neo-plasticisme. De Woning — De Straat — De Stad, in: *i 10* **I** (1927) 1, p. 18.
14. *Ibidem*, pp. 15, 16.
15. P. Mondrian, Natural reality and abstract reality (1919, 1920), in: M. Seuphor, *Piet Mondrian — Life and Work*, Amsterdam, n.d., pp. 303–306.
16. J. J. P. Oud, Over de toekomstige bouwkunst en haar architectonische mogelijkheden, lecture for 'Opbouw', printed in: *Bouwkundig Weekblad* (June 11, 1921); translation by R. Banham, in: *Theory and Design in the First Machine Age*, London 1960, p. 159.
17. J. J. P. Oud, *Holländische Architektur*, Munich 1926, p. 97.
18. J. J. P. Oud, *op. cit.* (note 16), p. 162.
19. J. J. P. Oud, Massabouw en straatarchitectuur, in: *De Stijl* (1919) **2** 7, p. 80.
20. Th. van Doesburg, Tot een beeldende architectuur, in: *De Stijl* **6** (1924) 6, 7, p. 78. Translation by Th. M. Brown, in: *The Work of G. Rietveld, Architect*, Paris 1923, p. 73.

21. Le Corbusier, *Vers une architecture*, Paris 1923, p. 73.
22. M. Stam, M-Kunst, in *i 10* (1927) 1/2, pp. 41, 42.
23. Wat is de 8? in: *i 10* (1927) 1, p. 126.
24. M. J. Granpré Molière, Bouwkunst en verwante kunsten, 1935, printed in: *Woorden en werken van Prof. Ir. Granpré Molière*, Heemstede 1949, p. 40.
25. J. B. van Loghem, *bouwen — bauen — bâtir — building*, Amsterdam 1932, p. 8.
26. M. J. Granpré Molière, *Woorden en werken, op. cit.* (note 24), p. 74 (1944).
27. *Ibidem*, p. 99 (1947).
28. *Ibidem*, p. 31 (1930).
29. J. B. van Loghem, *op. cit.* (note 25), p. 10.
30. *Ibidem*, p. 45.
31. A. Boeken, *Architectuur*, Amsterdam 1936, p. 40.
32. M. J. Granpré Molière, Schoonheidsleer (roneographed), Delft 1940, p. 29.
33. M. J. Granpré Molière, *Woorden en werken, op. cit.* (note 24), p. 119.
34. *Ibidem*, p. 63 (1943).
35. *Ibidem*, p. 28 (1921).
36. M. Stam, in: *ABC* **1/2** (1924), p. 4.
37. M. J. Granpré Molière, *Over mijn terugkeer tot de moederkerk*, 's-Hertogenbosch 1939, p. 6.
38. M. J. Granpré Molière, Het tuindorp (1921), in: *Woorden en werken, op. cit.* (note 24), p. 26.
39. N. L. Prak, De ontwikkeling van het Nieuwe Bouwen, in: *Bouwen '20–'40* (exhibition catalog), Eindhoven 1971, p. 38.
40. *Ibidem*, pp. 37, 38.
41. *Ibidem*, p. 45, 46.
42. *Ibidem*, pp. 46, 47.
43. S. D. Neter, in: *de 8 en Opbouw* (1939), pp. 152, 153.
44. Lecture by van Loghem to 'Opbouw' in 1928, printed in: N. L. Prak, *op. cit.* (note 39), p. 35.
45. Personal communication by C. H. van der Leeuw.
46. W. Boesiger, *Richard Neutra. Buildings and Projects*, Zurich 1951, pp. 26, 27.
47. H. de Haan and I. Haagsma, De paleizen van de Bijenkoningin, in: *De Architekt* **80** (Sept. 1980) 9, pp. 117–122.
48. J. Gratama, Het gebouw van 'De Bijenkorf' in Den Haag, in: *Architectura* **29** (1925), p. 9.

9. European and US Architecture Today

1. Team 10 Primer, London 1965, p. 15.
2. From the statement of the CIAM committee on the role of the aesthetic in Habitat, prepared for the conference in Aix-en-Provence in 1953, reprinted in: *Forum* (Neth.) (1959), p. 226 by an editorial board comprising van Eyck and Hertzberger.
3. A. van Eyck, in: *Forum* (Dutch) **14** (1959), p. 243.
4. A. van Eyck, De milde raderen van de reciprociteit, in: *Forum* (Dutch) **15** (1961), p. 205.
5. M. Safdie, *Beyond Habitat*, Cambridge, Mass. 1970, pp. 52–53. Safdie writes that he was also influenced by van Eyck's work.
6. W. Ruhnau and Y. Klein, Projekt einer Luftarchitektur, originally published in: *Zero* **3** (1960), reprinted in: U. Conrads, *Programme und Manifeste zur Architektur des 20. Jahrhunderts*, Berlin, etc. 1964, p. 164.

7. P. Cook, Archigram, in: P. Cook (ed.), *Archigram*, London 1972, pp. 27–29.
8. *Ibidem*, p. 32.
9. M. Culot and L. Krier, The only path for architecture, in *Oppositions* (Fall 1978) 14, pp. 39–43.
10. Royal Barry Wills Associates, *More Houses for Good Living*, New York 1976, p. 43.
11. A. Forty and H. Moss, A housing style for troubled consumers: the success of pseudo-vernacular, in: *Architectural Review* **CLXVII** (Feb. 1980) 996, pp. 73–78.
12. See A. Hahn, *Soziologie der Paradiesvorstellungen*, Trier 1976.
13. H. Hertzberger, De Traditie van het Nieuwe Bouwen en de nieuwe mooiigheid, in: *Intermediair* **16** (Aug. 8, 1980) 32, pp. 9–15.
14. J. Jacobus, *Philip Johnson*, London 1962, p. 118.
15. P. Rudolph, in an interview in: J. W. Cook and H. Klotz, *Conversations with Architects*, London 1973, p. 95.
16. H. Hentrich, in an interview in: H. Klotz, *Architektur in der Bundesrepubliek*, Frankfurt 1977, p. 140.
17. A. L. Huxtable, The troubled state of modern architecture, in: *The New York Review of Books* (May 1, 180), pp. 23–26.
18. B. Diamonstein, *American Architecture Now*, New York 1980.
19. *Ibidem*, p. 232.
20. H. Hardy, quoted in: C. Ray Smith, *Supermannerism*, New York 1977, p. 108.
21. R. Venturi, *Complexity and Contradiction in Architecture*, New York 1966, p. 22.
22. C. Moore, Personal statement, in: *The Work of Charles Moore*, Tokyo 1978, pp. 15, 16
23. *Ibidem*, pp. 14, 15.
24. Denise Scott Brown, in an interview in: J. W. Cook and H. Klotz, *op. cit.* (note 15), p. 251.
25. R. Venturi, D. Scott Brown and S. Izenour, *Learning from Las Vegas*, Cambridge, Mass. 1977, p. 163.
26. J. W. Cook, H. Klotz, *op. cit.* (note 15), p. 248.
27. *Five Architects. Eisenman, Graves, Gwathmey, Hejduk, Meier*, New York 1975, p. 15.
28. R. Maxwell, The Venturi effect, in: *Venturi and Rauch. The Public Buildings*, Architectural Monographs 1, London 1978, pp. 7–29.
29. R. Venturi, *op. cit.* (note 25), p.xiii.

Appendix A   A Note on Methodology

1. P. DiMaggio, Review essay: on Pierre Bourdieu, in: *American Journal of Sociology* **83** (1978) 6, p. 1467.
2. Management Communications Services, *Communication Needs of Ontario Architects*, Toronto 1971 (mimeographed), p. 56.
3. *Ibidem*, p. 71.
4. *Ibidem*, p. 70.
5. Th. van Doesburg and C. van Eesteren, Toward a collective Construction, in: *De Stijl* **VI** (1924) 6–7, (text dated 1923). Translated by S. Bann, in: S. Bann (ed.), *The Tradition of Constructivism*, London 1974, pp. 115–118, quote on p. 118.
6. Erwin Panofsky has argued that a coherent interpretation of data of doubtful provenance or relevance may actually confer some credibility on these data themselves. See: E. Panofsky, Introduc-

tion: the history of art as a humanistic discipline (1940), reprinted in: E. Panofsky, *Meaning in the Visual Arts*, Garden City 1955, pp. 23–50.
7. B. Russell, *Human Knowledge. Its Scope and Limits*, London 1948, pp. 359–360.

References

A.I.A., *Architect's Handbook of Professional Practice*, Washington 1963.

Alberti, L.B., *Ten Books on Architecture*, London 1955.

Alloway, L., *Topics in American Art since 1945*, New York 1975.

Ashton, D., *The Life and Times of the New York School*, Bath 1972.

Atelier 5, Wertherberg 4 Jahre später, in: *Der Baumeister* **69** (1972) pp. 1410, 1411.

Baird C.L., and C. Jencks (eds.), *Meaning in Architecture*, London 1969.

Bandmann, G., *Mittelalterliche Architektur als Bedeutungsträger*, Berlin 1951.

Banham, R., *Theory and Design in the First Machine Age*, London 1960.

Bannister, T.C. (ed.), *The Architect at Mid-Century*, New York 1952.

Bann, S. (ed.), *The Tradition of Constructivism*, London 1974.

Battcock, G., *Minimal Art. A Critical Anthology*, New York 1968.

Baume, M., *The Sydney Opera House Affair*, Melbourne 1967.

Behrman, S.N., *Duveen*, New York 1952.

Benton, C. (ed.), *Documents. A Collection of Source Material on the Modern Movement*, Milton Keynes 1975.

Berlage, H.P., *Gedanken über Stil in der Baukunst*, Leipzig 1905.

Berlage, H.P., *Studies over bouwkunst, stijl en samenleving*, Rotterdam 1910.

Berlage, H.P., *Amerikaansche reisherinneringen*, Rotterdam 1913.

Berner Beiträge zur Stadt und Regionalforschung, Berne 1974.

Bernhardt, K. (ed.), *Housing, New Trends and Concepts*, Ann Arbor 1972.

Blaser, W., *Mies van der Rohe — Principles and School*, Basle, Stuttgart 1977.

Blunt, A., *Art and Architecture in France: 1500–1700*, Harmondsworth 1953.

Boeken, A., *Architectuur*, Amsterdam 1936.

Boericke, A., and B. Shapiro, *Handmade Houses, A Guide to the Woodbutcher's Art*, San Franciso 1975.

Boesiger, W., and H. Girsberger, *Le Corbusier 1910–1965*, Zurich 1967.

Bolte, K.M., and H.J. Richter, Der Architekt; sein Beruf und seine Arbeit, in: *Detail 8* (1965) 5, pp. 885 f.

Bongard, W., *Kunst und Kommerz*, Oldenburg 1968.

Bonny, J.B., and J.P. Frein (eds.), *Handbook of Construction Management and Organization*, New York 1973.

Bonta, J.P., *Architecture and its Interpretation*, London 1979.

Boorstin, D.J., *America and the Image of Europe*, New York 1960.

Booz, P., *Der Baumeister der Gotik*, Munich 1956.

Bondon, P., *Pessac de Le Corbusier*, Paris 1969.

Borsi, F., *Leon Battista Alberti*, Milan 1975.

Bourdieu, P., Le marché des biens symboliques, in: *L'année sociologique* (1971), pp. 49–126.

Bourdieu, P., *Esquisse d'une théorie de la pratique*, Geneva 1972.

Bourdieu, P., *La distinction. Critique sociale du jugement*, Paris 1979.

Bourdieu, P., L. Boltanski, R. Castel and J.C. Chamboredon, *Un art moyen. Essai sur les usages sociaux de la photographie*, Paris 1965.

Bourdieu, P., and A. Darbel, *L'amour de la'art. Les musées et leur public*, Paris 1966.

Bourdieu, P., and Y. Delsaut, Le couturier et sa griffe, in: *Actes de la recherche en sciences sociales* (1975) 1, pp. 1–108.

Bourdieu, P., and M. de St. Martin, Anatomie du goût, in: *Actes de la recherche en sciences sociales* (Oct. 1976) 5.

Bouwen '20 — '40 (exhibition catalog), Eindhoven 1971.

Bowley, M., *The British Building Industry*, Cambridge 1966.

Boyd, R., *The Australian Ugliness*, Victoria 1968.

Briggs, M., *The Architect in History*, New York 1974.

Broadbent, G., R. Bunt and C. Jencks, *Signs, Symbols and Architecture*, Chichester 1980.

Brown, Th.M., *The Work of G. Rietveld, Architect*, Utrecht 1958.

Building and Civil Engineering Economic Development Committee, *The Public Client and the Construction Industries*, London (HMSO) 1975.

Candilis, G., *Bâtir la vie*, Paris 1977.

Carter, P., *Mies van der Rohe at Work*, London 1974.

Cassidy, R., Home owners taken for a ride, in: *New York Times Review* (Jan. 12, 1975) VII, p. 28.

Cassimatis, P.J., *Economics of the Construction Industry*, New York 1966.

Chipp, R.E. (ed.), *Theories of Modern Art*, Berkeley 1969.

Class, R.E., and R.E. Koehler (eds.), *Current Techniques in Architectural Practice*, Washington, New York 1976.

Collins, P., *Changing Ideals in Modern Architecture*, London 1965.

Columbia University School of Architecture, *A Report on Registered Architects*, New York 1953.

Conrads, U., *Programme und Manifeste zur Architektur des 20. Jahrhunderts*, Berlin, Frankfurt 1964.

Cook, J.W., and H. Klotz, *Conversations with Architects*, London 1973.

Cook, P. (ed.), *Archigram*, London 1972.

Copland, A., *What to Listen for in Music*, New York 1953.

Corbusier, Le, *Vers une architecture*, Paris 1923.

Cowley, M., *Exile's Return*, Harmondsworth 1976.

Craig, L. (ed.), *The Federal Presence*, Cambridge, Mass., London 1978.

Cram, R.A., *My Life in Architecture*, Boston 1936.

Creighton, T.H., The client, poor soul, in: *RIBA Journal* **56** (Sept. 1959), pp. 502–503.

Culot, M., and L. Krier, The only path for architecture, in: *Oppositions* (1978) 14, pp. 39–43.

Cutler, A., The tyranny of Hagia Sophia: notes on Greek Orthodox church design in the United States, in: *Journal of the Society of Architectural Historians* **XXXI** (March 1972) 1, pp. 38–50.

Demerath, N.J., and G.W. Baker, The social organization of housebuilding in: *Journal of Social Issues* **7** (1951), pp. 86–99.

Depaule, J.C., *L'architecture sauvage*, Paris 1970.

Diamonstein, B., *American Architecture Now*, New York, 1980.

DiMaggio, P., Review essay: on Pierre Bourdieu, in: *Am. Journal of Sociology* **84** (1978) 6, pp. 1460–1474.

Dow, J. Wheeler, *American Renaissance. — A Review of Domestic Architecture*, New York 1904.

Drew, P., *Third Generation. The Changing Meaning of Architecture*, London 1972.

Drexler, A., *Ludwig Mies van der Rohe*, New York 1960.

Duncan, J., Landscape taste as a symbol of group identity, in: *Geographical Review* (1973), pp. 334–355.

Eaton, L.K., *Two Chicago Architects and Their Clients. Frank Lloyd Wright and Howard van Doren Shaw*, Cambridge, Mass. 1969.

Egbert, D.D., *Social Radicalism and the Arts. Western Europe*, New York 1970.

Eichner, A.S. (ed.), *A Guide to Post-Keynesian Economics*, New York 1978.

Elbern, V.H. (ed.), *Das erste Jahrtausend*, Dusseldorf 1964.

Elias, N., *Was ist Soziologie?*, Munich 1970.

Erlande-Brandenbourg, R., La facade de la cathédrale d'Amiens, in: *Bulletin Monumental* **135** (1977), pp. 253–293.

Eyck, A. van, De milde raderen van de reciprociteit, in: *Forum* (Dutch) **15** (1961), pp. 197–235.

Ferber, C. von, *Soziologie für Mediziner*, Heidelberg, New York 1975.

Finer, A., and G. Savage, *The Selected Letters of Josiah Wedgwood*, London 1965.

Five Architects. Eisenman, Graves, Gwathmey, Hejduk, Meier, New York 1975.

Fogarty, F., How today's clients pick architects, in: *Architectural Forum* **110** (Feb. 1959), pp. 114, 115, 182.

Forty, A., and H. Moss, A housing style for troubled consumers: the success of pseudo-vernacular, in: *Architectural Review* **CLXVII** (Feb. 1980) 996, pp. 73–78.

Foxhall, W.B. (ed.), *Techniques of Successful Practice for Architects and Engineers*, New York 1975.

Frank, S.S., Michel de Klerk's design for Amsterdam's Spaarndammerbuurt, in: *Nederlands Kunsthistorisch Jaarboek* **22** (1971), pp. 175–213.

Frankl, P., *The Gothic. Literary Sources and Interpretations through Eight Centuries*, Princeton 1960.

French, R.M., and J.K. Hadden, An analysis of the distribution and characteristics of mobile homes in America, in: *Land Economics* **XLI** (May 1965) 2, pp. 131–139.

Gaber, B., *Die Entwicklung des Berufsstandes der freischaffenden Architekten*, Essen 1966.

Gans, H.J., *The Levittowners*, New York 1967.

Gans, H.J., *People and Plans*, London 1968.

Gibbs, J., *A Book of Architecture containing Designs of Buildings and Ornaments*, London 1728.

Gifford, D. (ed.), *The Literature of Architecture*, New York 1966.

Giurgola, R., The discreet charm of the bourgeoisie, in: *Architectural Forum* (May 1973), p. 57.

Gleichmann, P.R., Ein Problem kontrovers gesehen. Neue Wage der Architekturkritik, in: *Der Architekt* (1977) 6, pp. 239–242.

Goldberger, P., Architects meet to note failures of Modernism, in: *New York Times* (Dec. 11, 1980).

Goldstein, B. (ed.), *Architecture: Opportunites, Achievements*, London 1977.

Granpré Molière, M.J., *Over mijn terugkeer tot de Moederkerk*, 's-Hertogenbosch 1939.

Granpré Molière, M.J., *Woorden en werken van Prof.Ir. M.J. Granpré Molière*, Heemstede 1949.

Gratama, J., Het gebouw van 'De Bijenkorf' in Den Haag, in: *Architectura* **29** (1925), p. 9.

Greif, M., *The New Industrial Landscape. The Story of the Austin Company*, Clinton 1978.

Groot, A.D. de, *Methodologie*, The Hague 1961.

Gropius, W., Die Kunst in Industrie und Handel, in: *Jahrbuch des Deutschen Werkbundes*, Jena 1913, pp. 21, 22.

Guggenheim, P. *Confessions of an Art Addict*, London 1960.

Haan, H. de, and I. Haagsma, De paleizen van de Bijenkoningin, in: *De Architekt* **80** (Sept. 1980) 9, pp. 117–122.

Hahn, A., *Soziologie der Paradiesvorstellungen*, Trier 1976.

Halper, J.B., The influence of mortgage lenders on building design, in: *Law and Contemporary Problems* **32** 1967) 2, pp. 266–273.

Harvey, J., *The Mediaeval Architect*, London 1972.

Hecht, K., Zur Masstäblichkeit der mittelalterlichen Bauzeichnung, in: *Bonner Jahrbücher* **166** (1966), pp. 253–268.

Hecht, K., Mass und Zahl in der gotischen Baukunst, in: *Abhandlungen der Braunschweigischen Wissenschaftlichen Gesellschaft* **XXI** (1969), pp. 215–326; **XXII** (1970), pp. 105–263; **XXIII** (1971–1972), pp. 25–236.

Heery, G.T., *Time, Cost and Architecture*, New York 1975.

Hendriks, A., *De prijsvorming in het bouwbedrijf*, Rotterdam 1957.

Hertzberger, H., De traditie van het Nieuwe Bouwen en de nieuwe mooiigheid, in: *Intermediair.* **16** (Aug. 8, 1980) 32, pp. 9–15.

Hess, T.B., *Barnett Newman*, London 1972.

Heyer, P., *Architects on Architecture*, New York 1978.

Hitchcock, H.R., and W. Seale, *Temples of Democracy. The State Capitols of the USA*, New York 1976.

Holland, L.B. (ed.), *Who Designs America?* Garden City 1966.

Hunt, W.D., *Total Design. Architecture of Welton Becket and Associates*, New York 1975.

Huxtable, A.L., The troubled state of Modern Architecture, in: *New York Review of Books* (May 1, 1980), pp. 23–26.

Jackson, B., *Working Class Community*, Harmondsworth 1972.

Jacobus, J., *Philip Johnson*, London 1962.

Jaffé, H.L.C., *De Stijl — 1917–1931*, Berlin 1965.

Jenkins, F., *Architect and Patron. A Survey of Professional Relations and Practice in England from the Sixteenth Century to the Present Day*, London 1961.

Johnson, P.C., *Mies van der Rohe*, New York 1953.

Kahn, M., *The Design and Construction of Industrial Buildings*, London 1917.

Keddie, N. (ed.), *Tinker, Tailor... The Myth of Cultural Deprivation*, Harmondsworth 1973.

Klotz, H., *Architektur in der Bundesrepublik*, Frankfurt 1977.

Kooning, E. de, Subject: What, how or who? in: *Art News* **LIV** (April 1955) 4, pp. 26–29.

Kostof, S. (ed.), *The Architect, Chapters in the History of the Profession*, New York 1977.

Kramer, F., Die Wohnung für das Existenzminimum, in: *die Form* **24** (1929).

Krautheimer, R., The Carolingian revival of Early Christian architecture, in: *Art Bulletin* **24** (1942), pp. 1–38.

Lapidus, M., *Architecture: a Profession and a Business*, New York 1967.

Lipman, A., The architectural belief-system and social behaviour, in: *The British Journal of Sociology* **XX** (June 1962) 2, pp. 190–204.

Lipman, A., Architectural education and the social commitment, in: *The Sociological Review* **18** (1970), pp. 5–27.

Loghem, J.B. van, *bouwen — bauen — bâtir — building*, Amsterdam 1932.

McCue, G., and W.R. Ewald Jr, The Midwest Research Institute, *Creating the Human Environment*, Urbana 1970.

MacEwen, M., *Crisis in Architecture*, London 1974.

McQuade, W., The architects: a chance for greatness, in: *Fortune* (Jan. 1966), pp. 151, 158, 196, 200–202, 206.

McQuade, W., Why all those buildings are collapsing, in: *Fortune* (Nov. 19, 1979), pp. 58–66.

Management Communication Services, *Communication Needs of Ontario Architects*, Toronto n.d.

Mankowitz, W., *Wedgwood*, London 1953.

Mannheim, K., *Ideology and Utopia*, London 1976.

Marquart, F., and C. de Montlibert, Division du travail et concurrence en architecture, in: *Revue Francaise de Sociologie* **XI** (1970), pp. 368–389.

Mendelsohn, E., *Russland Europa Amerika*, Berlin 1929.

Merton, R.K., *Social Theory and Social Structure*, New York 11968.

Mies van der Rohe, L., Address to the Illinois Institute of Technology, 1950, in: *RIBA Journal* (Feb. 1959), p. 113.

Mies van der Rohe, L., Interview, in: *Interbuild* **6** (1959) 6, pp. 9–11.

Mitford, N., *Noblesse Oblige*, Harmondsworth 1963.

Moles, A., *Théorie de l'information et perception esthétique*, Paris 1973.

Mondriaan, P., Neo-plasticisme. De Woning — De Straat — De Stad, in: *i10* **I** (1927) 1, pp. 12–16.

Moore, C., *The Work of Charles Moore*, Tokyo 1978.

Moos, S. von, *Le Corbusier. Elemente einer Synthese*, Frauenfeld, Zurich 1968.

Morgenthaler, N., *Atelier 5 — Terrace Houses: Flamatt, Halen and Brügg*, Tokyo 1973.

Moulin, R., *Le marché de la peinture en France*, Paris 1967.

Moulin, R., F. Dubost, A. Gras, J. Lautman, J.P. Martinon and S. Schnapper, *Les architectes*, Paris 1973.

Nederlandse architectuur. 1880–1930. Americana, Otterlo 1975.

Nederlandse architectuur 1910–1930. Amsterdamse school, Amsterdam 1975.

New York School. The First Generation, Greenwich, Conn. 1965.

O'Donoghue, M., The Liberal Book, in: *Evergreen* **14** (Nov. 1970) 84, pp. 33–39.

Oud, J.J.P., Massabouw en straatarchitectuur, in: *de Stijl* **2** (1919) 7, pp. 79–82.

Oud, J.J.P., *Höllandische Architektur*, Munich 1926.

Panofsky, E., *Meaning in the Visual Arts*, Garden City 1955.

Parry Lewis, J., *Building Cycles and Britain's Growth*, London 1965.

Pawley, M., *Mies van der Rohe*, London 1970.

Perin, C., *Everything in its Place. Social Order and Land Use in America*, Princeton 1977.

Perkins, B., Marketing architectural services, in: *Architectural Record* (April 1972), pp. 65–66.

Perrinjaquet, R., *Elements pour une sociologie de la production architecturale*, Paris 1978.

Pevsner, N., *An Outline of European Architecture*, Harmondsworth 1945.

Phillips, H.E., Comprehensive architectural services for the large corporate client, in: *AIA Journal* (May 1964), pp. 74–86.

Porter, S.G., White House for Tokio, in: *American Architect* **CXVIII** (Oct. 1920) p. 484.

Portman, J., and J. Barnett, *The Architect as Developer*, New York 1976.

Prak, N.L., Measurements of Amiens Cathedral, in: *Journ. Soc. Arch. Hist.* **XXV** (1966), pp. 209–212.

Prak, N.L., *The Language of Architecture*, The Hague, Paris, 1968.

Proshansky, H., W.H. Ittelson and L.G. Rivlin (eds.), *Environmental Psychology*, New York 1970.

Pugin, A.W., *An Apology for the Revival of Christian Architecture in England*, London 1843.

Ray Smith, C., *Supermannerism*, New York 1977.

Reichsforschungsgesellschaft für Wirtschaftlichkeit in Bau- und Wohnungswesen E.V., *Bericht über die Siedlung in Stuttgart am Weissenhof*, 1929.

Reinink, A.W., *K.P.C. de Bazel — architect*, Leiden 1965.

Reise, B., Greenberg and The Group: a retrospective view, in: *Studio International* **175** (May 1968) 900, pp. 254–257.

Richardson, H.W., and D.H. Aldcroft, *Building in The British Economy between the Wars*, London 1968.

Ricken, H., *Der Architekt. Geschichte eines Berufs*, Berlin 1977.

Roesch, M., The making of an architect. A look at architectural education in Chicago, in: *Inland Architect* (Sept. 1979), pp. 7–11.

Rosenberg, H., *The Tradition of the New*, London 1970.

Rosow, I., *Modern Architecture and Social Change* (unpubl. MA Thesis, Univ. of Michigan), Ann Arbor 1948.

Roth, A., *Begegnung mit Pionieren. Le Corbusier, Piet Mondrian, Adolf Loos, Josef Hoffman, Auguste Perret, Henry van de Velde*, Basle 1973.

Roth, R., High rise down to earch, in: *Progressive Architecture* (June 1957), pp. 196, 197.

Royal Barry Wills Associates, *More Houses for Good Living*, New York 1976.

Royal Institute of British Architects, *The Architect and his Office*, London 1962.

Rudovsky, B., *Architecture without Architects*, New York 1964.

Russell, B., *Human Knowledge. Its Scope and Limits*, London 1948.

Saarinen, E., *Search for Form*, New York 1948.

Safdie, M., *Beyond Habitat*, Cambridge, Mass. 1970.

Salaman, G., Architects and their work, in: *Architect's Journal* **21** (1970) 1, pp. 188–190.

Salzman, L.F., *Building in England down to 1540*, Oxford 1952.

Scully, V., *Louis Kahn*, New York 1962.

Seuphor, M., *Piet Mondrian — Life and Work*, Amsterdam n.d.

Smithson, A. (ed.), *Team 10 Primer*, London n.d.

Soane, J., *Plans, Elevations and Sections of Buildings*, London 1788.

Staff of *Arts Magazine* (eds.), *The Museum World*, New York 1967.

Stam, M., M-Kunst, in: *i10* **1** (1927) 2, pp. 41–43.

Steinmann, M. (ed.), *CIAM Dokumente 1928–1934*. Basle, Stuttgart 1979.

Stern, R., Stompin' at the Savoye, in: *Architectural Forum* (May 1973), pp. 47, 48.

Summerson, J., *Architecture in Britain: 1530 — 1830*, Harmondsworth 1953.

Summerson, J., *Inigo Jones*, Harmondsworth 1966.

Summerson, J., *Georgian London*, Harmondsworth 1969.

Swenson, G.R., Interview with Tom Wesselmann, in: *Art News* (Feb. 1964), pp. 41, 64.

Tafel, E., *Apprentice to Genius; Years with Frank Lloyd Wright*, new York, 1979.

The International Competition for a New Administration Building for the Chicago Tribune. MCMXXII, Chicago 1923.

Thormann-Wirz, E., and F. Thormann, *Wohnort Halen*, St Gallen 1964.

Tolzmann, R., *Objective Architecture: American Influences in the Development of Modern German Architecture* (unpubl. PhD Thesis, Univ. of Michigan), Ann Arbor 1975.

Tomkins, C., *The Scene. Reports on Post-Modern Art*, New York 1976.

Trilling, L., *The Liberal Imagination*, New York 1950.

Venturi, R., *Complexity and Contradiction in Architecture*, New York 1966.

Venturi, and Rauch — The Public Buildings, London 1978.

Venturi, R., D. Scott Brown and S. Izenour, *Learning from Las Vegas*, Cambridge, Mass. 1977.

Wampler, J., *All Their Own*, New York 1977.

Ward, C. (ed.), *Vandalism*, London 1973.

Wat is de 8? in: *i10* (1927), p. 126.

Webster's New Collegiate Dictionary, Springfield 1976.

Wells, H.G., *A Modern Utopia*, London 1905.

Wharton, E., *A Backward Glance*, New York 1964.

Willis, P., L'école des ouvriers, in: *Actes de la recherche en sciences sociales* (Nov. 1978) 24, pp. 50–62.

Wolfe, T., *From Bauhaus to Our House*, New York 1981.

Yeomans, J., *The Other Taj Mahal. What Happened to the Sydney Opera House*, London 1968.

Credits for Illustrations

Australian Information Service: 23, 32
W. Blaser, Basle: 14, 15
J.S. de Boer, Philadelphia: 18, 24, 71
D. Bowers, Minneapolis: 70
Cambridge Newspapers Limited: 13
© H. Cartier Bresson, *Magnum*: 33
G. Cassel, Johannesburg: 28
City of Montreal: 38
P. Eisenman, New York: 75
© ESTO (Ezra Stoller Photo), Mamaroneck, New York: 1, 2, 74
Gemeentelijke Archiefdienst Amsterdam: 48, 49, 61
Gemeentelijke Archiefdienst Rotterdam: 42, 57
M. Ghisalberti, Como: 44
P.R. Gleichmann, Hanover: 9
R. Herron, London: 67
E.J. Jelles, Amsterdam: 21
F. Keuzenkamp, Pijnacker: 10, 17, 51, 52, 54, 63, 68
A.M. Key, The Hague: 65
KLM Aerocarto, Schiphol: 66
L. Krier, London: 69
© Le Corbusier, Spadem, Paris/Beeldrecht, Amsterdam: 6, 8, 34, 35, 36, 37
Museum of Modern Art, New York: 46
Nederlands Documentatiecentrum voor de Bouwkunst, Amsterdam: 19, 20, 62, 63
New York Public Library: 43
Penrod Hiawatha Co., Holland, Michigan: 39
N.L. Prak, Rotterdam: 3, 30, 40, 41, 50, 53, 56, 60, 64, 76, cartoons
Provinciaal Electriciteitsbedrijf van Noord-Holland, Velzen: 58
Roche, Dinkeloo and Associates, Hamden, Connecticut: 73
D.J. de Ruiter, Delft: 29
J.E.N. de Senerpont Domis, Delft: 25, 26
SMU Foundation, North Dartmouth, Mass.: 72
Stedelijk Museum, Amsterdam: 11
F. Thormann, Berne: 5, 7

Index